# Media Transparency in China

# Media Transparency in China

*Rethinking Rhetoric and Reality*

Baohui Xie

LEXINGTON BOOKS
Lanham • Boulder • New York • London

Published by Lexington Books
An imprint of The Rowman & Littlefield Publishing Group, Inc.
4501 Forbes Boulevard, Suite 200, Lanham, Maryland 20706
www.rowman.com

16 Carlisle Street, London W1D 3BT, United Kingdom

Copyright © 2014 by Lexington Books

*All rights reserved.* No part of this book may be reproduced in any form or by any electronic or mechanical means, including information storage and retrieval systems, without written permission from the publisher, except by a reviewer who may quote passages in a review.

British Library Cataloguing in Publication Information Available

**Library of Congress Cataloging-in-Publication Data**

Xie, Baohui, 1971–
Media transparency in China : rethinking rhetoric and reality / Baohui Xie.
pages cm
ISBN 978-0-7391-8326-7 (cloth : alk. paper)—ISBN 978-0-7391-8327-4 (electronic) 1. Mass media—Political aspects—China. 2. Freedom of the press—China. 3. Mass media policy—China. 4. Government and the press—China. 5. Censorship—China. I. Title.
P95.82.C6B37 2014
302.23'0951—dc23
2014025279

∞ ™ The paper used in this publication meets the minimum requirements of American National Standard for Information Sciences Permanence of Paper for Printed Library Materials, ANSI/NISO Z39.48-1992.

Printed in the United States of America

To Shengguo Priscilla

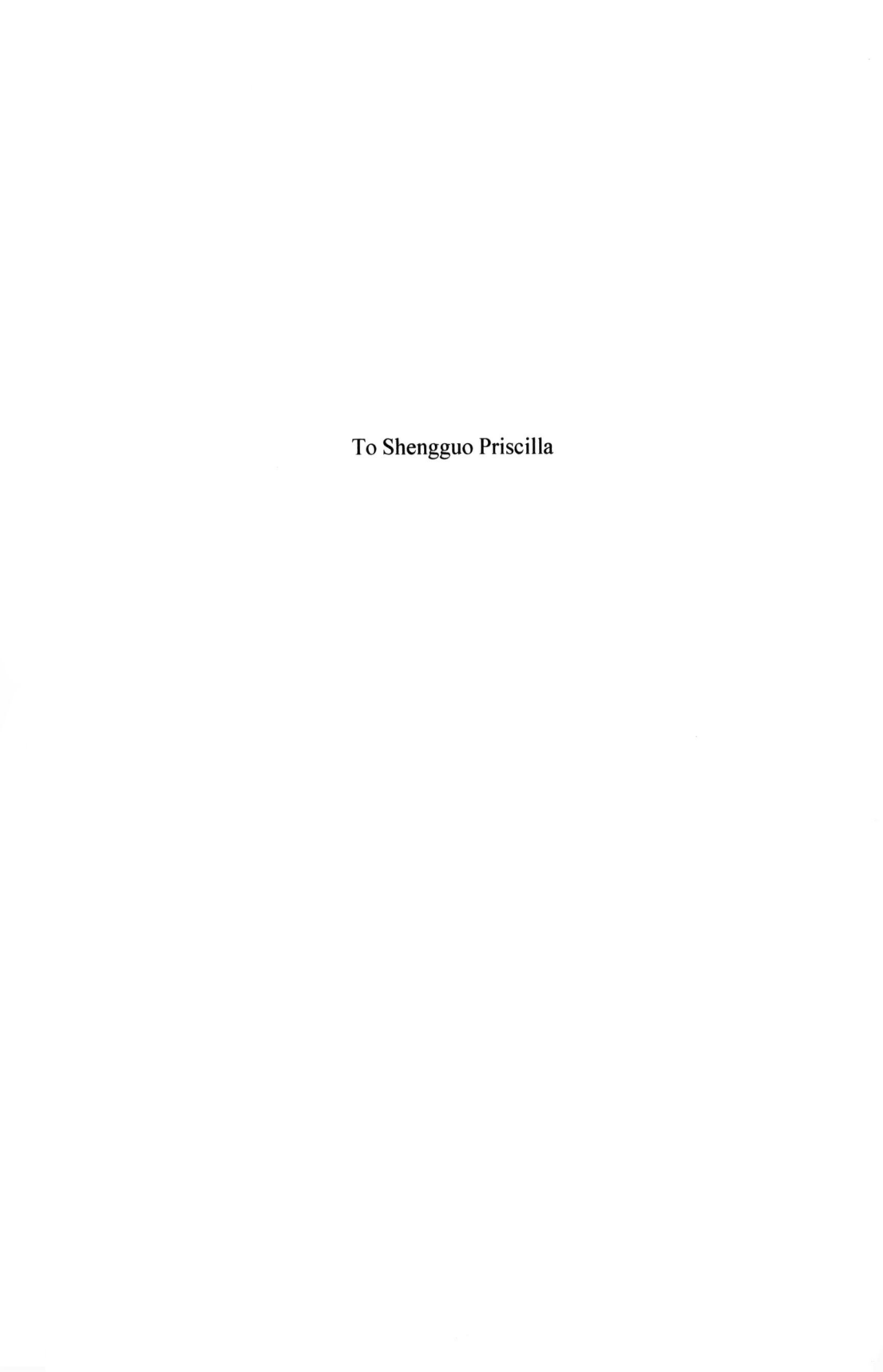

# Contents

| | | |
|---|---|---|
| Foreword | | ix |
| Acknowledgments | | xiii |
| Introduction | | xv |
| 1 | Press Freedom and Transparency in China: Rhetoric, Reality, and Rationale | 1 |
| 2 | Media Transparency | 29 |
| 3 | Meta-Censorship: A Justification Problem | 53 |
| 4 | Pandemic Media Corruption: An Ownership Problem? | 77 |
| 5 | Marketization and Conglomeration of State-Owned Media: A Market-Oriented Corporate Governance Myth? | 101 |
| 6 | "Opening a Skylight": Media Activism Revived? | 123 |
| 7 | Transparency Illusion and Disjuncture of Representation | 149 |
| Afterword | | 165 |
| Bibliography | | 167 |
| Index | | 191 |
| About the Author | | 195 |

# Foreword

Contemporary China is often, if not always, referred to as an authoritarian state, or one-party state. One of the defining features of Chinese authoritarianism is pointed out to be the overwhelming control of the media by the Communist Party of China. Chinese government's suppression of freedom of expression is often analyzed in terms of the goodness of liberal democracy and benefit of the market. In other words, the problems of not having a healthy media in contemporary China are interpreted as a direct consequence of the state's intervention and control. If and when China practices liberal democracy and market freedom, the problems will go away.

However, a careful examination of the media situation in contemporary China will demonstrate that the framework of media freedom is not adequate enough (adequate to some extent in that there is a lack of freedom, there is censorship, and there is crackdown on dissidents from time to time) to explain the complexity of how the media is structured and how media works in contemporary China. There are at least the following that cannot be easily explained by the freedom model:

- There is an increasing freedom for the media in China, especially in social media.
- It is the government's official policy to encourage the media to hold some power holders accountable.
- There does not seem to be a conflict between the marketized media and state. In fact the media is marketized, but the market is managed by the state.
- There is a whole set of what Dr. Baohui Xie calls malpractices in the Chinese media which are promoted by market freedom and supported by the party at the same time.

- Though the term *propaganda* is still used in Chinese officialdom, such as "the Minister of Propaganda," it is not meant to mean the same as it is understood in the West. The Chinese government could easily change the term and call their propaganda ministry "the Ministry of Information" for instance. For the Chinese state, media should play a role of education in encouraging positive values and attitudes. Criticism can be offered but must be constructive. Exposure for the sake of exposure and for sensationalism should not be allowed.
- There have been a series of media reform purporting to commercialize the media and to reduce direct party control.

How to explain the complexity of the Chinese media in a more nuanced and adequate way is the main purpose of this book. To do this Dr. Xie avoids the most convenient, cliché model of liberal democracy and market freedom. Instead, he focuses on the issue of media transparency. With this focus Dr. Xie ties together several theoretical issues and practical problems in contemporary Chinese media. Practical problems include of course the lack of freedom of expression, the censorship, corruption, commercialization of news, fabrication of news and event, and various malpractices. Theoretical issues include what is media transparency, why marketization leads to corruption and a whole set of malpractices, the relationship between the state and the market, and crucially the disposition, or what Dr. Xie calls "disjuncture," of political representation. The CCP does not represent what it claims to represent politically and economically. The party is not the party of the people or the working class but the party of the capital. The media is not the media of the party or the state but the media of the corporate. The book therefore offers a nuanced explanation of the development of the Chinese media from the tool of the state to person of the corporate, the development of the state from that of the country to that of the capital, of how marketization has failed to lead to media pluralism and of how the media collaborates with state to undermine the voices of the weak and the marginalized. The media problem is no longer a black-and-white issue of censorship and state control. Rather, the contemporary Chinese media is a bastard of capitalization of the Party and the marketization of the state.

Let me finish this brief piece by recounting something personal about the author of this important book. Baohui was a lecturer of English at Jiangxi Normal University in Nanchang, the capital of Jiangxi Province, before he was given a scholarship by the University of Adelaide to carry out a PhD program at the Centre for Asian Studies. Baohui was the first from Jiangxi to win an international scholarship for a doctorate degree in social sciences from The University of Adelaide. He was also the first from mainland China in the field of social sciences to have been awarded the Dean's Commendation for Doctoral Thesis Excellence at The University of Adelaide. This reflects Dr. Xie's excellent diligence and talent, which are clearly shown in the book.

—Mobo Gao
Professor and Chair of Chinese Studies
University of Adelaide
Adelaide, September 2013

# Acknowledgments

This book is based on my doctoral thesis completed at the University of Adelaide in 2012. I am very grateful to the University for its generous full Adelaide Scholarship International (Research), which made it a lot easier for me to come to Australia in February 2009.

I would extend my sincere gratitude to my supervisors Professor Mobo Gao and Dr. Gerry Groot, who have been inspiring and encouraging during my study. A number of Australian friends also offered generous help with proofreading. They are Mr. Colin Schumacher, Mr. Darren Loechel and Mrs. Helen Dunkley. I also feel much indebted to Dr. Zhang Shaoquan who introduced me to the field of Chinese studies.

I would like to thank my family, including my parents, sister, my dear wife Ling, and son Shengjia for their unreserved helping hands and understanding, especially during my busiest days over the past few years.

# Introduction

Democracy and freedom are something that many like to demarcate China and the West with. The absence of the western liberal democracy, in particular, is considered by many as the root of the stifling information control and other problems of the media in China, and hence, the liberal free market and free press as the solution. However, when it comes to such a dark side of the story as the blatant collusion between the private media and the American government in silencing the voice against the Iraqi War in 2003, the News International phone-hacking scandal fermented in the United Kingdom in 2011, and most recently in January 2014, the Australian Prime Minister Tony Abbott's harsh criticism, with a threat of funding cuts, of the state-owned Australian Broadcasting Corporation for "taking everyone's side but Australia's" and of the creation of the latter's fact-checking team, the viability of the Western model as a cure-all solution turns out to be questionable. Furthermore, proposals of copying the western libertarian model usually rest on a state-versus-media dichotomy, which considers the media as a natural and inherent enemy and, therefore, martyr of state control. As a result, much attention and sentiment has been paid to the Chinese censorship apparatus and clampdown stories. However, it does not take a genius to realize that the relationship between the Party-state and the reformed and profit-seeking media in the post-Mao era can hardly qualify a confrontational one, although the media may sometimes grumble about lack of "press freedom" when information controls intensifies upon the occurring of some particular media events. In effect, the Party-state and the media have developed a mutually accommodating framework within which both are beneficiary players vying for power and profits, at the cost of the voice of the weak and poor.

In light of the inadequacy of Western liberal democracy and press freedom rhetoric for framing the problems of the media in China, this book turns to the perspective of media transparency. Targeting political and market control, media transparency aims to hold both politics and the media responsible to the public sphere in terms of openness, credibility, accountability and relevance. While the ideas of transparency and supervision by public opinion seem to have gained increasing popularity and to be offering a potential solution to the pandemic problems that are plaguing the media, there exists a significant distance between the positive connotations of the rhetoric and a gloomy version of the reality as these concepts have yet to be substantiated.

Thence, this book aims to answer a number of questions related to the failure of official transparency rhetoric and increasing market incentives and prosperity to generate substantial transparency and sets out to identify the undermining causes of the problems. Media transparency, the center of this discussion, is a multi-faceted prism that reflects the policy environment, the roles of the market, management, and professional activities. The media administration and the media should be transparent, and the practices should offer an unobtrusive and penetrating lens through which truth can be presented to the public, also in a transparent manner. Moreover, media transparency is closely related to business and professional activities that are affected not only by government policies and rules but also by management and corporate governance in a vibrant market environment. Meanwhile, the discussion dismisses the state-versus-media cliché and demythologizes the market discourses as it is paradoxical to take for granted that the marketized media outlets and their senior management, which have benefited both financially and politically, would rise up against the system in which their benefits are rooted.

The question of media transparency is almost as broad as the complexity it has to get through:

- What is media transparency?
- How and why the censorship reality is rampant yet denied both by the government, and interestingly, by the media as well?
- What has resulted in media corruption that has hampered media transparency?
- Why has the post-Mao media boom failed to lead to adequate media transparency?
- Why has the skylight phenomenon failed in reviving the pre-1949 media activism?

Answering these questions, I will argue that China's media transparency illusion, or the gulf between official transparency rhetoric and censorship reality, should not be simply understood as the conflict between state power and the media, or only a matter of censorship. Instead, it demonstrates the discrepancy between what the Party-state and the media are and what they claim themselves to be. The discrepancy has led to their refusal to substantiate the concept of transparency and supervision by public opinion. The Party-state and the media have largely reached a consensus on political control and pursuit of profits, and the media system is reformed to suit this consensus. This discrepancy and consensus have led to various problems that have hampered media transparency. Finally, I will put the question of media transparency in its socio-political context to bring out the notion that the transparency illusion results from the disjuncture of political representation of both the Party-state and the media. The very first step toward media transparency is a substantial debate over its substance and causal implications to political representation, which is the main concern of this study.

This book draws on David Heald's discussion of "transparency illusion" (Heald 2006b, 34) and points out that such illusion prevails in the Chinese media system. Identifying the political and market control to be the cause of the gulf between transparency rhetoric and reality, the chapters analyze the political factors underpinning the illusion and reveal a "disjuncture of representation" (H. Wang 2011a, 85) of the Party-state and the media. The media administration policy rationale, problems concerning media management and the rising media activism are discussed herein. Further, the disjuncture of political representation is addressed to explain why the market success of the media has failed to lead to pluralism and empowerment of underrepresented voices. Such a representation problem has beset the macro environment in which policy making, business management, and professional activities are involved.

This book proposes that the lack of substance does not necessarily result from the conflict between state power and the media but should be considered more panoramically by looking at the political and market control exerted on the public sphere jointly by the Party-state and the media outlets, and its implications resulting from the disjuncture of their political representation. For this purpose, various sub-themes are discussed regarding meta-censorship, media corruption, business management and conglomeration, and media activism. Each chapter carries a sub-theme or sub-argument. Various perspectives are adopted individually or combined to allow a qualitative exploration into the sub-themes in these chapters.

In doing so, this book adopts a multi-thematic approach and develops a number of sub-themes from chapters 2 to 6 to support the main argument. A combination of conceptual analysis and historical comparative case study is adopted to support this approach so that the multi-faceted implications of media transparency can be examined carefully. This approach regards "concept as a system of interrelated concepts," a methodology that is more popularly used in the study of linguistics (Goldstone, Feng, and Rogosky 2005, 287). A concept, as expounded by Goldstone et al., "can only be understood if an entire system of interrelated concepts is acquired." As "the content of each concept is wholly determined by implicational relations to other concepts of the system," the task of conceptual analysis, according to C. I. Lewis, is to "map out these relations" (Brown 2007, 131). Such a process of "explication" as "the first business of conceptual analysis" sees the breaking up of a multi-faceted concept or terminology into a number of thematic concepts that provide explicit explanation to the top concept in return (Schilpp 1968, 29). This approach has a significant role to play in that the lack of transparency in the conceptual domain more often results from a concept that bears taken-for-granted good connotations being deliberately distorted, manipulated, and hollowed out by the elite politics and the media.

Moreover, a historical comparative case study is made in analyzing media phenomena that have a comparative significance. Case study is an empirical approach to verify a theory in the real world (Andrew, Pederson, and McEvoy 2011, 132). As Robert K. Yin (2003, 1) argues, it is a generally preferred strategy for answering "how" and "why" questions, particularly when the focus is on a contemporary phenomenon within some real-life and historical context. Comparative case study can be used to compare a case procured by conventional means with another similar case (Dubben and Williams 2009, 88). Furthermore, a historical comparative case study aims to identify causal patterns that are associated with distinct historical occurrence which bears historical resemblance (Onyegam 2006, 11). This method allows for selecting cases for comparing phenomena in different historical contexts so as to identify manipulated interpretation of the past and to avoid misinterpretation of the present.

This methodology is useful particularly when history is involved in interpreting the present, imagining the future, or "the focus on contemporary as opposed to historical phenomena" (Yin 2003, 1). As Peter C. Rollins suggests, misinterpretation of the present is largely attributable to inaccurate understanding of the past when one relies on the past to understand the present (Rollins 2003, xiv). The deepening effect on investigation by comparative case study, as Charles C. Ragin (1987, 77) suggests, is the explanatory effect of the variables on various cases that share common features. Given that cases in different historical stages may share such common features, overconcentration of these features may lead to exaggeration of similarity, ignorance of key variables and hence misinterpretation. To avoid this misinterpretation and engage in historical comparative case study, identifying cases and comparability are essential. According to Kaarbo and Beasley (1999, 379–380), selection of cases is "to establish the relationship between two or more variables," and "comparability depends on the theoretical basis of the study." Therefore, comparing variables between these cases can reveal their different implications for a certain investigation especially when there exists a prevailing misunderstanding caused by simplistic or uncritical association of the past in interpreting the present.

For example, chapter 6 uses a historical comparative case study to select and analyze media activisms in different historical stages. The chapter gives a historical account of the pre-1949 media activism and analyzes various blank spaces left on publications, dubbed "skylights," in the reform era. These blank spaces are often interpreted as protest against censorship and paralleled with the anti-censorship and pro-democracy media activism before 1949. The analysis with comparative perspective distinguishes the skylights of the reform era from the pre-1949 activism so as to demythologize the transparency illusion borne on misinterpretation of the key variables of the media activisms in the past and present. These key variables are political engagement, participatory elements, and ideological consensus. The relationship between the variables of the activisms in the two periods is established upon the similarity in their historical backdrops, namely the one-party-rule political system and heavy censorship. The comparability of these variables lies in their implications for press freedom and democracy. This chapter will show that misinterpretation of the pre-1949 media activism is attributed to the ignorance of the broad participation and the ideological consensus on press freedom and democracy among the participants. Such broad participation and consensus is tellingly absent in the reform era, especially after 1989, which determines the major weaknesses of the media activism among the marketized media.

This book consists of seven chapters. Following the introductory chapter 1, chapter 2 outlines the theoretical framework in which the definition of media transparency is discussed in order to set up the targets and realm of the study. Drawing on the general principles of transparency, this chapter develops the concept of media transparency and identifies the impact of the current rules, the degrees of transparency, and various constraining elements.

Chapter 3 analyzes how and why censorship is applied yet denied by various discursive strategies. This chapter argues that censorship is censored because the Party-state and the media are unable to justify their censorship regime. The justification problem is rooted in the incompatibility of communist ideology and the capitalist economic base, a matter of political economy. As a result, the Party becomes increasingly disjunct from its communist values and the media from its public nature, breeding the current censorship apparatus geared around secrecy and uncertainty.

Chapter 4 discusses the current phenomena of professional malpractice including fabricated and misleading news, a rampant problem that not only renders the prolonged official *"Sanxiang Xuexi Jiaoyu Huodong"* [Three Learning and Education Programs] void and futile but also hampers the further development of media transparency.[1] Instead of looking at the professional malpractice as a problem of individual and ideological weakness that official discussion intends us to believe, the chapter shows that the problem is rooted in the market, and the ethical and the identity dilemmas for the grassroots professionals. These dilemmas result from political control and market forces and further demonstrate the disjuncture of political representation of the Party-state and the media.

Chapter 5 discusses media marketization and conglomeration. It asks why business management and conglomeration have failed to lead the media from financial prosperity and autonomy to expanding the public sphere. Instead of being marginalized, Party leadership has been duly reinforced and consolidated *through* conglomerated corporate governance. Meanwhile, the line between the state-owned media's commitment as public institutions and their role of a mechanism of power as Party assets becomes increasingly blurred. This chapter demythologizes the predication of press freedom on market forces, arguing that the consensus on political control and pursuit of profits, which is reached between the Party-state and the media, leads to nowhere but rhetoric and illusion.

Chapter 6 explores media activism such as leaving blank spaces on newsprints. Using historical comparative case study, this chapter argues that the media activism today is drastically different from that in the pre-1949 period in terms of participatory elements and ideological consensus. These differences have determined the major weaknesses of the media activism in the post-Mao era. As a result, the Party-state remains coercive; profit-driven outlets loathe challenging the censorship apparatus; activist professionals and editorial practice are vulnerable to both political and market control. This analysis dethrones deliberate misinterpretation of the present by borrowing the legacy of the past, and further reveals the disjuncture of political presentation of the commercialized media.

Finally, chapter 7 is concluding as well as pointing to future discussion. This chapter argues that the transparency illusion revealed herein derives from the lack of substance of officially defined concepts such transparency, freedom, and democracy. Underneath the misleading gloss of these concepts are deliberate emptiness, obscurity, and confusion so that state and market control can be attained and maintained at the discretion of the powerful. The lack of substance is determined by the Party-state and the media's disjuncture of political representation and their collusive joint suppression of the voice of the weak and poor. This disjuncture of representation is entrenched in official rhetoric, market discourses, and restructured relationships within the media system. Rethinking the freedom of information in China, therefore, cannot afford to bypass the problem of political representation.

This book, made as a preliminary quest for substantive transparency in a highly state-controlled and market-oriented environment, is an invitation to debate and further study. The complexity of media transparency and especially of its relationship with politics and the market, like many other contemporary ideals and concept, however, prohibits any uncritical reverence crowned to its nominal value. The main goal of this book, which seeks to identify the causes of the concept being blurred, emptied, and hollowed out, and subsequently attempts to substantiate it, will have been realized if this preliminary quest can be further developed by those who are interested in similar topics.

## NOTE

1. The TLEP was launched in October 2003 by the CPD, aiming at massive education of socialist journalistic values and ethics among the media professionals. It is an ongoing program for all journalists and editorial staffers who are requested to participate in the program in form of on-site and off-site training courses. The CPD, GAPP, and SARFT also organize officials and specialists for lecturing tour nationwide.

## Chapter One

# Press Freedom and Transparency in China

*Rhetoric, Reality, and Rationale*

### THE GULF BETWEEN TRANSPARENCY AND PRESS FREEDOM RHETORIC AND INFORMATION CONTROL REALITY

Never before have the Chinese people been able to get access to as much information as they can today.[1] A media boom has gained momentum since the start of the reform era in the late 1970s. As shown in figure 1.1, The media industry has grown into a multi-billion dollar business with 1,937 newspapers, 251 radio stations, and 272 television stations by the end of 2009 (Cui 2009, 4). The number of radio and TV stations,[2] which provide combined radio and television broadcasting services, mounted to 2,579 (GAPPRFT 2013a). Media's overall turnover reached 246 billion yuan in 2005, went up to 422.08 billion yuan in 2008 (Cui 2009, 7), surged to 637.88 billion yuan in 2011 (D. He, Zhang, and Wang 2012, 22) and maintained its momentum in 2012 by growing to 760 billion yuan (Cui 2013). The availability of daily newspapers per 1,000 people reached 97.6 copies in 2012, an increase of 2.7 percent from the previous year (GAPP 2013). The digitalized media has also experienced a dramatic growth at the threshold of the second decade in the new millennium. The revenue of the online video businesses alone surged from 3.14 billion yuan in 2010 to 9.25 billion yuan in 2012, with a twofold relayer of 6.27 billion yuan in 2011 (GAPPRFT 2013b). As of the end of June 2013, China remains the world's biggest nation of netizens with an Internet population of 5.91 hundred million, and among the 26.56

million new online users in the first half of 2013, 70 percent are of the smart phone generation (CNNIC 2013). It is against this backdrop that the news media are able to play an increasingly important role, not only as a platform for information, but to some extent, also for expression. More importantly, the editorial content is no longer uniform.

One of the media's roles is as a watchdog acclaimed by the Chinese government in official documents and speeches, particularly after the Hu Jintao–Wen Jiabao Administration's proposal of "Constructing a harmonious society" in 2005. This proclaimed a shift of priorities from economic growth to resolving the problems resulting from increasingly prominent social tensions (Saich 2006, 37). The media is crucial to this call because it is hard to imagine social harmony without adequate mass communication and relatively open public discussion. To achieve these aims, the Chinese government has added "openness" to the official parlance as a demonstration of its efforts to improve government-citizen relations and ultimately its legitimacy. In the *Report of the Work of the Government* (2009) presented in the annual session of the National People's Congress[3] on March 5, 2010, Premier Wen Jiabao, on behalf of the State Council, stated that:

> We will promote transparency of administrative affairs, improve regulations for transparent governance and administrative review, create conditions for the people to criticize and oversee the government, let the news media fully play their oversight role, and exercise power openly. (Crossick 2010; Wen 2010)

Apart from Wen's pledge, many new regulations have been stipulated to promote an ostensibly journalism-friendly environment. The *Measures for*

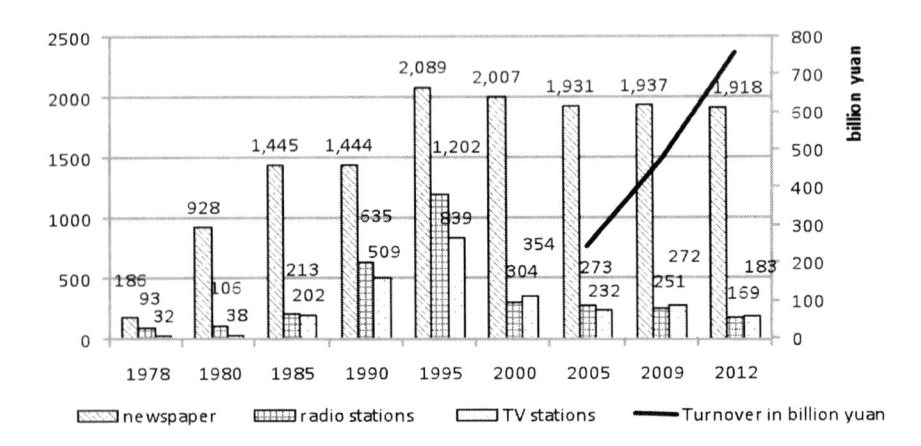

**Figure 1.1.** Number of newspapers, radio stations, and TV stations from 1978–2012.

*the Administration of Press Cards* (MAPC), for example, was issued by the General Administration of Press and Publication (GAPP) in 2004 and revised in 2009. This administrative regulation declares in article 5 the protection of journalists and their professional activities by law, and requires government agencies and their staff members at all levels to provide necessary facilities and protection. It states that "Any organization or individual shall not interfere in or obstruct the lawful activities of the press institutions and journalists" (GAPP 2009). Ostensive restraints on activities of foreign journalists were also reduced in 2008 as a signal to the international community that China is becoming more open and tolerant (Olesen 2011, 121). To exhibit the government's welcome of supervision by public opinion [*yulun jiandu*],[4] the idea of *transparency* was for the first time included in the *Twelfth Five-Year Plan* in March 2011.[5] President Xi Jinping, on behalf of the new top leadership succeeding the Hu Jintao–Wen Jiabao Administration, reiterated the significance of "maintaining honest and clean by keeping transparency [*yi touming bao lianjie*]" at a meeting of the Central Political Legal Commission in January 2014.[6]

These official pledges and actions might be taken as increasing transparency. However, there is an obvious gap between the official transparency rhetoric and information control reality. On the one hand, increased government transparency through supervision by public opinion is positively affirmed in official discourse, while on the other, the public sphere is from time to time stifled (M. Gao 2004a, 2110). It is not uncommon that open discussion of sensitive issues is banned and outspoken journalists suspended, fired, or even jailed. Censorship and self-censorship mechanisms are employed to filter sensitive key words, ban public discussion of sensitive issues, and block access to foreign databases such as wikipedia.org and social networks such facebook.com (H. Wang 2010, 40). The government has sponsored a number of firewall projects such as the Great Firewall, the Green Dam Project and the Golden Shield Project to monitor and control online content and activities (Deibert, Palfrey, Rohozinski, and Zittrain 2011). Also, some China-based websites such as sina.com, tudou.com, and youku.com have classified part of their video content to make it unavailable for viewers outside China's borders.

The official transparency parlance is defined here as rhetoric because the Party-state has hardly specified, despite its ongoing promotion of this concept, what transparency is and to what extent transparency can be realized through supervision by public opinion. At best, while implying it is an unmitigated good word in and of itself, the official concept of transparency is no different from the better known catchword of openness. This explains why the adoption of e-government and promulgation of *Decree of Government Information Openness*[7] are described officially as symbolic moving toward transparency (Weifeng Liu 2007). At worst, transparency is no more than a figure of speech and a meaningless subject of cynicism. Yet, as hollow as it is, this concept can nevertheless be manipulated by elite politics that holds the discourse power to employ and manipulate any concept and to resist any attempt toward substantiating the concept, including that of transparency.

The difficulty in substantiating the concept of transparency and materializing it through journalism is rooted in the Party-state's fear for and consequent limit of both transparency and journalism. At a symposium on journalism organized by the Central Publicity Department (CPD) on November 28, 1989, Jiang Zemin in his capacity as General Secretary of the CCP, defined press freedom and transparency as well as their connection as follows:

> Under the socialist system, journalism is no longer the business of private owners, but that of the Party and the people. It is to maintain the fundamental interest of the people that no freedom will be given to any illegal journalistic activities that attempt to change the socialist system, and these activities must be punished according to law. Press freedom is an important method of "peaceful evolution" for the international hostile forces and bourgeois liberalization advocates.

I would also like to address the popular question of *transparency*. . . . Some things should be and must be transparent; some other things cannot be transparent immediately and can become transparent only when the right time comes; some things are not meant to be transparent at all. . . . Some people are either naive and ignorant or conspiratorial to request transparency by all means and think this is democracy and freedom. What can be transparent, what cannot be transparent, what can be more transparent than it is, are by all means determined by the interests of the Party, of the nation and of the people and by whether such transparency is conducive to the stability of the society, political order, economy, and public opinion (Z. Jiang 1999, 258).[8]

Jiang's talk is a telling demonstration of the Party logic of journalism, by which "the CCP insists that the media are its mouthpiece" (Yuezhi Zhao 1998, 2). Despite the ongoing conglomeration and restructured corporate governance, the state-owned journalism, posing as increasingly marketized and reader-oriented public institutions, remain Party-state assets. Firstly, according to Jiang, both press freedom and transparency are not something laudable unless they serve the interests of the Party because they can also be used against the Party-state and the political system. Secondly, the Party logic rejects any causal connection between press freedom and transparency because freedom and transparency beyond the Party's definition are considered to be no more than fantasies for "naïve and ignorant" people or "conspirators." Thirdly and most importantly, the definition of press freedom and transparency is determined at the discretion of the Party because the scope of the *nation* and the *people* is too vague while the Party is the only definite entity that holds the power and has the ability to define the concept. Therefore, any interpretation or specification of the concepts of transparency and press freedom beyond the interest of the Party-state is not legitimate, and consequently unwanted.

On the other hand, the substance of transparency has not been a concern of outsider observers. Central to most concerns about press freedom in existing discussions has been censorship and the information control reality. This reality exists despite the increasing marketization and prosperity of the media industry. It is this which seems to have attracted attention from many liberal observers in the West. According to liberalism, which is grounded largely on the belief in liberty and equality of individuals (R. Song 2006, 45; Young 2002, 39), censorship is a vehicle of authoritarian state power which not only suppresses dissident voices but also threatens "the ideal of transparency" (Vernon 1998, 115). The resistance to censorship that Vernon mentioned is also manifested in the condemnation of the Chinese censorship system because the rights of individuals to free expression and access to information are strangled.[9] Criticism of censorship in China can easily be found in opinions in Western media such as the British Broadcasting Corporation, the Voice of America, and the Cable News Network,[10] reports by non-government organizations such as Reporters Without Borders and China Human Rights Defenders, and articles and books by Diaspora Chinese dissidents such as Cao Changqing, and media such as *Epochtimes*, to name just a few.[11] But censorship-centered discussion often leads to bitterness and desperation because there seems to be an endless list of clampdowns by Chinese authorities, and the state-versus-media cliché more often pins its advocate on the subversion of the state. By listing the stories of censorship and its chilling effect, focus is fixed on the censorship apparatus to such an extent that this "harping on about censorship" considers censorship as the center subject of all problems.

This constant refrain leads many to the belief that eliminating censorship and embarking on Western liberal democracy and free market will be the solution. Unfortunately, this perspective neglects other critical facets of the complexity that constitute freedom and transparency. More often than not, liberal discussions of the censorship reality subscribe to free market and privatization (Ang and Wang 2010; X. Zhu 1998, 2006). The market discourses of press freedom usually start with a censorship problem and conclude with a proposed predication on free market and privatization.

## IT IS NOT ALL ABOUT CENSORSHIP

In a 2010 CNN online report (Facsar 2010), for example, a number of university students in Hong Kong from the Mainland were interviewed to give their comments on Chinese information control. They attributed the increase in

Chinese students studying abroad and the success of universities in Hong Kong, Singapore, and Japan over their counterparts in the Mainland to the help of the Party-state censorship system. "I love my country, but I don't want to give up on my right to access information," said one to explain his not returning to the Mainland in the report. By delivering concerns over the fractured freedom of information in China, the article creates the impression that it is the censorship system alone that is responsible if a patriotic Chinese student chooses to leave home and stay overseas.

But one's motives to seek a personal future overseas can hardly be a simple equation of liking or dislike of censorship. China became the world's biggest exporter of international students in 2006, with 14 percent share of the internationally mobile students worldwide.[12] To most of those who have left the Mainland to study or work in places like Hong Kong and other Western countries, seeking better opportunities for education, employment, business, living conditions, and academic and professional development is the overwhelming motivation. As stated in an IDP Education report, there is "a clear positive relationship between education attainment and future wage earnings."[13] Wealthier destinations such as the United States, the United Kingdom, and Australia are on top of the choice list followed by Japan, Canada and New Zealand.[14] Domestic economic growth, expectations of parents, better proof of competence with a foreign degree, positive attitudes of the Chinese government toward studying abroad, or the inadequacies in Chinese higher education, and the physical and cultural attraction of Western societies constitute a "push and pull effect" for those students (M. Yang 2007, 3–4). The study of Li and Bray (2007) and Varghese (2008) also shows that students from the mainland in Hong Kong are attracted mainly by the better education quality there. The relatively free access to information is part of the agreeable environment, which understandably, is preferable. However, there is little research evidence to support the claims that it is the censorship system per se that has driven these promising youth to go and stay overseas or that it should take the blame for a "brain drain."

Such focus-on-censorship perspective takes censorship as the kernel of the problem of freedom of information. This is a minimized and oversimplified conflict between the censorship apparatus or state power and "the media." Journalism is also simply divided into two opposite sides, with one having "abandoned professional ethics and participated actively in the all-out promotion of the Party's interests" and the other having "risked being fired or jailed in the process" to win the increase of press freedom (Reporters Without Borders 2009). Any fault found with press freedom is therefore redirected to the "original sin" of censorship as a whole.

Such a perspective, however, usually fails to address the fact that censorship is not something exclusive to China. It tends to stress the CCP clampdown and futility of the media under political pressure, implying that there cannot be press freedom in a communist regime. This "all or nothing" approach increases resentment of the government's administrative role, particularly that of a communist regime. Yet, it fails to explain the far greater information accessibility, availability, and diversity today despite the presence of this censorship regime. This approach has not produced an ideal pattern of what transparency through journalism might become in the future, nor can it provide a valid solution to the existing problem in that it is very unlikely that censorship or centralized state power is ready to give in within the short run.

Such censorship-focused perspective avoids discussion of censorship as a controversial issue that involves arguable facts (Vernon 1998, 116). One of the facts is that censorship still exists in highly developed democracies such as the United Kingdom,[15] the United States,[16] Australia,[17] Canada and Germany.[18] Furthermore, over-concentration on censorship per se significantly lacks consensus on how changes should be made. Some dissidents such as Cao Changqing (2010a, 2010b) advocate overthrowing the Communist regime with violence, and many others, such as Zhu Xueqin (1998), hold belief in "expansion of incrementalism" in social reform. However, neither of these perspectives has been able to go any deeper in addressing why censorship has not been eliminated in the much freer and more democratic West, nor has it hampered the prosperity of the media industry in the much more intensively controlled China.

The over-concentration on censorship is based upon the narrow perspective that the free flow of information and transparency is hindered by the censorship apparatus and communism. These approaches are rooted in the approval of Western liberal democratic system and are more often than not based on "privatization of the state-owned media" (Ang and Wang 2010). The understanding of press freedom and transparency is simplified as journalism without censorship in a Western style democratic system and free market. It is considered to be a limited perspective because it deals with only part of the problem of Chinese media, an issue no more than the "operational component" of "process transparency," or the "nominal" aspect of the "transparency illusion," which David Heald (2006b, 32) describes as a matter of "application of rules, regulations and measures to a particular case." This book, nevertheless, is by no means defending censorship or trivializing censorship with relativism. While it is largely true that censorship exists and government clampdowns stand in the way of free flow of information, the issue of media transparency is a matter that should be observed from a more panoramic view.

## PRESS FREEDOM AND THE HABERMASIAN PUBLIC SPHERE

Free press is regarded as an indispensible part of democracy from liberal perspectives.[19] However, it is critical "to clarify what press freedom and whose press freedom we are talking about" (Hardt 2000, 93; Yuezhi Zhao 2011, 122) and in what way this freedom is possible. The following discussion explains why liberal perspectives of press freedom are problematic in discussing the Chinese media and why media transparency instead is essential so as to prepare the ground work to develop the narrative.

The liberal concept of press freedom dates back to John Milton's argument of unlicensed publication in the seventeenth century.[20] Press freedom implies freed communication and expression through the media. According to article 19 of the Universal Declaration of Human Rights adopted by the United Nations in 1948, it means that:

> Everyone has the rights to freedom of opinion and expression: this right includes the freedom to hold opinions without interference and to seek, receive and impart information and ideas through any media and regardless of any frontiers.[21]
>
> To preserve these rights, constitutional and legal provisions are usually adopted by liberal states to assert minimum interference from coercive state power. Among the best known are the 1689 English Bill of Rights and 1791 First Amendment to the United States Constitution.[22] The liberal perspective of press freedom is celebrated in established Western democracies to such an extent that M. Rodwan Abouharb and David L. Cingranelli (2007, 212) claim that "Only a liberal democracy with a bill of rights and an independent judiciary to uphold it can prevent the tyranny of the majority" in protection of "certain liberties such as freedom of speech, association and press." Other liberals, John Whale (1977, 154) and Zhu Xueqin (X. Zhu 1998, 2006), for instance, have argued for a free market because they believe that market imperatives enable the press to write *whatever* they like freely.

Apart from its ideological stem, the neoliberal claims of press freedom also draw heavily on the Habermasian argument of "cultural and political public sphere made possible and supported by the mass media" (Habermas 2005, 289). Habermas's belief in the public sphere and the mass media lies in his approval of the dominance by experts of "professional abilities" and intellectuals who supposedly "consider . . . all relevant points of view impartially" and "take all interests involved equally into account" (Habermas 2005, 290). Many of these "experts," however, are paid or sponsored intellects, who more often claim themselves to be independent and impartial, within the elite conceptual system. This system sustains the official or mainstream ideology, ideals, and various concepts in a much depoliticized manner, which, in turn, constantly update and support the system. The experts are able and equipped to coin, systemize, and manipulate ideals and discourses, including the popular concept of transparency itself, in favor of the elite politics by gearing up the linguistic innovation borrowing the afterglow of the Enlightenment legacy. The carefully and wisely designed conceptual system, as hollow and empty, as lofty and reverential it may seems to be, constitutes an effective ideological defence for the elite politics and its legitimacy, and suppresses substantial expansion of the public sphere.

In addition, the source of the acclaimed experts' impartiality and equality has hardly been identified whatsoever and, therefore problematic and unaccountable. Such so-called impartiality and bias-free professionalism stance usually pay no attention to the internal relationships within the media system. Such internal factors as labor relationships, journalist subjectivity, public nature of the public sphere, and political representation usually are not research subject from market or professionalism perspectives or within state-media binary frameworks. This is a typical problem of the elite ideal system that keeps producing sophisticated concepts, transparency, for instance, and yet refrains from and even prevents engaging substantive exploration intensively and extensively. Likewise, not only has the Habermasian proposal of public sphere created a phantasmic romance of free media as an actual entity occupying a particular space, his presupposition of elite idealism has in effect mystified the nature, purpose and value of public sphere. As Vincent Mosco (1996, 154) has insightfully pointed out,

> What we call the public media is public not because it occupies a separate space, relatively free from market considerations, but because it is constituted out of a particular patterning of processes that privilege the democratic over commodification. To the extent that it does not, the expression public media diminishes in value.

The problems of media transparency in China, for the same reason, can hardly be solved without further looking into the elite ideal system and being revealed in the way that Michel Foucault questioned and rejected the "blackmail of Enlightenment" (Foucault 2000, 312).

The problems of transparency and press freedom in China, therefore, can hardly be tackled without questioning why these ideas always allude to positive connotations but fall short of practicality. Shall we accept the new ideas and concepts as markers of modernity, or should we go beyond their superficial suggestions and question their causes and purposes? Just because an idealistic concept or principle may sound divine and promise some universal value does not mean any default significance substantive and operational to those struggling at the bottom of the social strata whose voice has been muzzled and representation absent in the Habermasian public sphere. However, while the substance of public discourse, such as public media, public sphere, transparency, and press freedom, keeps diminishing in the elite conceptual system, questioning such lack of substance may evoke interrogations like "Don't you want transparency?" or "Are you trying to go against press freedom?"

Such rhetorical questions are pointless. Habermas's trust in the reverend of expertise and experts echoes the trend of rationality in the modern European political culture and coincides with the fashionable elite culture in China's politics and niche market oriented media as well. Actually, it demonstrates the source of the "crisis of rationality" that Max Weber antithesized (H. Wang 1997, 5). In this crisis, all lofty ideals and concepts such as freedom, democracy, and transparency, once manufactured, manipulated, and emasculated in the elite conceptual system, can be deceptive and suppressive. One has to ask more profound questions before gulping down these ideas without thinking beyond their appealingly implied denotations and connotations. Rightfully, Wang Hui (1997, 9) has asked a question of "Modernity? Whose agenda of modernity?" Mobo Gao (2011) has also interrogated the popular idea of democracy by asking "Democracy? What democracy?" Likewise, this book attempts to provoke thinking, beyond the state-versus-media dichotomy, of the political causes that have frustrated the ideas of freedom of information and transparency in the reformed China.

As Kaarle Nordenstreng (2011, 85) opines, the concept of "freedom of the press" is "misleading" because it stresses and stretches the libertarian rights of the media and ignores those of the people expressing their voices *through* the media. Hence, uncritical use of the notion of press freedom can also be misleading without specifying the potential problems that cannot be adequately solved within the liberal press freedom framework.

Firstly, political influence on the free media is inevitable even in liberal democracies, let alone in an authoritarian context. While any liberal government can play a strong role in setting the press agenda (Bennett 1990; Norris, Kern, and Just 2003, 23), the media, public or private, does not necessarily regard this agenda as unfriendly or antagonistic. In a liberal democracy like the United States where there exist "independent media ownership, legally sanctioned press freedom, and formal institutional independence from the state" (Yuezhi Zhao 1998, 152), the media can be highly associated with the government's political agenda. This has been demonstrated in the fact that neither the idealized nor the institutionalized press freedom has been able to prevent the U.S. mass media from becoming a loyal messenger of the government and capital, as tellingly demonstrated in the media's rampant promotion of the 2003 Iraqi War and their curious absence of supervision over the Wall Street before the 2008 financial crisis hit (Yuezhi Zhao 2011, 122). Other examples include how the free and privately owned [New York] *Times* has been consistently silencing reporters and stories which may cause the government discomfort (M. Gao 2004a, 2106)[23]; and that Dan Rather,

CBS's former anchor for *Evening News*, openly uttered his unswerving loyalty in 2003 to then President George Bush (M. Gao 2004a, 2107).

Furthermore, the impossibility of press freedom in avoiding political influence can be seen in how Western liberal governments and courts, including those of the United States, Germany, the United Kingdom, and Canada, to name just a few, have been trying to exert impact on cyberspace content. According to Google's 2012 *Transparency Report*, the U.S.-based international search engine continues to be "disheartened" by removal requests from the United States, which, during the period from January to June 2011, increased by 70 percent comparing to the period between July and December 2010 during which Google deleted 1,100 search results according to six U.S. court orders (Burgess 2012). China also lodged three requests regarding 121 search results, during the period between January and June 2011, apparently less from those from the United States. Moreover, removal requests from the United States increased by 103 percent between July and December 2011 (Google 2012). The U.S. law enforcement departments and courts requested Google to remove search results regarding at least one blog, 1,400 videos on youtube.com, and 218 websites. In contrast, Google does not reveal any removal requests from China during this period (Google 2012). In terms of political influence over the media, the Google report shows that the liberal United States, where press freedom is highly developed and celebrated as one of its core value of libertarian human rights, is doing no better than China.

Google is also widely criticized for its possible misuse of search results including page ranking manipulation, violation of people's privacy, and self-censorship. Particularly, since Google announced its abandonment of a strict separation between search results and advertising in May 2012, rankings of search results have been given priority over non-advertisement information, and the advertisers simply bid for invisibility on the Google interfaces. Users will not be able to distinguish commercial advertisements from normal search results as one may be well misled by the Google's rationale of its search engine as one "that used links to determine the importance of individual webpages" (Google 2014). Its profit-driven rationale, however, is nowhere to be identified in its stated mission, which is "to organize the world's information and make it universally accessible and useful" (Google 2014). Its do-it-yourself ad, or AdWords, was introduced in 2000 as a self-service program for advertisers to create their own online advertisement campaigns. While advertisements are mixed up with regular search results and the ranking is determined by highest offers rather than importance and relevance, it is practically up to the users to judge the importance or relevance of the search results when they are actually relying on the Google interface. This way, Google is able to make profits with minimum accountability and responsibility for its possible misleading effects. Lack of transparency helps Google thrive in a culture of legally sanctioned business secrecy as much of the related criticism on its transparency problems pertains to issues that have not yet been addressed by the United States legal provisions that govern digital dissemination of digital information and information technology (Maurer et al. 2007).

Secondly, a literally independent press is not necessarily free of collusion with market forces and politics (Yuezhi Zhao 2011, 120). As James Curran and Jean Seaton (2010, 346) have critiqued, liberal theorists tend to argue that the freedom to publish in a free market guarantees pluralism and democracy and would deny the pitfalls of the market when expression of *certain* viewpoints is "missing." In a liberal context, the triangle relationship among commercialism, politics, and privately owned media may be established upon as much consensus on political influence and profits as possible in an authoritarian country. Amy Goodman and David Goodman (2006) have well illustrated such a triangle relationship in their 2006 book, which reveals in detail how the government deception, corporate profiteers, and media hypocrisy have become rampant in such a liberal state as the United States. This reality is contrary to John Whale (1977, 85) claim of reader's influence and reader-oriented content in a free marketplace. In an authoritarian context, the market per se is not adequate for realizing democracy and supervision by public opinion. As Chin-Chuan Lee (2000, 35) once commented, "The market may betray the ideals of democracy and Habermas's 'public sphere,' but from the pluralistic perspective it is also a necessary yet insufficient condition for checking on authoritarian state power."

Thirdly, a free media is not necessarily a transparent one, nor does it necessarily aim for transparency. Susan D. Moeller and her research team (2006) investigated twenty-five major news outlets, among which twenty-four are in liberal democracies including the United States and the United Kingdom, to examine these outlets' degree of transparency.[24] The investigation concludes that these outlets are keen to call for transparency but reluctant to practice transparency on themselves. According to Moeller's study, what these outlets manage best is "grudgingly" admitting to who owns them, and where they really do poorly is disclosing their guidelines for writing and editing stories. Lack of transparency in both practice and intention among the free media in liberal democracies has demonstrated that the notion of press freedom alone is inadequate to realize the freedom of communication and expression and, more importantly, inadequate to substantiate transparency.

The Party-state has borrowed the liberal market discourses in commercializing the media under close state supervision and in effect reinforced dominance by the state, capital and powerful interest groups. The official statistics over the reform decades has consistently shown the media industry spearheading market success. While the media spare no efforts in trumpeting the tone set by the Party-state (Yuezhi Zhao 2008a, 93), their content becomes increasingly irrelevant to everyday struggles of the disenfranchised groups (W. Sun 2008b), which include not only the vast rural population but also low-income, urban, working-class families and migrant workers (Yuezhi Zhao 2008a, 93). This has created a twofold problem. One is that while the media stay unswervingly in line with the Party line, they pose to have been forced to do so; the other is that while the media largely have no interest in voicing for the weak and the poor, they tend to lead us to believe that they have been prohibited to do so. The liberal market logic, as Lu Xinyu and Yuezhi Zhao (2010, 8) have pointed out, often attributes such problems to censorship and "incomplete marketization" and subsequently proposes further de-politicization and privatization. As a result, the media have increasingly subscribed to the class containment dimension and displaced class antagonism, and in turn, become in itself a "power of the market on behalf of the dominant political, economic, and cultural forces" (Yuezhi Zhao 2008a, 124) that shape the normative expectations and moral foundations paralleled with the thriving capitalist economy.

Lu and Zhao (Lu and Zhao 2010, 6) also suggest that liberal theories of journalism are inadequate to explain why the politically submissive and market-oriented media, both the Party outlets and non-Party ones, have "significantly marginalized the subjectivity of the workers and peasantry" in post-Mao journalism. Such marginalization is seen, at least in part, in the urbanization and middle-class orientation of the media content imposed on the rural community, which has in effect dismantled the social base for the rural subjectivity (Lu and Zhao 2010, 6). Endorsed by the WTO membership as a backdrop for de-politicization, naturalization and normalization of the neo-liberal market agenda (Yuezhi Zhao 2003, 36), editorial attention has been dedicated to the affluent urban elites and middle-class consumers as they are advertisers' marketing target groups (Yuezhi Zhao 2005, 70). Given that the media play a special role in forming subjectivity, Wanning Sun (2002, 33) also argues that the arrival of television broadcasting in rural China, which carries commercialized programs full of vicarious life in foreign and unknown places, marks the beginning of formation and transformation of a transnational imagination among rural residents who have not, will not, and cannot leave their rural premises for the overseas destination of that imagination. The irrelevance of the programmed content to the rural life and concerns has demonstrated the marginalization of the subjectivity of the poor and disenfranchised in commercialized content production and led to a deep gulf between the urban and rural realities as well as the commercialized media and the marginalized subjectivities.

## MORE FREEDOM TODAY?

Nevertheless, it is obvious that there is more freedom in the Western liberal democracies than in China, but also that there seems to be more freedom in China now than before. There is also much more flexibility in the new media, particularly social media such as *weibo* microblogs, than in the traditional media like newspapers, radio and television broadcasting services.

However, the talks on liberal press freedom are usually framed in terms of Western liberal democratic system, which is absent in China. This absence has made the idea of liberal press freedom even more irrelevant because this idea does not find a relevant social political environment to grow in, as metaphorized by Hu Zhifeng, a plant cannot grow properly without a right soil and environment (Yuezhi Zhao and Hu 2011, 14). This does not mean that China is not a suitable land for freedom and democracy but that a problem cannot be properly solved by introducing another problem or by a problematic solution. At best, the liberal talks call for copying the Western political and market systems and inevitably lead the Chinese media to the same problems in the West. At worst, these talks ignore the political and capital control in both Western democracies and capitalized autocracies, and justify and reinforce such control by promoting the bandwagon of elite conceptual rhetoric and market discourses.

Furthermore, despite the new openness demonstrated by the Party-state, tolerance of topics once considered taboo and increase of public choices of media outlets and content, journalism is still experiencing what McNally has called "a period of significant contraction" (McNally 2008a, 132). The increased freedom and flexibility result from adaptation rather than any significant changes of the Party-state's media administration regime. The increase of diversity is mostly seen in the non-political areas such as entertainment, sports, and finance that are not considered a threat to social stability and the political status quo. However, as Chin-Chuan Lee (2000, 9) argues, content diversity as the result of marketization is vulnerable to the distorting and restricting market forces in both liberal democracies and illiberal China.

Such distorting and restricting potential is demonstrated in how cultural and political boundaries are constantly being created by the media, and how such boundaries are negotiated between the media and state power as well as between the media and the market rather than between the media and those in need of faithful representation in the public sphere. As Wanning Sun (2009a, 2009b) has insightfully observed, the image of the workers and peasants from less educated, financially worse-off, and geographically discriminated backgrounds is shaped and stereotyped to be low human quality [*suzhi*] people and the urban middle-class as high *suzhi* people. Such depiction is often seen in stories that carry description of violence, murder, and sexuality. Sun (2009a, 128) maintains that such depiction is a manifestation of all politics and practicalities, because the way in which these stories are narrated epitomizes the way in which the image of the vast poor and weak is created in politics and the media. Sun (2009a, 127) cites and analyzes, for example, the media coverage of murder stories, including one that took place in April 2005 in Changzhi, Shanxi Province where a sexually abused *baomu* [nanny] killed a couple who had employed her. The report, instead of interrogating the politics of social inequality behind the case, spent words generously on detailed playback of the alleged sexual relationship between the *baomu* and her employer and the bloody crime scene. Sun (2009a, 128) highlights "the fact that the media's predilection for stories about transgressive maids does scant justice to the complexity and breadth of the *baomu*'s quotidian behavior and experience" and critiques that the media's *suzhi* discourse and image-shaping have inscribed the discourse of danger and risks onto the *baomu* and hence justified panoptic scrutiny of the *baomu*'s political activities by the state, the industry and their employers. This is how the media have resorted to solve the twofold problem mentioned previously: indulging or fostering the market appetite for spicy stories while shunning class antagonism to embrace for-profit reportage and to avoid political implications.

The distorting and restricting potential of the profit-driven media, as suggested in Sun's ethnographic study, lies in the media's "fertile imagination and voracious appetite for spectacle" that amplifies violence and stereotypes to define the low *suzhi* people to be sources of danger and social instability rather than the oppressed and victimized "whose actions are intended, however unrealistically, to improve their lives and working conditions" (W. Sun 2009a, 129). The publishers care more about marketability than the everyday struggle of the weak and poor (W. Sun 2008b), and discussion of the life and concerns of "the poor" virtually does not exist in the trend of tabloidization of the media (Yuezhi Zhao 2002, 113). This explains why media stories related to these disenfranchised groups are more often than not mixed up with sex, crime, and other spectacles, if one wants to call this content diversity and increased freedom of the press. Such kind of media narration fits well into the Party-state agenda of political control because the more dangerous and unstable the poor and victimized are pictured to be, the more such control can be legitimized.

Moreover, the flexibility in the new media is more a result of active mass participation than the benevolence of the Party-state and the social media. When one way is blocked, it is the users who always manage to find circumvention. The cat-and-mouse-game is played largely between the media users on one side and the cohort of Party-state and the media on the other. A recent example took place in April 2012 when Sina *weibo*, a Chinese microblog platform home to 324 million registered users, suspended commenting for three days in response to the Party-state's request to quiet down online discussion of the Bo Xilai incident.[25] As many would admit, Sina *weibo* is too big and too influential for the government to blatantly shut down. Yet, the biggest concern of this cyberspace giant (in terms of the size of its users and consequent implications for profit-making opportunities) remains that "its failure to police the site itself will provoke the authorities to close it" while its least concern is the users' complaint about the limits imposed upon their activity (Weisberg 2012). For these varied concerns, Sina *weibo* started to recruit "monitoring editors" to strengthen its "rumour control team" in May 2012 (Muncaster 2012). Sina *weibo* practice shows that the new media is just as politically alarmed and profit-driven as any other traditional media. The limited increase of content diversity and flexibility does not change the fact that the new media remain under both political and market control, no different from any traditional media.

Hence, the liberal notion of press freedom is not adopted in this study nor is it considered as the center topic here as much as in liberal discussions of censorship and press freedom. Predictions of systematic changes on liberal democracy and free market are just unwarranted speculation. Banging on about Western liberal press freedom and increases in content diversity and flexibility is not relevant to framing and solving the problems of political and market control of the media in the post-Mao China.

Nevertheless, this book is not rejecting the idea of press freedom per se, but suspicious of any uncritical predication of press freedom on a liberal political system and free markets when discussing the media problems in China. Should the phrase *press freedom* appear in the following chapters, it carries connotations of freedom as an "absolute good" that combines "harmony, unity, stability and lack of contradiction" (Curtis 1997, 121), a value against unrestrained capitalism (Singer 1980, 89), and a weapon in the service of an emancipatory struggle for the disenfranchised workers and peasantry (Hardt 2000, 37; X. Sun and Michel 2001, 11).

## TRANSPARENCY ILLUSION

David Heald (2006b, 34) defines the discrepancy between nominal transparency and substantive transparency as "transparency illusion," a term that helps us understand the gap between the official transparency rhetoric and information control reality. It suggests that rules and the fairness of transparency rhetoric cannot determine the outcome of substantive transparency while media practice can also impact on the transparency effect, not necessarily in a positive way. Heald (2006b, 34) maintains that:

> There can be a divergence between the path of nominal transparency and that of effective transparency, the gap being described as the "transparency illusion." The intuition behind the transparency illusion is that, even when trans-

parency appears to be increasing, as measured by some index, the reality may be quite different.

In terms of policy environment and rationale, the questioning of the nominal fairness of transparency versus effective transparency in recent decades also suggests that rules and rhetoric, the aforementioned article five of the MAPC, for instance, should not be regarded as a sufficient factor of transparency. These rules, even when claiming to uphold transparency and public supervision, do not necessarily substantiate the public nature of journalism and empower its obligations of facilitating openness, credibility, accountability, and relevance. The relationship between journalism, politics, and the market is ambiguous and evasive and, therefore, is hardly able to hold the Party-state and the market accountable.

Similar situations happen in Western democracies such as the United States as well. There can be numerous rules and notions in place granting press freedom and advocating transparency, but, as Chomsky (2003, 30) opines, the procedural and political correctness of these rules does not prevent the U.S. mass media from becoming the propaganda tool and "bought priesthood" for the national terrorism of the U.S. government and blacking the American people out.

Heald's transparency illusion argument brings forth the importance of substantiating the concept of media transparency. It shows that transparency is not an abstract concept or ideal that is manufactured with any taken-for-granted Holy Grail. It should not be used as a shield for elite politics or corporations that try to use this ideal to glorify or gloss over their interest or power-driven behaviors. Instead, transparency involves process, procedures, and activities that aim at generating substantive openness, credibility, accountability, and relevance in the interests of the public, particularly the disenfranchised groups.

There has been a shift from deification of transparency as a sacred notion (Bentham [1790s] 2001; Hazell 1998; Lamble 2002, 8; Shrader-Frechette 1991), to futility (Stasavage 2006, 177), jeopardy (O'Neill 2006, 89; Power 1997), to a perversity argument (McDonald 2006, 134), and then to an instrumental view of transparency (Heald 2006a, 71). The functional perspective, in particular, regards procedural fairness implied in this notion as no more than a means to other primary goals. Even when laws, regulations, rules, and policies in favor of transparency are, to some extent, in place, the rhetoric fairness is inadequate to conceptualize the profound changes in the social context to produce a more substantive certainty of what transparency is all about. In an authoritarian context, rule makers are as powerful as the rules themselves (NG'Weno 1978, 131). In terms of facilitating editorial autonomy for transparency purposes, rhetoric concept without substance does not necessarily lead to substantive outcome when the public sphere is plagued by political and market control. This uncertainty has actually accentuated the critical significance of the substance of the concepts of transparency and transparency through journalism in holding the politics and the media responsible to public interests.

Moreover, proclamation of transparency and its rhetoric in-and-of themselves do not guarantee substantive transparency. Transparency will be at stake when rules in the name of openness are meant to draw a line to confine rather than to allow exploration in media practices. As Christopher Hood (2006a, 219) points out:

> Policy measures such as transparency laws can achieve the very opposite of their intended goals and not merely null effects or undesired side-effects. . . . Citizens would end up knowing less rather than more as a result of the introduction of transparency provisions.

Without substance, the notion of transparency will remain an abstract and hollow ideal and only leave the public frustrated, a result likely to culminate in a crisis of public trust.

Even when checked by ethical morality, media practices may still militate against transparency. When the interests of a particular media or a professional in relation to their clients (i.e., organizations, government agencies, and individuals) is left unclear, media corruption such as bribery for news coverage is very likely to occur even when there exists an unspoken agreement against corruption (Tsetsura 2009, 665). Transparency in media operations is of crucial significance because media corruption, like that in other industries, thrives on "cultures of secrecy" (Eigen 2002, 188). Media ethics consist of not only professional integrity, objectivity, impartiality, honesty and disclosures of conflicts of interests (Soley and Feldner 2006, 228) but, more importantly its commitment to the representation voice of the public. All of these aspects can be affected by various pressures and pursuits. Faked news, paid news, and bribed news are no longer sins crouching at the door but already inside the Chinese media house. Withholding of news reports under pressure from the government and commercial interests also hinders media from upholding their ethical standards. Over the first decade of the twenty-first century, pervasive media malpractice has diminished public trust in journalism to new low with "a poor image with the public" (Belsey 1998). What's the point then of media exposures of corruption when the media themselves are corrupt?

The account of the transparency illusion has explanatory power when used to describe the gap between transparency rhetoric and censorship reality because it focuses on the easily neglected rhetorical nature of *transparency* as political parlance. Without substance, any political ideal can be conveniently manipulated by elite politics and changed into a mere conceptual mechanism to resist the substantive obligation of such an ideal. On the other hand, transparency is rich with meanings entailing openness, credibility, accountability, and relevance in general. Each of these aspects is associated with many positive connotations. For example, openness is positively related to candour, transparency, freedom, flexibility, expansiveness, engagement, and access (Tapscott and Williams 2010, 9). It involves policy rationale, professional activities, media operations, the market, and all other participatory elements in journalism that influence transparency. These factors are far too complex to be simplified into the idea of "journalism without censorship in a liberal democracy." Therefore, without adequate substance, transparency rhetoric will remain just that even when overt information control is alleviated.

## A NEW-LEFTIST PERSPECTIVE

Karl Marx opposed censorship. What makes him different from the liberals is his historical materialist approach that takes an insight into the internal factors of a contradiction in the "real conditions of the social, economic and political environment" (Hardt 2000, 87) rather than elaborating the formative part of it. This insight is still much needed today because the development of modern sociological theory owes its relevance to the "ghost of Karl Marx" (Farganis 2000). Modern critical theory can also find its roots in Marxist philosophy (Ritzer 2008). The influence of historical materialism is so immense today that, as Jennifer Kretchmar propounds, "it is to Karl Marx and his work that we now turn" (Kretchmar 2009). In the same line, when addressing the contradictions embedded in the modernity, Wang Hui (2009, 74) maintains that "Marxism is a modernist project that critiques modernity—it too is established upon the logic of historical teleology." Not only does Marxism remain the best way to understand the world but also the only theory that can empower human liberation (Sparks and Reading 1998, xii). In the trend of pervasive de-politicization since the 1980s (H. Wang 2009, 6), as important contributions and correctives have been made to the Marxism as Yuezhi Zhao (1993, 71) has argued, "it is premature to write off Marxian perspective entirely." As the social struggles and the media's absence in addressing these struggles are political and ideological issues, the symptoms reflected in the fractured public sphere cannot be explained and mitigated by depoliticized rhetoric and market discourses. In this regard, neo-leftism offers a valid perspective for critique and analysis.

The press (news media in broader sense today) was regarded by Marx as "a determinant of political process" which "produces and reinforces specific ideological positions" (Hardt 2000, 94). The media plays its role as "an extension of public sphere," as Marx defined the purpose of freedom of speech to be "in the spirit of the people" (Hardt 2000, 95). For this purpose, the press is seen as a collectivized social instrument for social cooperation and community building (Merrill, Gade, and Blevens 2008, 83). The freedom of the press, therefore, is considered by Marx as the fundamental basis for all other freedoms instead of in the interests of the press itself (Marx 1967).[26] He denounced censorship not only because it suppressed the rights to challenge orthodox, but more importantly it jeopardized the ideal of freedom for all. According to Marx's comments on the Prussian censorship law, "the press law is a right and the censorship law is a wrong."[27]

Marx rejected the belief that people were born imperfect and therefore in need of guidance and education (Kamenka 1962, 26). From his point of view, there is no justification for censorship that is applied in the name of producing good results. As he wrote:

> The censored press is bad even if it brings forth good products, for these products are good only in so far as they represent the free press within the censored press, and in so far as it is not part of their character to be products of the censored press. The free press is good even if it brings forth bad products, for these products are apostates from the character of the free press. (Kamenka 1962, 27)

For Marx, there is no such a thing as censorship in the interest of the public whatsoever. Censorship is no more than a mechanism of confinement that limits the press within the boundaries drawn by the censors. While press freedom embraces respect, tolerance, and mutual accommodation, censorship is engendered by disrespect, intolerance, and suppression.

However, Marx was not just talking about censorship as a suppressing regime. He saw the self-contradictory nature of censorship and the possibility that it could be applied in the name of good and against the good in essence. He was well aware that censorship had significant difficulty in seeking justification. In discussion of press freedom and censorship, He wrote:

> From the standpoint of the Idea (of freedom), it is self-evident that freedom of the press has a justification quite different from that of censorship, in so far as it is itself a form of Idea, of freedom, a positive good, whereas censorship is a form of bondage, the polemic of a *Weltanschauug* of appearance against the *Weltanschauug* of the essence. It is something merely negative in character. (Kamenka 1962, 27)

This negative nature is usually glossed over by the censors, and censorship discourse will more often than not lead the public opinion to the belief that too much freedom is dangerous and unhealthy. Unlike the Roman censors who targeted individuals, as Margarete A. Rose (1978, 20) maintains, the censorship system since the industrialization era aims to stifle the public spirit of society. Such a system suppresses the voices of the oppressed. A censorship system that posits its justification on "guiding public opinion correctly," or in whatever name, is by all means against the public opinion in essence.

Censorship is bad in a civil society because it distorts the government-public-media relationship. It hinders the public access to certain information and prevents the media from facilitating public access to that information. The balance within this trilateral relationship, if considered in terms of substantive transparency, can be attained only when the weaker party has adequately accommodated access to policies, decision-making process, and relevant information, has their voices heard and their demand properly realized. In the same line, David Heald (2006b, 38) also suggests that effective transparency cannot be achieved before the public can process, digest, and use the information.

In China, the censorship reality reflects the distorted relationship between the Party-state, the media and the public. As being constantly proclaimed, the Party-state itself represents the public that is the source of state power. The Three Represents rhetoric is an example of such proclamation.[28] According to this rhetoric, the Party-led public media, as part of the superstructure, at least nominally, represents the voice of the public. The market takes up an interactive role between the media and the public in connecting what the public need and what the media offer in response. The role of the market is relatively external because it is not supposed to exert direct impact on the representational relationship between the public media and the public. Nor is the market expected to affect the representational relationship between the public and the Party-state because the market is not supposed to be the source of state power.

However, such a public-centered relationship, as shown in figure 1.2, exists and functions only when there is at least an ideological consensus on, and preferably an existence of, the representation of the public by the Party-state and the public media. The higher the level of the consensus, the less contentious the trilateral relationship will be. Unfortunately, this consensus

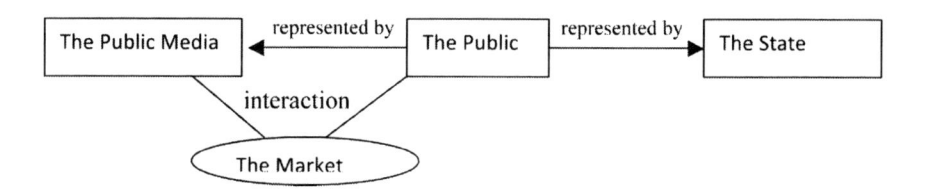

Figure 1.2. Public-centered representational relationship between the public media, the public, and the state.

on the public nature of the state and the state-owned media has virtually diminished in the post-Mao era, particularly since 1989.

Instead, the public media is managed and operated under both the official "throat and tongue for the Party and the people" parlance and market discourse. In reality, the relationship between the three is Party-state-centered at the cost of the representation of the public, a *de facto* commitment from which the state and the media are disjunct.

Figure 1.3 shows that the proclaimed representation relationship between the Party-state and the public and between the state-owned media and the public virtually does not exist. The public media and the public are segregated by the Party-state's political and market control.

Thus, journalism is controlled in many ways. The state-owned media is mandated to assume the role of constructing the Party's ideological positions hindering the public questioning, discussing, and contributing to these positions without permission. The media, the news production section which remain exclusively state-owned in particular, must follow the government decrees and documents because these rules are made legally binding by the *PRC Legislation Law* and the *PRC Administrative Approval Law*. In terms of market diversity, journalism has no place for non-state capital (Jieyun Xu 2010). The marketized media outlets, particularly those financially successful and editorially influential, are restructured into conglomerates, each of which is without exception headed by a Party mouthpiece. Senior management are ultimately appointed by Party authorities. Censorship is intensified to clamp down media activities that are likely to intrigue mass incidents [*qunti shijian*] and considered a threat to social stability and the political status quo. Moreover, the public is controlled as attempts to facilitate the voices of the disenfranchised groups lead inevitably to warnings, harassment, arbitrary detention, and even jail sentences. The public media, and the public are relatively remotely connected via the market, which again, is subject to government intervention at any time. Profit-driven and politically submissive

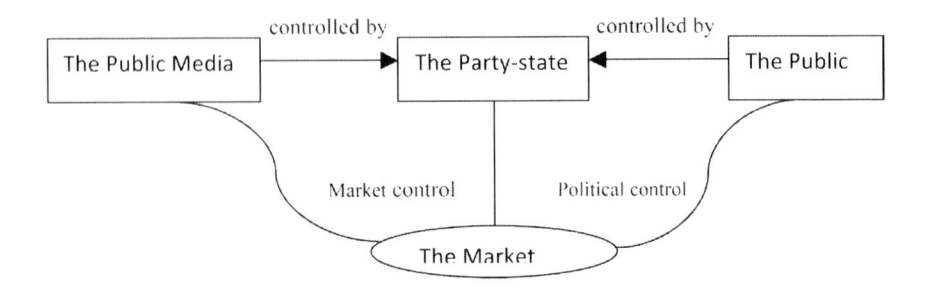

Figure 1.3. Party-state-centered relationship between the public media, the Party-state, and the public in the Reform Era.

media management usually loathe risking their positions and interests in pushing boundaries beyond the Party-state's envelop. In result, there is no such thing as a substantial representational relationship between the Party-state, the public media, and the public as proclaimed in or inferred from either the "Three Represents" rhetoric or "Throat and Tongue" parlance.

At the media operational level, the substance of journalistic values of truth and objectivity are implanted with a mixture of what Yuezhi Zhao (1998) has called "Party logic" and "market logic." Party logic defines journalism as part of the Party cause notwithstanding the ongoing growth of non-political content diversity. The market logic places profit-seeking on top of the editorial priority list. Between the Party line and bottom line (Yuezhi Zhao 1998), there are "ambiguities and contradictions" (Lee 1994), which generate room for political and market forces against openness and accountability. Thus, the media reform has turned media outlets into profit-seeking businesses that tend to prioritize market performance over the media's public nature. The increased freedom and flexibility has been invested heavily in profit-generating content, such as sex and crime, rather than the "everyday struggle" of the weak and poor (W. Sun 2008b, 23). Should any struggle be covered, it is more often than not the downside of this struggle, treated as a spectacle for ratings and profits (W. Sun 2002, 105). Consequently, the political significance of the life and concerns of the public is largely ignored, and the transparency of politics and media operations is hindered. As J. M. Balkin (1999, 1) argues, "mass media can hinder political transparency as well as help it."

The problematic representation relationship between the Party-state, the public, and the media is an ample example of the "disjuncture of representation," a marker of China's post-1989 modernity argued by Wang Hui. According to Wang (2011a), the problems of modern politics are rooted in the disjuncture of representation [*daibiaoxing duanlie*], the disconnection of political system from social reality, an unprecedented crisis that threatens the political system per se. With regard to the difficulties in democratizing China, Wang (2011b, 69) defines "disjuncture of representation" as follows:

> I believe that "disjuncture of representation" is the best way to generalize the crisis of the practice of democracy at this stage. . . . The social base of the disjuncture of representation lies in the disconnection of the political elites, economic elites, cultural elites and their interests with the public. This disconnection is directly demonstrated in the fact that political parties, the media and legal system (whatever universally acclaimed names they may use) cannot represent correspondingly the social interests and public opinions. This disjuncture of representation are shown in three crises, namely that of the party politics (as demonstrated in party statification), that of the public sphere (as demonstrated in the expansion of the media irrelevant to the space of public

sphere), and that of the legal system (as demonstrated in procedural fairness manipulated by interests).[29]

To further explain the legitimacy crisis of China's Party-state, Wang argues (2011b, 70) that "the legitimacy crisis originates from the disjuncture of representation of the political system, that is, the disconnection of the political system and social reality."[30]

The representation problems, shown in the figure 1.3, are rooted in the discrepancy between what the Party is and what it claims itself to be. The post-Mao Party-state posits its practical legitimacy largely on capital-driven economic growth rather than the fundamental interests of the people, the weak majority of whom remain the workers and the peasantry. Unfortunately, most of the societal imbalance and social stability issues arise between the powerful capital and political elites on one side and the weakest strata of the society at the bottom on the other (M. Gao 2005). These societal problems are caused by and reflect the disjuncture of representation and subsequently culminate in a legitimacy crisis. Public discussion of these problems may lead to collective protests and movements, which are perceived as a direct threat to the social stability and more significantly, the political status quo. Consequently, as Xiao Qiang (2011, 209) argues, the most important aim of censorship becomes preventing large-scale distribution of information that may lead to collective action, especially offline actions such as mass demonstrations or signature campaigns. As a result, public expression of and access to certain information, particularly that which is related to incidents in which the workers and peasants are victimized, is considerably hindered.

Given the obvious tendency for state power and ruling party to control the media (H. Wang and Xu 2006, 236), the nature of the representation of Party-state has evident impact on its relationship with the media. In the post-Mao China, both political dominance and economic success are powered by a capitalist economy, which has inevitably led to revision of the ideological system (Fewsmith 2001, 36). The media, maintained as part of the superstructure, is also subject to the same political or ideological commitment and market incentives as the Party-state. The media's representation problem is the result. In reality, the media businesses peg their success to political patronage and profit-seeking incentives and disconnect from their public nature. This disjuncture problem has inevitably resulted in rampant pursuit of profits and abuse of media power such as bribery, blackmailing, and sensationalism. Reciprocally, corruption incurs an endemic loss of professional integrity and accountability which justifies as well as invites interference by state power and constitutes the social base for state control (H. Wang and Xu 2006, 248).

Post-Mao China is full of contradictions because the Party-state finds it difficult to justify capitalism with an ideology labelled communism. Marxism has to be significantly revised in the name of domestication (Fewsmith

2001, 18). Maoism and Maoist social systems are totally abandoned (M. C. F. Gao 1999, 91). Although the Party-state holds a dominant position in the government-citizen-media relationship, it fails to "protect the life-world from erosion and confinement by the market and the bureaucratic system" (H. Wang 2009, 73). The failure has given rise to the necessity for the Party-state to control and use journalism to conceal and gloss over this disjuncture, which has led to the Party-state's reluctance to substantiate transparency. As Joseph Fewsmith (2001, 18) maintains, "On an ideological level, openness undermines the antagonistic relationship presumed to exist between socialism and capitalism." The control of the media, borrowing from the Soviet idea of "newspaper as a collective tool" (Lenin 2005, 12),[31] has in turn inevitably led to the media's disjuncture from journalistic values and representation of the public, regardless of the latter's ownership status in the public ownership system.

Therefore, media transparency has a significant role to play in addressing political and market control and aims to hold both politics and the media transparent and accountable to their commitment to the public in the public sphere. By questioning the rhetoric and market discourses legitimized in liberal framework, the discussion of media transparency will form an interesting ground for exploring the nature, essence and ultimate goal of transparency and supervision by the public as well as their connection with democratization in contemporary China's social political context.

## NOTES

1. Discussion is limited to the situation in the Mainland China.
2. According to the *2010 China's Radio and Television Year Book* (Yuming Zhao 2011), an annual publication dictated by the SARFT, the statistics on the number of radio and TV stations in the period between 1998 and 2009 has been adjusted due to the change of the internal statistical policy of the SARFT. As a result, the *2010 Year Book* carries the number of three kinds of broadcast services, that is, that of radio stations, of TV stations, and of radio and TV stations (Yuming Zhao 2010). As defined by the SARFT's *Annual Report on the Development of China's Development of Radio, Film and Television* (2010), a radio station is one that broadcasts radio programs only, and a TV station is one that is specialized exclusively in TV broadcasting while a radio and a TV station provides a merged service of both radio and TV broadcasting. For example, there were 298 radio stations, 347 TV stations, and 1,304 radio and TV stations in 1998; and 251 radio stations, 272 TV stations, and 2,087 radio and TV stations in 2009.
3. NPC is the legislative branch of Chinese state power.
4. There are various Chinese terms to describe the watchdog role of the media in China. Most commonly used versions include *yulunjiandu, meitijiandu*, meaning supervision by the media and supervision by public opinion, respectively. See Sterling 2009, 290.

This book looks at the idea of "supervision by public opinion," questioning the common perception of the public media as a default representative of the public and public opinion.
5. The *Twelfth Five-Year Plan* is released in March 2011. See Xinhua 2011.
6. Yang, W. 2014. *Xi Jinping Chuxi Zhongyang Zhengfa Gongzuo Huiyi: Jianchi Yange Zhifa Gongzheng Sifa [Xi Jinping Attending the Central Political and Legal Commission Meet-*

*ing: Adhering to Strict Law Enforcement and Judicial Justice]* [Online]. Available: news.xinhuanet.com/politics/2014-01/08/c_118887343.htm [Accessed February 20, 2014].

7. *Zhengfu Xinxi Gongkai Tiaoli* was promulgated on April 5, 2007. It came into effect on May 1, 2008. According to this Decree, governments at various levels are required to release information that "affects the immediate interests of individuals and groups" or which "ought to be widely known and demands public participation." See State Council 2007.

8. Translation by author.

9. Amnesty International 2006.

10. For example, see BBC.

11. For example, see C. Cao and Seymour 1998.

12. According to the UNESCO report of *Global Education Digest 2006*, the term "internationally mobile students" refers to "those who study in foreign countries where they are not permanent residents" (UNESCO Institute for Statistics 2006, 38).

13. IDP Education Pty Ltd (IDP) is an international institution based in Sydney that offers "student placement and English language testing services." Viewed on June 23, 2010 from www.idp.com/about_idp/about_us/welcome_to_idp.aspx (Maslen 2007).

14. Also see Verbik and Lasanowski 2007, 4.

15. Wary of the News Corporation scandal and the London riots in 2011, the British government has been tightening up its information control. Prime Minister David Cameron's Conservative-Liberal-Democrat coalition government introduced a filtering system so that, by the end of 2013, anyone signing up a new broadband account will have the filters automatically switched on by default, which will block all online material the government deems objectionable. This was done in the name of "protecting the most vulnerable in our society, protecting innocence, protecting childhood itself." But, alluding to protecting children from pornography, this censorship scheme does not define clearly whom to protect and what to protect from. This has given the government and the Internet service providers the possibility to extend the use of the censorship regime at their discretion.

Please see BBC 2013.

16. For example, under the rule of Alien Registration Act (Soley and Feldner) of 1940, any attempt to "knowingly or willfully advocate, abet, advise or teach the duty, necessity, desirability or propriety of overthrowing the Government of the United States or any State by force or violence . . ." is defined as a crime, which provided legal support for McCarthyism against Communists in the United States in the 1940s to 1950s. While ARA was rolled out in 2008, the Federal Communications Commission takes the role in broadcast censorship and the Child Online Protection Act was passed by the Congress in 1998 to target internet pornography and other information defined unhealthy. Media outlets also play a censorial role to some extent. Voice of America stopped broadcasting an interview of M. M. Omar, former Afghanistan's Taliban leader after receiving a decision from the federal government not grant "a platform to terrorists." Viewed on May 4, 2010 from www.serendipity.li/cda.html.

17. The Australian Office of Film and Literature Classification censors publications according to "the standards of morality, decency and propriety generally accepted by reasonable adults" in the *Publications Guidelines* of the Office without giving clear and specific definition of "standards generally accepted by reasonable adults," which may result in banning of certain publications without having the public reasonably informed.

18. Please see Zittrain and Palfrey 2007, 2.

19. Western democracies such as the United States, the United Kingdom, France, and Australia boast press freedom as institutionalized human rights embedded in electoral politics and free market (Feldman 2008).

20. John Milton published his long-celebrated article *Areopagitica* in 1644 in condemnation of the English pre-publication censorship. This article is still cited widely by liberal discussion of press freedom as relevant to the *First Amendment to the United States Constitution* (Douglas A. 2000, 1) (Blasi 1996).

21. Green and Karolides 2005, 87.

22. The First Amendment to the U.S. Constitution is part of the Ten Amendments to the U.S. Constitution, which are commonly referred to collectively as the U.S. Bill of Rights (Pearson and Polden 2011, 28).

23. Also see the discussion of "the Silenced Majority" in (Goodman and Goodman 2003, 8). Nevertheless, it is worth noting that the *Times* also practices objectivity and from time to time produces investigative reports that reveal the dark side of the politics and corporate businesses. However, this professionalism is far from consistent and persistent because, as Yuezhi Zhao and Zhifeng Hu have pointed out, this professionalism is rooted in the post–World War II consensus and value system that engenders the discourse myth and hegemony sustained by capitalism. Also, as opined by Hackett and Zhao, journalists themselves have important stakes in the ethos of objectivity, dismissing rigid correlation between the capitalist economic context and any particular mode of journalism. The professionalism that appears on and off in the U.S. media does not justify the validity of liberal democracy in generating and safeguarding objectivity. See Yuezhi Zhao and Hu 2011, 14, and Hackett and Zhao 1998, 71.

24. The only outlet in non-liberal country is Al Jazeera English located in theocratic Saudi Arabia. However, Al Jazeera English, according Moeller's research, is by no means the least transparent outlet. It ranks fourteenth among the twenty-five outlets on Moeller's transparency list.

25. Bo Xilai, former member of the Politburo and head of CCP Chongqing Committee, was removed from his offices in late March 2012 and later stripped of his Party membership for alleged involvement in charges of "breaching of Party rules." In September 2013, he was found guilty of corruption, accepting bribes, and abuse of power and sentenced to life in prison. Unlike other high-ranking officials who were found guilty for corruption and abuse of power, Bo denied all charges against him in the trial (S. Jiang 2013).

26. The book *Writings of the Young Marx on Philosophy and Society* collects several articles that reflect Marx's perception of press freedom and his denouncement of censorship. These articles include "Comments on the Latest Prussian Censorship Instruction," "The Leading Article in No. 79 of the KolnischeZeitung: Religion, Free Press and Philosophy," and "From Defence of the Moselle Correspondent: Economic Distress and Freedom of the Press." Also see X. Sun and Michel 2001, 11.

27. See Curtis 1997, 121.

28. The Three Represents is a theory of representation produced by Jiang Zemin Administration on February 25, 2000 during his visit to Guangdong Province. This theory proclaims that the CCP has always represented the development trend of advanced productive forces, the orientation of advanced culture and the fundamental interests of the overwhelming majority of the people in China (Z. Jiang 2001, 71).

29. Translation by author.

30. Translation by author.

31. Lenin defined newspaper as not only a means of disseminating information, but also a collective propagandist, collective agitator, and collective organizer. However, there are differences between a collective tool and an authoritarian tool. The differences, nevertheless, are not the focus of this study.

## Chapter Two

# Media Transparency

Despite its heavy hand of censorship, the Party-state could not really object to the common sense that transparency is something laudable. In fact, the idea of *touming*, the Chinese term closest in meaning to "transparency," has been increasingly officially promoted over the reform era. At the same time, supervision by public opinion, particularly for anti-corruption purposes, is encouraged in various official documents and talks. Such promotion in recent memory is the inclusion of the concept of transparency in the Twelfth Five-Year Plan in March 2011.

However, there is an apparent gap between transparency rhetoric and information control reality. The performance of the Chinese news media has been dubbed as "dancing while wearing fetters" (Fang and Chen 2002, 560). With the prevalence of the notions of transparency, supervision by public opinion and constructing a harmonious society during Hu-Wen administration escalated critical sentiments and cynicism that the word "harmony" lost its commendatory connotation but was found to describe how unwanted voices are silenced by censorship (Holden and Scrase 2006, 100).

Apart from the censorship reality, a significant cause of the aforesaid gap lies in the fact that the concept of transparency and supervision by public opinion has been kept as rhetoric with empty substance. The Party-state holds on to the sole authority of defining press freedom and transparency, as emphasized from time to time by the CPD and Party leadership such as Jiang Zemin (1999, 258). Yet, Party-state officials loathe specifying what transparency is and what the key elements of supervision by public opinion are. As a result, the boundary for journalism between what is forbidden and what is allowed has been uncertain for media professionals (McNally 2008a, 129). Meanwhile, discussions on press freedom, officially in Jiang Zemin's talk (1999) and academically in published scholarship such as Wang Shoucheng

(2008), for example, more often than not try to massage public opinion to the belief that an unchecked flood of information may give too much room for confusion, rumor, and instigation, and thus jeopardize social stability. Such discussions aim to limit the substance of transparency and supervision by public opinion within the scope of what a dictionary can tell and to justify the Party-state's monopoly over defining and interpreting these terms.

Taking an opposite route, this chapter discusses "media transparency" in an effort to substantiate the notion of transparency facilitated in and by journalism because journalism, as a major vessel in the public sphere, offers a multi-lateral communicative window for government and citizens, both domestic and overseas, for professionals and non-professionals, the insiders and the outsiders, to observe and be observed, to inform and be informed, to voice their views and to have their voices heard. Addressing the problem of transparency rhetoric is important not only because an empty concept more often than not fails to lead to realization of its ideal but because it usually generates opposite effects. Instead of simply taking "transparency" as a figure of speech meaning openness, or "media transparency" as journalism without censorship, this chapter tries to answer the question: What is media transparency?

The discussion commences with a brief account of the general principles of transparency and develops into defining media transparency. This account will also lead us to the discussion of related phenomena in the following chapters.

## GENERAL PRINCIPLES OF TRANSPARENCY

Both as a term and doctrine of modern governance, transparency consists of various expressions of meaning (Hood 2006, 1). The concept of transparency today puts together the pre-twentieth-century ideas of rule-governed administration, candid and open social communication, and methods of making organizations and society knowable (Hood 2006, 5). Its origin dates back to the eighteenth-century English philosopher Jeremy Bentham in his belief in good governance by rule of law against secrecy and conspiracy (Hood 2006, 9). The popularity of the transparency terminology today is rooted in expectations and efforts to reduce government and business corruption (Ball 2009, 295).These ideas revolve around the general principles of rule of law for generating certainty and predictability, press freedom as a watchdog over government and politics, and development of means that enable supervision by the public. This chapter argues that the implementation of these ideas is usually concerned with openness, credibility, accountability, and relevance of the governance behaviors.

Openness involves both attitude and actions. An open attitude will exhibit willingness to adopt interactivity between the government and the public. Open actions lead to adequate disclosure and public participation. The Organization for Economic Co-operation and Development defines openness as governments listening to their citizens and businesses and taking their suggestions into account when designing and implementing public policies (Kondo 2002, 7). While openness might be a one-way offer by governments and businesses to the public, interactivity unmistakably facilitates two-way communications and mutual accommodation for all parties. This interactivity has to be based on adequate access to information and expression relevant to the focus of the interactions. Information made available to the public is a means towards transparency and the effect of information disclosure leads to participation (Edelmann, Hochtl, and Sachs 2012, 34). This way, openness fulfilled with interactivity makes it possible for what Cotterrell (1999, 414) describes as the citizens' participation in political decision-making processes. Similarly, Richard Oliver's *active disclosure* (2004, 4) argues that "the old transparency (being open and forthright, should anyone happen to ask) has given way to new transparency, more active in calling attention to deeds, both intentional and unintentional." This suggests a move for the idea of transparency from information availability to public participation, from an abstract concept and vague understanding to real connections and actions.

With the demand by the public of substantive openness comes the obligations on part of the government to fulfill its pledges. This is why the notion of transparency is often, if not always, accompanied by that of accountability. Although almost everyone tends to prefer confidentiality to accountability, it is the rulers and overseers who have the power and resources to claim "a cloak of privacy" (Hood 2006, 6). The disequilibrium between the government and the public in possessing and using power and resources accentuates the importance of making accountability an explicit responsibility. In addition, governments assume responsibility because the process of government is carried out by people in charge, and these people must be held responsible (Dykstra 1939).

To enable this responsibility in a liberal context, accountability is maintained, and to some extent vindicated, by external supervision over the rights of authority through electoral retribution, legislative scrutiny, and public seeking redress from government and its officials (Mulgan 2000, 555). Accordingly, those held accountable must respond to the wishes and needs of their citizens and facilitate public discussion in this regard (Mulgan 2000, 556). The nominal value of accountability proclaimed from electocracy diminishes when the Center for Public Integrity, Global Integrity and Public Radio International in the United States (2012) concluded in their 2012 *State Integrity Investigation,* a data-driven assessment of transparency and accountability in all American state governments, that eight out of fifty earned failing grades, none got A, only five got a B, nineteen received Cs, and eighteen earned Ds. In an authoritarian context, on the other hand, the absence of effective electoral retribution and legislative scrutiny raises to a greater extent both the difficulty and the significance of holding the government agencies and officials accountable by effective public discussion. Whether in a liberal or authoritarian context, the question remains largely the same: accountability, accountable to whom? How? Electocracy does not seem have been able to hold the Western liberal governments more accountable to the voters than to the bankers and consortia while political and business tycoons just go blatantly with their power to control. This is where journalism committed to transparency in public interests comes into play, to substantiate the concept of accountability through facilitating the efficacy of public opinions in both Western liberal communities and a less democratized country like China.

Moreover, accountability cannot be substantiated without adequate credibility. Credibility often refers to accuracy and reliability of disseminated information, an ability to make or generate belief, particularly among one's counterpart (Freund 1992, 77). Positive government credibility reduces political uncertainty and meets expectations of its future behavior. Government credibility, as maintained by Ben Ross Schneider and Sylvia Maxfield (1997, 11), most likely generates positive consequences with the help of sound policies. Also, we must bear in mind the fact that building credibility through the media can be of high priority in the eyes of government officials because of the media's "third-party endorsement effect" (Hallahan 1996, 322). Government credibility, therefore, is intertwined with the media criteria of usefulness, the capacity to produce information that is reliable, interesting, and timely and in a form that can be used (Palmer 2000, 50). In practice, the credibility of the news media is often used by governments to test the public response to a certain policy and maintain public faith at moments of crisis management (Palmer 2000, 50). As a result, the credibility of the media is unavoidably affected by its relationship with state power.

The usage of *transparency* and other related terms, largely seen in describing government institution and behavior, can and does frequently extend into areas that previously subscribed to different terminologies. This extension, as Richard Mulgan (2000, 556) recognizes, is not necessarily unhealthy but also helps add significantly to the understanding of public institutions.

Thereby, this book shifts the discussion of press freedom from liberal individual freedom to a discussion in the substance of and constraints on transparency and supervision by *public* opinion, which is largely ignored both in official discourse and by liberal perspectives. The central importance of transparency does not lie in its taken-for-granted positive connotations but in the power of its substance and how it is substantiated. The original core of accountability, for example, signifies external scrutiny, justification, sanction, and control (Mulgan 2000, 557). However, this signification does not carry substantive significance unless it enables fair participation of the disenfranchised groups in the public sphere to have their voice heard without being harassed by political and market control.

To sum up, the idea of transparency embraces the following substance and principles:

> *Openness*, meaning proactive attitude and actions toward transparency of the authority that listens to its people and involves the public in decision-making process.
> *Accountability,* meaning that the authority takes responsibility, is answerable and liable for its action, policies and governance, subjects itself to public supervision and suffers punishment in the case of eventual misconduct.
> *Credibility,* meaning the authority is trustworthy, reliable, and responsive to public requests.
> *Relevance,* meaning the information is available in a direct, precise, complete, and timely manner.

## THREE ASPECTS OF MEDIA TRANSPARENCY

Based on the above understandings, this chapter incorporates the principles of transparency into the discussion of journalism as the authority that is to be held transparent refers to not only government but also mass media. Ben H. Bagdikian (1997, xxvi) argues that the mass media becomes the authority at any moment for its unparalleled capability to shape public mind by defining what is important, true, and reality and what is trivial, false, and fantasy. This capability, or power (Couldry and Curran 2003; Curran 2012), if deployed in a non-transparent manner, can blatantly make certain ideas and values present while others absent while shunning public responsibilities beyond the collusion between the media, market forces, and politics (Curran and Seaton 2010; Z. Pan 2005). Jurgen Habermas (1991) ordains a public sphere to check the domination of state and non-state organization. However, the Habermasian ideal collapses when the boundaries between the key players blur to the extent that the powerful becomes dominant and the public nature of the public sphere diminishes.

Given the role and the power of state, the media, and the market forces in the public sphere and the necessity to hold them transparent, the features of openness, credibility, accountability, and relevance are to be substantiated in the concept of *media transparency* in the following three aspects:

- *Policy environment for media transparency*, meaning that the policy environment should be transparent when the media is regulated by a rule-governed administration. The media rules, including laws, regulations, policies, and guidelines with binding effect should be in place, accessible, accountable, and relevant. The policy environment covers public accessibility to and discussion of the intention, formulation, and implementation process of the rules. For example, the intention of a law is not to be considered transparent when it is stated, promoted, and proclaimed to be granting and ensuring more rights, while it is used to restrict the rights of the media institutions, participants, and their activities.

- *Transparency of the media*, meaning that the media should be open, accountable, and credible in terms of its ethical integrity, operating policy, business structure, and corporate responsibility (Moeller, Melki, Lorente, Bond, and Cutler 2006). Media is not considered transparent unless it adopts a welcoming attitude and actions toward pluralism and objective reporting, discloses conflicts of interest and the policies that govern its activities and business structure, upholds its publicized journalistic values, and maintains a readiness to recognize and rectify mistakes without shaking off its responsibilities.
- *Transparency produced by the media*, meaning the extent of transparency to which the media is capable of delivering information to its users in a timely, relevant, and objective manner, and of facilitating the understanding between the government, citizens, and other parties involved in media activities.

Each of the three aspects of media transparency entails the basic principles of transparency mentioned above: the first one related to the rules and policy environment; the second to the media practice; and the third to transparency efficacy. Any lagging behind of any part of these essential aspects will result in a transparency reality distant to its ideal and hence to an uncertain future. These three aspects are interrelated and interactive, all involved with reciprocal connections between rules and media practice.

## POLICY ENVIRONMENT FOR MEDIA TRANSPARENCY

Policy environment has direct impact on media transparency because rules prescribe the scope and limit of media activities. Chinese media policies are mainly composed of government rules and regulations that enshrine the popular official slogan of *rule of law*. Since Jiang Zemin urged to "govern the country according to law" in his February 1996 speech, China has embarked on the "bandwagon" of rule of law (Lubman 1999, 128). The rhetoric effect of the official rule of law parlance is boosted by Premier Wen Jiabao's pledge (2010) of "creating conditions for the people to criticize and supervise the government." The phrase "according to law [*yifa*]" is mandatory to precede every official decision, whether the "law" refers to a statutory act or government document. Given the information-control reality in the presence of increasing number of government rules and regulations administrating the media and in the absence of a press law, Zhou Ze (2008), a high-profile scholar in journalism in China, evinces that there have been enough laws in place and there is no need for a specific press law for ensuring free journalism because only rights including that of press freedom need legal sanction while no law is needed to define or confine freedom. Such argument suggests that judiciary justice plus the established legislation is essential to realize the freedom of the press, reducing the substance of this freedom to a matter of relativism subject to interpretation by some vaguely inferred universal value or standards. Such argument coincides with the fact that most government rules concerning journalism bear or imply a specious plea for protecting legal journalistic activities or facilitating transparency according to law while the lack of operational substance has lent much discretion to the government agencies, officials, and businesses to go right against such pleas.

However, the concept of rule of law invoked in Jiang's speech and Wen's vow is by no means what is commonly understood as "a means to restrain government and to secure the rights of the citizens" that "aims to minimize any discretionary power" (Bovard 2000, 51). According to Jiang Zemin, all government works must be legal-systematized [*fazhihua*] and standardized [*guifanhua*] in order to protect the nation's long-term peace and stability (Lubman 1999, 128). Lubman (1999, 129) points out that Jiang's proposal attaches more emphasis on creating a legal framework for government work than the need to clarify the relationship between the Party-state and law. This notion of rule of law in China does not aim at a civil society with a high degree of rule of law in which the government has little discretion. Rather, the Party-state's lack of intention to limit government power engenders confusion between *rule of law* and *rule by law*. This confusion has exerted considerable impact on transparency for the media.

Rule by law refers to a form of instrumentalism where law is merely a tool for the state to control others without imposing meaningful restraints on the state itself (Peerenboom 2002, 64). It aims at strengthening government control of the media so that the media can be used by political elites both at central and local levels for contests for power (Joseph Y.S. Cheng 1998, 13). As Brian Z. Tamanaha (2004, 3) quotes Li Shuguang,

> Chinese leaders want rule by law, not rule of law. . . . The difference . . . is that, under the rule of law, the law is preeminent and can serve as a check against the abuse of power. Under rule by law, the law is a mere tool for a government that suppresses in a legalistic fashion.[1]

36  Chapter 2

The connotations of rule of law, therefore, are confused to such an extent that promotion of rule of law results in facilitating expansion of state power.

The media policy environment is plagued by this confusion as it is dominated by government rules including decrees, rules, normative documents, and consequent ambiguity of the boundary between rule of law and rule by the Party-state. Although the draft of Press Law has been shelved for over twenty years since its first proposal to the National People's Congress in the mid-1980s, China is not short of government rules and regulations related to media administration.

According to the information disclosed by the SC, GAPP, SARFT, and MIIT,[2] there are 118 rules and regulations in effect related to journalism as of December 2011. Fifty-four rules are directly concerned with newspapers, twenty-six with radio and television broadcast services, seventeen with online and digital media, and twenty-one with all media. These rules are classified hierarchically as follows:

- One NPC resolution as a statutory law passed by NPC Standing Committee;
- Two Party resolutions issued by the CCP Central Committee;
- Twenty-one administrative regulations [*xingzheng fagui*] passed by the State Council and ministries in form of decrees [*zhengfuling*];
- Twenty-nine ministry rules [*bumen guizhang*];
- Sixty-five normative documents [*guifanxing wenjian*] including all legislation passed by governments other than mentioned above.[3]

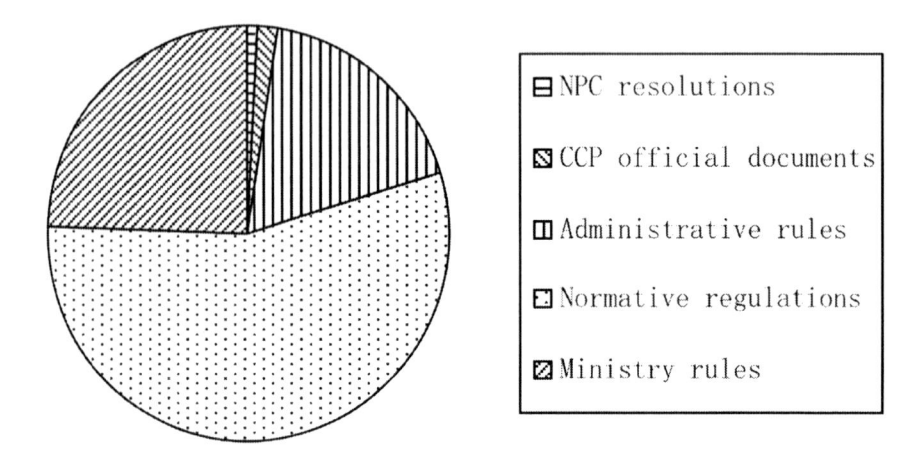

Figure 2.1.  Types of rules and regulations for journalism in China.

Apart from only one NPC resolution and two CCP resolutions distributed in form of notification, the rest of the rules and documents are produced by the government or jointly by the government and the Party publicity department. Twenty-one administrative regulations, sixty-five normative documents, and twenty-nine ministerial regulations take up the most provisions. In the obvious absence of a specific statutory law, the rule bylaw refers to the governance of the rules, regulations, documents, and orders issued by the State Council, ministries, and local governments (Peerenboom 2002, 138). When referring to law-abiding administration, it is more like *rule by the Party-state* than rule of law, a legalized version of confusion between rule by law and rule of law.

The confusion has advanced since the PRC Legislation Law (LL) and PRC Administrative Approval Law came into effect in July 2000 and July 2004, respectively. The former endowed government decrees and normative documents with the status of administrative law. The latter proclaimed to clarify the boundary of government regulations and prevent the abuse of government power and protect human rights. The State Council and ministries are empowered to enact administrative regulations to implement basic laws as well as normative rules regarding matters within their administrative power (Lo and Tian 2009, 11). The making and revision of these rules is subject to the discretion of the issuing authorities without having to obtain prior approval from the NPC. The public hearing prior to promulgation, an important community consultation procedure, is basically nominal and lacking substantive significance, recognized Cao Kangtai, director of the Legal Office of the State Council at the National Conference of Directors of Legal Offices and Departments on December 2, 2009 (L. Li 2009).

The confusion over rule of law is largely the result of the popularized legalism in post-Mao China which, according to John Gray, assumes that the executive and legislative branches of state power will be determined by constitutional and legal boundaries (Gray 1996, 76). It is also notable that the inadequacy of legislative law and dominance of government rules have enabled the Party-state and political elites' "self-interest seeking within the boundary of law" (Graen and Graen 1992, 200). The procedural fairness embedded in such legalism leads to the Party-state's indifference toward the result that the media is futile in carrying out its role of supervision by public opinion (Tomkins 2002, 162).

This confusion has exerted considerable impact on transparency for the media because it entails difficulties in making the intention of the government rules and regulations transparent, particularly when these rules aim to strengthen government power. For example, the following analysis on the *Measures for the Administration of Press Cards* (hereinafter referred to as the MAPC) illustrates how government control over the media professionals is strengthened and this intention is concealed in the name of protecting journalists and their professional activities.

The press card is a professional identity granted by the GAPP to journalists and editors to lawfully carry out journalistic jobs including collecting and editing news and interviews. The intention of the MAPC, as Zhu Weifeng, deputy director of the Department of Journalism, Newspapers and Periodicals of the GAPP stated in an interview with the *China Press and Publication Newspaper*, is to "facilitate and protect the journalists' rights to collect news and report, which to some extent represents the people's constitutional rights to know, to express, to participate and to supervise" (Zeng 2009).

Although the MAPC is supposed to facilitate and ensure these rights, the promise does no more than gloss over the prescribed restrictions. One restriction lies in the eligibility for applying for the press card (B. Xie and Gao 2013). Portals and smaller websites, except those attached to traditional state-owned media that carry news, are not categorized as "news media" by the MAPC and are not allowed to collect news according to the Administrative Regulations on the Internet News Information Services jointly promulgated by the Information Office of the State Council and the Ministry of Industry and Information Technology in 2005. Many of these media, such as the NASDAQ listed sohu.com, netease.com, and Hong Kong–listed tencent.com, have hundreds of millions in their audience. Editorial employees from these online media are not eligible for press cards. One of the reasons, according to Zhu, is that "most countries including the United States do not define websites as independent media" and "none of the Olympic Games or World Expos has issued formal journalist permit to any website" (Zeng 2009).

To justify its refusal to grant journalism licenses to non-state-owned websites by referencing the United States is ironic to say the least. What Mr. Zhu did not or chose not to mention is that the Chinese, Japanese, U.S., and Australian branches of yahoo.com, a detached Internet-based global media, "were proudly issued dozens of journalist permits for the Beijing 2008 Olympic Games" (F. Huang 2008). Also, tencent.com, a Chinese Internet service provider based in Shenzhen, established a high-profile strategic partnership with the Shanghai Expo authority by producing a special news column titled "2010 Shanghai Expo Online" featuring a 3D version live transmission (Shibowang 2010). Moreover, netease.com has secured an exclusive deal to collect news and report both in text and video for the 16th Asian Games in Guangzhou in 2010. And, by introducing baidu.com, it was the first time that a Chinese Internet search engine has been involved in the official report of the Asian Games (Dayangwang 2010).

Despite disqualification of reporters from detached Internet service providers to apply for accreditation, the MAPC has been unable to stop the online media from rapidly disseminating extensive news products, especially on significant and profit-generating media events. In effect, the excluded reporters and editors from online media undertake responsibilities no different from those with traditional outlets who are eligible. The MAPC's restriction on press card eligibility has demonstrated the obvious intent of the government and its policies to control journalist professionals by limiting their eligibility for journalistic activities. This restriction sheds doubts on the MAPC's vowed purpose stipulated in Article One "to safeguard journalists' normal professional activities and ensure legal rights of journalists and social public." Without the press card, the news-making activities by online media and its professionals are defined as "illegal" and consequently dangerous. Punishment of these illegal activities is, therefore, subject to the discretion of the administrative power of the authority. Reciprocally, this discretion increases the coercive effect of the government rules.

Furthermore, public accessibility to decision or policy-making process also has implications for transparency of the policy environment. Policies and rules such as the MAPC are drafted and promulgated by the government including the State Council, GAPP, SARFT, MIIT, and Party publicity authorities. There are few opportunities for the vast majority of grassroots professionals to engage themselves in the policy-making process. Either there has been no specific channel for professionals to express their concerns regarding these rules or the lack of adequate participation in the policy-making process has, at least in part, resulted in difficulties in making the policy intention transparent. The difficulties explain to some extent why fewer than 220,000 journalists and editors are eligible to apply for press cards when there are around four million professionals sustaining the booming news industry.[4]

Building up a favorable policy environment for news media professionals gives rise to the need for transparency as it is not a spontaneous result of any rhetoric or of top-down decisions made behind closed doors but the outcome of a much wider community engagement. Adequate interactivity between the governing and the governed on an informed basis is the first step toward transparency, and to release control is a pathway, similar to promoting corporate governance in the spirit of transparency (Fitton, Gruen, and Poston 2010, 213; Holtz, Havens, and Johnson 2009, 7). Not only should adequate rules be in place, the whole process including intention, proposal, drafting, discussion, ratification, execution, and revision must be an accessible, accountable, and relevant to, at least, the vast majority of professional practitioners.

## TRANSPARENCY OF THE MEDIA

Transparency of the media, at its most simple, is about transparency in corporate governance within the media, regarding the process of editorial decision-making and management policies. Moeller et al. (2006) established five categories coded for Corrections, Ownership, Staff Policies, Reporting Policies, and Interactivity, respectively, in order to examine how transparent a media outlet can be. These categories are designed to evaluate the outlet's willingness to openly correct mistakes and give information about its corporate owners, the outlet's candor about its internal staff policies, and its internal reporting and editing policies, as well as the outlet's openness to reader comments and criticism.

Moeller et al. (2006) concludes that of twenty-five major news outlets in the United States, the United Kingdom, and the Middle East that have been studied, "most news outlets are unwilling to let the public see how their editorial process works" while "what most news sites manage best . . . is admitting to who owns them." Although Moeller's research did not involve the news media in China, the understanding of the criteria for evaluating transparency of the media is in common: "It is not only important to demand accountability of the subjects of news coverage, it is also important to demand accountability from those who do the coverage" (Moeller et al. 2006).

Moeller's first category is about correction policy. The purpose of examining an outlet's correction policy is to see whether it learns to use its past errors for future cordon under public supervision (Russell 2006, 137). It is understandable from a market reputation point of view that news outlets loathe recognizing their mistakes and subjecting themselves to public supervision. Reluctance to make an apology open and available exhibits an outlet's unwelcoming attitude to transparency of the media management in that it believes that public knowledge and memory of its misdoings will not only affect the ratings but more importantly its positions and career future.

Standardization of corrections in the West started in the early 1970s, before which corrections could be found scattered in different places in different papers, and often under different headlines in the same publication (Silverman and Jarvis 2009, 228). Modern correction standards were created by Abraham Michael Rosenthal, former senior editor with *Times*, in 1972, which gave corrections a place, a title, and a format (Silverman and Jarvis 2009, 229). Rosenthal's standard was soon accepted by most newspapers in the United States. Almost every North American city daily today, for example, carries corrections, if any, at the bottom corner of page two (Silverman and Jarvis 2009, 229). Chinese newspapers, also, are no strangers to corrections. For example, *New Hunan Daily* was one of the newspapers in the early 1950s that regularly published corrections. Its editors made open apologies in the paper when they were found responsible for errors (Hunansheng Difangzhi Bianzuan Weiyuanhui 1993, 231).

However, online technology today has altered the landscape of journalism so that there are more options regarding how corrections are to be made. Many Chinese newspapers now have established websites and make their reports available online. News contents are disseminated at the speed of electrons, being reprinted and reposted by other media and users. Publication of corrections is obviously outrun by the spread of the original messages that carry mistakes. Some newspapers in the United States have established specific corrections tally or resorted to external news database such as Nexis to gather the corrections (Silverman and Jarvis 2009, 232). But these methods are rarely used for error-prevention purposes (Silverman and Jarvis 2009, 232). Therefore, it is of crucial importance that the media, particularly those that provide online services simultaneously, have a correction policy that ensures its corrections reach the readers as quickly and broadly as the original messages. Such a policy must be open, explicit, and able to hold the media accountable.

Few Chinese media today have made their correction policies open and available to the public, if they have any. The attitudes toward their mistakes vary among the press. For example, Xinhuanet.com, the portal of Xinhua News Agency, apologized on September 26 for publishing an article that had reported stories about China's first spacewalk on September 25, 2008, two days before the walk actually took place (Telegraph 2008). As of May 30, 2012, the apology letter remains retrievable on xinhuanet (Xinhuanet 2008). Another example is an apology missive issued by *Huaxi Metropolis Daily* (HMD) in 2010 for its admitted inaccurate report of China Writers Association (CWA) Annual Presidium Conference. In the report, the HMD accused the CWA of extravagance including using presidential suites and luxury cars for the conference participants. The HMD was ordered by the GAPP to openly apologize to the CWA. The apology was made in the form of an official missive addressed to the CWA so that it was treated only as a bilateral dispute between the HMD and the CWA rather than sensationalism that has misinformed the readership. However, this missive is not available to the public from any HMD sources.[5]

Secondly, disclosure of information about ownership is included in the discussion of transparency in that it indicates the possible influence of the owners over editorial practice, which imposes implication on the editorial independence of a news outlet. The Council of Europe urged its member countries in September 1993 to pass policies to mandate disclosure of media ownership in order to improve knowledge of level of media concentration (Jakubowicz 2011, 316).

In China, journalism remains exclusively state-owned. However, it does not mean that disclosure of ownership and corporate structure of the market-oriented outlets becomes superfluous. Yuezhi Zhao (1998, 158) has pointed out that while market discourses keep hinting at more credibility generated by market-driven content production, the possibility that the market will eventually drive the media away from their political obligations is largely overestimated. Media outlets are willing to boast their non-official status and market-oriented editorial style. In particular, introduction of non-state capital to the profit-making sector such as logistics, distribution, and advertising is usually claimed to endorse a non-official background. The oppositional nature of commercialized media is more often than not exaggerated (Y. Zhao 1998, 158). The reality is that not only does the commercialized media trumpet the tone set by the Party-state (Y. Zhao 2008a, 93), it has also targeted the urban elites and new rich, the wealthiest fraction on the top of the social ladder, as their key market (Sun 2009; X. Wang 2003, 276).

Despite the tide of commercialization and organizational restructuring, journalism remains a no-go zone. Each media conglomerate, without exception, is headed by a Party media. Each outlet is governed by its parent official media. In conglomerated outlets, it almost goes without saying that the newsroom is under the direct leadership and guidance of the senior management. Senior management positions are appointed by the Party and answerable to both the Party and the market (E. L. Davis 2005, 780). But, disclosure of ownership, particularly participation of non-state stakeholders, should not be used to endorse the market discourses of the profit-seeking editorial style. As the public as the nominal owner has far less influence on editorial content production than the Party-state-media joint venture does, such disclosure is more like a formality or gesture of openness. Declaration of ownership does not carry substantive significance if it does not rationalize effective measures to hold the stakeholders and their influence transparent and accountable.

Thirdly, internal staff policies specify responsibilities of employees and management and the implications of these responsibilities for editorial processes. These policies usually include employment conditions, training programs, incentive and discipline policies, and other policies related to staff management. Likely are these policies considered as internal affairs, and consequently are not necessarily released to the public.

However, what many are not aware of is that these policies are closely related to who are making the news and therefore significant to the resulting news production. The recruitment criteria impact the professional quality of the editorial employees. In addition, training programs should also be in place to keep the employees updated to the latest standards. Incentive and discipline policies motivate the professionals and the management, impose critical impact on management policies, and bring journalistic behaviors under the jurisdiction of professional ethics.

These policies have a strong implication particularly when there is a choice to be made between money and journalistic values. Who is most likely to get the journalist's or editor's job? Is it someone with satisfactory expertise, professional convictions and experience, or others capable of securing advertising sales contracts? Is the salary and welfare system fair enough for grassroots professionals? Are the training programs designed to improve reporting and editing skills, or will they reinforce ideological brainwash? Can reporters accept gratuity or seek sponsorship during an interview or news collection? What are the discipline measures in place to ensure ethical standards? What is the authority and discretionary power when judging professional misconduct? To what extent can professionals be supported by their organizations when there is a conflict or legal case incurred from a report? These questions are just a few of many in the complex media environment in which the professionals and their news products may be involved.

Fourthly, reporting policies or standards with regard to the process of news production have direct impact on the news products. It is generally understood that a news article or report is either assigned as a top-down task or initiated by a reporter based on his or her own resources. The finished article or report will then have to go through bottom-up procedures and be approved by the chief editors before getting published. Reporting policies, however, are more than procedures that can be inferred from a topological graph or similar. These policies specify what to report and how to report, what not to be reported and why, "how many sources it takes to confirm a story" (Moeller et al. 2006), with an independent supervisory system or equivalent to be alert to possible corruption and misconduct.

For example, few know how the newsrooms operate at the CCTV and how the editorial staff are guided and instructed in everyday work. A senior editor from the CCTV Social News Department described in a private conversation with the author how their daily routine starts in the morning.[6] The very first thing every reporter, journalist, and editor must do when they get to their offices is switch on their desktop computer. Having logged on the system with the unique ID number and password assigned to each staff member, they will receive a message popping out on the screen from the chief editor. It is a dot-point list instructing the particular staff specifically what he or she MUST NOT do on that day. These instructions are usually based on the chief editor meeting on the previous night immediately after the *Xinwen Lianbo* [CCTV News] finishes at 8:00 p.m. Only senior editorial staff are allowed to attend the meeting, and the chief editors decide what particular restrictions should be applied the next day regarding sensitive events or censorship orders from the Party publicity authority. Any editorial staff, no matter how popular they may be among the audience, who dare to disobey the instructions will be warned, suspended, shifted to other positions, or even fired. For example, Bai Yansong and his *News 1+1* program were suspended on July 26, 2011 for his sarcastic criticism on July 25 of Wang Yongping, the spokesperson of the Ministry of Railway, who defended the high-speed train technologies after the Wen-Yong high-speed train collision on July 23, despite that Bai had been specifically warned not to do so.

The purpose of explicit and open policies or rules governing the news production process is to tackle ambiguity and discretion that may give rise to secret sub-rules [*qianguize*] prone to generate media malpractice and hinder transparency. Only when the rules and policies are open can the news outlets, and their management in particular, be held accountable. One of the sub-rules that helps the management reduce personnel cost and shed editorial responsibility is to outsource news collection so that the outlets do not have to consider salaries and welfare cost. Casually employed news providers, usually "special reporters [*teyuejizhe*] or "special editors [*teyuebianji*]" get paid on word-count basis and undertake substantive responsibilities for their stories (Mente 2012, 116). When things go wrong, the "special" professionals become dispensable (B. Xie and Gao 2013). By outsourcing a considerable part of the news collection and editing without disclosing relevant reporting policies, the editorial accountability of chief editors is reduced to that of an OEM contractor.

Fifthly, interactivity reflects the extent to which the news outlets take readers' opinions into their editorial consideration. It should be, according to common sense, at least two-way communication and mutually responsive. It functions not only as a channel for the readers and viewers to complain but also an important source of information to the news room and editorial decision. Both traditional forms of interactivity, such as letters to the editors, and digital platforms based on real-time communication technologies can serve that purpose, as long as they adhere to two-way communication. From readers' points of view, they should be able to lodge complaints, ask questions, demand verification of information sources, make suggestions, and provide information. From editors' point of view, on the other hand, they should respond to the readers' complaints, meet the request for answers and authenticity, appreciate and take seriously suggestions and information, and more importantly, keep the interactivity transparent to all rather than keep it as a mere source of feedback.

Transparency of media outlets is important because an outlet achieving remarkable market success may not necessarily be as transparent and responsible as it claims to be. Pippa Norris (2010, 131) maintains that the media watchdog cannot be effective if it is not credible and accountable for what it does. Corporate transparency is not all about making catchy slogans that highlight the transparency rhetoric but about demonstrating the way openness, accountability, credibility, and relevance of corporate governance is materialized. The goals of media reform should aim at "making media organizations more transparent about their ownership, their editorial decision-making process, and the pressures and restraints on reporting" (Norris 2010, 133).

It is not a question of whether the media truly wants transparency or not. Transparency of the media does not come without a cost. A transparent media will not be able to manipulate the editorial content to the advantage of its own or its major stakeholders, as easily as a non-transparent outlet can. Its editorial policies will be placed under public supervision. The news room will be held accountable to its commitment to the public in the public sphere. The media will have to disclose its relationship with the political and commercial interests, making blatant political and market control more difficult. The outlets will have to place their personnel management under public surveillance so that exploitation and career blackmail are no longer a convenience for keeping the editorial staffers in line. The management will have to observe the open reporting policies and therefore make censorship orders open and disclose self-censorship procedures. Editors will have to be responsive to transparent interactivity with the readers and audience, which means that public opinions, particularly those critical ones, will have to be facilitated in a pluralistic manner. This is the price a media will have to pay for being transparent. Such a price, of course, is worthwhile when the voices of the underrepresented groups can be uttered, heard, and taken seriously.

## HOW MUCH TRANSPARENCY CAN BE PRODUCED BY THE MEDIA?

The extent to which transparency can be made possible through journalism lies in the degree of openness, accountability, credibility, and relevance that the media is able and willing to push forward. Susanne Nikoltchev (2004, 57) maintains that media organizations play a vital role as an essential factor in pluralistic communication and are supposed to honestly present facts and events and encourage free formation of opinions. However, this vital role does not necessarily suggest any connate quality facilitating commentaries sympathetic with the muzzled voice of the disenfranchised groups or allowing free expression of their opinions. Indeed, transparency by the media signifies how far journalism can go in expanding the public sphere in the interests of these underrepresented weak and poor.

This role, apart from common factors such as size and scale of investment, technologies, and level of professional skills, is affected by policy environment and how the media is managed. Policy environment is restrained by institutional control by the Party-state. Business management is subject to both Party-state control and profit-seeking incentives (W. Tang 2005, 80). At best, media products are the result of negotiation and bargaining between profit-seeking outlets and the Party-state's efforts to maintain control (W. Tang 2005, 80). At worst, the media system created by fusion of Party-state and market power serves the interests of the political and economic elites while suppressing and marginalizing the voices of the oppressed and victimized (Y. Zhao 2004a, 179).

Figure 2.2 shows that Party-state control over the media is implemented by the CPD and the State Council at the top and editorial content at the bottom.[7]

According to Tang Wenfang (2005, 80), the CPD does not only censor material but also acts as the principal coordinator of the media industry. However, the CPD usually works behind the scenes. As shown in the previous discussion on policy environment, most administration work and policy-making is done by the government ministries and departments. The central government launched a new round of integration of ministries in March 2013, putting print media and broadcasting services in the hands of the GAPPRFT, an incorporation of the former GAPP and SARFT. Online services and communication networks continue to be governed by the MIIT. The integration of government agencies aims to improve the administration efficiency to cope with the increasing organizational diversification within the fast growing media groups. By becoming the only authority issuing administrative documents, decrees, and regulations governing the rich and powerful conglomerates, the new GAPPRFT is able to streamline its policy-making process and avoid delay and discrepancies caused by complex cross-department bureaucratic procedures. This way, much difficulty in coordinating regulatory efforts between the government agencies is reduced.

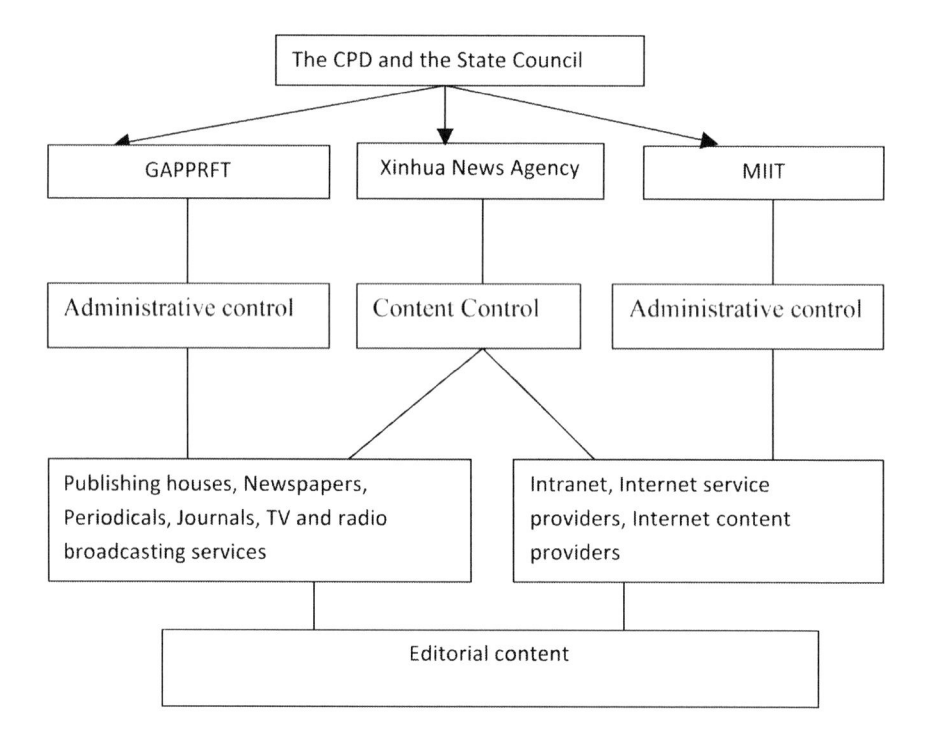

**Figure 2.2.  Media administration structure in China.**

The intensified Party-state control keeps the senior management of the conglomerates part of its bureaucratic officialdom and thus fosters editorial despotism within the state-owned journalism. Editorial despotism means that the power to make editorial decisions is concentrated in the senior management, which then hampers transparency within the media organizations. Most Chinese news outlets, including newspapers, radio, and television businesses typically are governed simultaneously by a board of directors and a Party commission. The chief editors decide what to publish while the chief executive managers make decisions for commercial activities such as advertising and distribution (Fischer 2009, 184). Senior management officials are appointed by the Party or the parent media group headed by a prominent Party mouthpiece (Y. Zhao 1998, 21).They form the top layer of the media management. Many of these chief editors, like the one with *Xinmin Evening Post* [*Xinmin Wanbao*], who proudly equalled himself with the Party, are so powerful that not only do they alone decide the content of each issue but their censoring power far exceeds even that of the external superiors.[8]

The senior management officials including chief editors and chief executive directors are usually within the publicity section of the Party personnel system. The level of their ranks usually corresponds to the level of the outlets. A division-chief level (*xianchuji*) official will be assigned to an outlet at the same level, such as a city newspaper. A bureau level (*sijuji*) official usually takes up a position as leader of a media conglomerate at the bureau level. These officials are Party bureaucrats whose appointment and transfer are strictly kept within the Party personnel system and are subject to the approval of the Party publicity authorities at the corresponding levels.

The problem of transparency arises when the management does not have to listen to its lower-level staff members internally and answer the demand for truth and relevance externally. The lack of openness reflects in the absolute management despotism which excludes the involvement of lower-level journalists and editors in the decision-making process. The situation deteriorates when the editorial work caters only for senior management decisions. The involvement of the lower-level media workers in the editorial decision-making processing is diminished to the extent that even in *Southern Weekend*, an outlet that boasts rebellious journalism, reporters are declined to partake in making decisions as to whether a report is publishable. According to Li-Fung Cho's investigation (2006, 137) of *Southern Weekend*'s internal policies, "Whether a story can be done is the reporter's problem, but whether a story can be published becomes the editor's problem." The internal policies, the "compensation policy," for example, which is meant to protect the reporters, are usually unwritten, and hence not open, accountable, or credible. These policies, at best no more than oral agreement out of goodwill, are made and executed at the discretion of the senior management, and therefore, unable to provide reliable, consistent, and substantive support for serious journalism.

On the other hand, media transparency has been deeply affected by rampant commercialization. Sensationalism takes the form of serious journalism, but denies its principles at the heart, dressing the "unverified information" with a convincing facade. Sensational reports manipulate with melodrama, emotion, and entertainment and reduce the importance of reason and information in media practice (Kolstø 2009, 27). The ultimate goal of sensationalism is profit (Montague 2010, 114). The role of sensationalism, as Gadi Wolfsfeld (2004, 44) opines, is destructive to media environment. Commercialization is also accompanied by rising rent-seeking corruption. High-profile corruption cases include the bribery of the eleven staff from official media including three from the Xinhua News Agency after a mining disaster took place in Fanzhi County, Shanxi Province, in June 2002.[9] Another similar scandal occurred in Hongdong County, Shanxi Province, where around two hundreds journalists from various media across the country lined up to accept cash gifts in trade for not reporting a mining accident in September 2008.[10] These corruption cases are just the tip of an iceberg that has led to increasing concern about corruption as part of the deteriorating media environment (Klyueva and Yang 2009; Tilt and Xiao 2010).

The money-making outlets have shifted their primary goal from serving the public toward earning profits (Stockmann 2011, 177). Media products are increasingly regarded as a cultural product or commodity that can be sold for money apart from meeting official publicity obligations (Hugo de Burgh 2003a, 48). Li Zeng (2008, 147) points out that the first priority of Chinese TV stations, like those in the West, is to rack their brains to produce programs that aim at enlarging advertising revenue. Also, much of the merit of senior management of media outlets is posited on profit turnover. This profit-oriented cultural market has been reinforced since Deng Xiaoping's Southern Cruise in 1992 (Z. Li 2008, 147). However, unfettered commercialization has engendered problems including sensationalism, corruption and media outlets' reluctance to invoke conflicts with the Party-state. These problems have inevitable impact on the transparency effect that journalism is devised to achieve.

As Christopher A. McNally (2008a, 143) maintains, China's capitalist transition has not only enabled market forces to reshape editorial content but also led to the rise of tabloidization and sensationalism. Sensationalism is common because it is the easiest way for the management to "search for higher ratings that generates greater revenue" (Guerrero 2009, 266). Fabricated and misleading news is a certain result of sensationalism when journalism goes so far that it becomes a maxim that "false news is better than no news" and "false news is better than true news" (Smith 1901, 881). If fabricated news happens frequently and sensationalism prevails in a media, it has to be what Lincoln Steffens would call "a systematic problem" for which the media system should be responsible (Palermo 1978, 43). Apart from political agenda and profit incentives, as Wanning Sun has argued, institutional routines of media production, technological imperative of news-making, encourage and reward the tendency to go sensational and spectacle, and as a result, the entire array of violation and disrespect of social, economic, and cultural rights in every life is largely ignored (Sun 2008, 32). Senior management will cling to profit-driven incentives in the game of sensationalism when they believe the gains by playing with non-political content outbid the risk of getting caught and bad public exposure.

Also, profit-seeking incentives give rise to the media's reluctance to invoke conflicts with the Party-state. As You-tien Hsing and Ching Kwan Lee (2010, 184) construed, the Party-state designs and enacts control policies around permission, prohibition, and various requirements, while the profit-seeking outlets implement, localize, or particularize these polices. In contrast with the incentives for profits and fame, the media seems to have little reason to offend the Party-state because the latter is apparently trading economic benefits for media loyalty (Chin-Chuan Lee 2000, 17). The fact that few senior management of the news outlets in China have openly condemned or even discussed the top-down censorship orders in an open and unreserved manner and that few news outlets have openly acknowledged practice of self-censorship illustrates how hard it is for the senior management of news outlets to engage themselves in conflict with the Party-state. The Party's publicity authority produces censorship orders and the senior management executes these orders and practices self-censorship. The obedience comes from the senior management's need for securing their positions because they are subject to the vetting system coordinated between the CPD, the GAPP, and the State Personnel Ministry (Brady 2008, 81). On the other hand, journalists are also increasingly influenced by the market force. Many of them have developed an unconventionally pragmatic attitude toward ethics and accepted their new role as part of the profit-seeking media business and hired publicity officers for the Party (Z. He 2000, 142).

## MEDIA TRANSPARENCY AS A PERSPECTIVE

Based on general principles of transparency, this chapter outlined media transparency in three aspects: policy environment, management, and transparency effect. These aspects are important because transparency of policy-making processes, media outlets themselves, and restrains on journalism have direct impact on the extent to which the idea of transparency can be substantiated. The news media, in particular, has responsibilities beyond many other industries in that its performance affects the integrity and transparency of the government and shapes the public's perception of the world (Sylvie, Hollifield, and Sohn 2009, 45). It is hard to expect transparency when the policy environment is full of uncertainty at unfettered discretion of the Party-state and its officials. There is growing dissatisfaction with the government officials for their delay, hesitation, wavering, and indecision in executing social responsibilities. Consequently, there has been a shifting of social expectation from the government to the media even in light of the fact that these outlets are highly state-controlled and profit-driven. But, one should not expect significant transparency from those that are managed in a deficit of openness, accountability, and credibility, or from a commercialization model that uses transparency rhetoric for making money and building brand rather than expanding the public sphere in the interest of the public.

In the public sphere, the function of journalism has moved from its preliminary phase of being informative to the constructive phase of "public problem solving" (Barlow 2010, 41), which indicates the increasing significance of public journalism in solving social problems. To enable this function, the news media must clarify and fulfill its commitment to citizens rather than the state or profit, particularly to those who are underrepresented and disenfranchised. For this commitment, there is a purpose in journalism to truth as a public watchdog to hold politics and the media themselves transparent and accountable (Friend and Singer 2007, 229; Kovach and Rosenstiel 2001). Without substantive legal provisions for transparency commitment, it is easy for journalism to fall to the hands of various levels of elite politics and become a political tool for political faction fights (J. Tong 2011, 54). And, with significant lack of transparency comes the discretion of censorship orders and self-censorship practice and hence frustration of public faith in promoting transparency through media efforts.

Moreover, transparency of internal management policies impacts the media's ability to enhance transparency externally. The concept of transparency will be no more than a market strategy if a media seeks to disseminate information about others while it keeps its own withheld, tends to hold others accountable while it remains unaccountable itself, demands credibility from others while being careless of its own, and makes decisions relevant to market success but irrelevant to enhancing transparency. The promotion of transparency will not be substantive unless the media holds this concept as a "higher purpose of benefiting relevant others . . . without calculating any personal gain in return" (Mendonça and Kanungo 2007, 73). Without adequate media transparency, press freedom may not be a valid indicator of transparency given the possibility that, same as some are concerned, the practice of a news media may fail to fulfill the ideal in its practices in a given place and time (Finel and Lord 2002, 260).

Nevertheless, the idea of transparency in itself does not guarantee fair and accurate reporting (Moeller et al. 2006). Not only should an outlet be able to openly admit to and correct its mistakes but it should also willingly subject itself to public supervision in order to avoid future failure. Also, not only should a media disclose its staff policies and reporting policies to the outsiders but must then make these policies operable, specific, and accountable. Interactivity is not an accessory to transparency rhetoric but an essential to build credibility among the audience and readers, particularly those most dedicated consumers of the news products. Media transparency, therefore, calls for transparent policy environment and management policies, which in turn, serve to facilitate public knowledge and expression through transparent journalism, build up media credibility, and promote transparency in greater depth and breadth. Above all, media transparency is of no practical significance if this concept is not substantiated for sustaining and expanding the public sphere to allow the voice of the weak and poor and to unleash their constructive potential.

## NOTES

1. Also see Graham and Tesh 2009, 30.
2. Please refer to the appendix for details including document titles, issuing authorities, and issuing dates.
3. Chinese legislative hierarchy is classified into Constitution, statutory laws, administrative regulations, local laws, rules, and normative documents. Also see Peerenboom 2002, 271.
4. The statistics come from the speech of Mr. Li Dongdong, deputy director of the GAPP, dedicated to the female workers in the news industry during the Lianghui period in March 2011. Viewed on November 11, 2011 from www.baoye.net/News.aspx?id=312945.
5. As of August 30, 2013, an electronic version is available at the Phoenix Network [*Fenghuangwang*], news.ifeng.com/mainland/201004/0406_17_1597127.shtml.
6. A private conversation between the senior editor and me in November 2013. Name of the editor and venue of the conversion, at request, are not released here.
7. See (W. Tang 2005, 80). This figure is different from Tang's, emphasizing that the media is not controlled by the Party alone but by the Party-state through administrative and content control.
8. *Xinmin Evening Post* is a Shanghai-based newspaper under the direct leadership of the CCP Shanghai Committee that assigns the position of *Xinmin*'s chief editor. According to White, the chief editor boasted there were no other censors because he was the censor himself. He considered himself as the CCP personified because he is highly consistent with the CCP leadership who assigned him the position. See White 1999, 122.
9. Viewed on January 10, 2011 from news.xinhuanet.com/zgjx/2006-12/26/content_5534553.htm.
10. Viewed on January 10, 2011 from news.qq.com/a/20081027/000536.htm.

*Chapter Three*

# Meta-Censorship

*A Justification Problem*

This chapter is not just looking at censorship per se, but how and why censorship is applied yet denied by the censor and the censored. The Party's publicity business increasingly finds itself in a dilemmatic situation in the post-Mao era. On the one hand, positive self-promotion through Party media is no longer able to doctor public opinions as effectively as it used to (S. Hu 2011, 77; Xinshu Zhao and Shen 1993, 314). On the other, societal problems including, but not limited to, increasing polarization (S. Fan, Kanbur, and Zhang 2009; M. Gao 2005), stratification (Chan, Ku, and Chu 2009), failure of the reform of public services such as education (N. Zhang 1992) and the medical system (Bunkenborg 2012), land seizure and forced relocation (Cai 2010), and mass incidents (Y. Cai 2008) arise at an alarming rate. Despite these problems, the media is called upon to play a *positive* role (Donald and Keane 2002, 6). Meanwhile, they are often requested not to publish negative news or report government mistakes (L. Li 1994, 231). Increasingly, these requests are funnelled through the censorship apparatus.

However, two questions need to be answered in observing the censorship reality: 1) How are the negative connotations of censorship managed in its information control commitment? 2) Why is the official talk of transparency incapable of changing the censorship reality?

Therefore, this chapter describes the discursive strategies permeated in the censored censorship reality and argues that the information control mechanism is not about censorship and its apparatus per se but censorship's justification problems. These problems are rooted in the disjuncture between and the incompatibility of what the Party is and what it claims itself to be.

Following this line, this chapter argues that the present censorship regime has little to do with safeguarding communist ideology or even the rule of the Party-state as believers of state-media dichotomy may postulate. In contrast to its damage to the CCP image, application and denial of censorship enhances control in the interest of the political elites and capital that has virtually disconnected the CCP from its communist representation, and the media from its public nature.

## CENCORSHIP AND CENSORSHIP REALITY

Censorship is the direct or indirect blocking of communication and access to certain information. It refers to "any attempt to limit or prevent free exchange of information" (Steele 1999, 7). Censorship rules are the doctrines, open or secret, upon which actions are taken against what is defined by the censors to be unpleasant, harmful, sensitive, or inappropriate. Censorship can be carried out by either coercive government authorities or spontaneously by the media or individuals who have the power or liberty to decide whether the content or implication of a certain piece of message or even its source should be withheld or blocked. The implementation of censorship may include a wide range of methods from mild warnings to brutal massacres.

The genres of censorship vary in terms of the type, value, object, and subject of the information to be censored (Marshall Cavendish Corporation 2010, 284). It rests on some rationale, usually for the purpose of protecting or defending the interests of the censoring authority and the power it represents. Moral censorship, typically related to the issue of pornography and violence, is carried out to defend a certain mainstream moral norm (Quinn 2006, 70). Military censorship forbids releasing of sensitive information that may jeopardise the national security, such as Section 798 of Title 18 of the U.S. Code that forbids the revelation of classified information about secret codes and other communications intelligence (Jamieson and Campbell 2000, 110). Religious censorship happens when the authority believes that certain heretical information is harmful to the dominant faith (Petersen 1999, 3). Political censorship covers more extensive areas and involves sensitive information that the government would like to control, more often than not pertaining to the ideological pillar of the state power. Self-censorship, in the form of self-discipline or conscious evasion of trouble, actually reinforces information control largely for political reasons (Castells 2009), and, in a market where transparency is hindered, for financial benefits.

To achieve a blocking effect, preventive measures or pre-emptive censorship is applied before the production, publication, and circulation of books, pictures, animated cartoons, or movies that may contain morally, religiously, or ideologically objectionable information. Classification or banning of products of pornography and violence is a common practice worldwide. Intellectual discussions, however, may also be targeted. For example, anything that "touches on the government organs and actions" was subject to heavy censorship by the German authorities in the 1910s against the rising democratic ideas and thoughts. Progressive newspapers such as *Frankfurter Zeitung* and one of its major contributors, Max Weber, found themselves constantly in a "difficult situation caused by the imposition of preventive censorship" (Mommsen and Steinberg 1984, 160).[1] In order to get any pro-democracy essays published, Weber had to "avoid a direct assault on the Monarch himself" (Mommsen and Steinberg 1984, 157). Chilling in effect, on the other hand, punitive censorship or post-publication censorship may be applied when a piece of work in question has been released to the public against the censorship rules. The measures range from prohibition or removal of the information to persecution of the writers and banning of the media sources, especially when the censoring authority senses direct or indirect threats to their fundamental interests.

All forms of censorship have a more or less political basis (Hübner and Kosicka 1988, 27), serving to either consolidate the power of the rulers or suppress that of their opposition. Generally, censorship is carried out in the interest of the censoring authority itself, such as a monarch, government, or political party in power, to protect or reinforce its own political legitimacy, state power or ideology. Even Max Weber, to assist in eliminating the monarchy, and in promoting his democratic ideology, proposed his own version of censorship, which was "a creation of criminal code against publication of royal speeches and programs" (Mommsen and Steinberg 1984, 161).

China's censorship apparatus as well as the way censorship is carried out, remains lacking transparency because there are few rules and regulations legitimizing censorship. The CPD, which is believed to be the highest level of the censoring apparatus, is one of the few, if not the only, CCP organs that has no official website or even public disclosure of its address. It assigns senior managerial officials of media outlets at all levels and issues guidelines and scrutinizes media products without disclosing any of its censorship orders (Kesselman, Joseph, and Krieger 2009, 91). Censorship, of course, is not included in its ostensible official duties.

Anne-Marie Brady (2008, 93) believes that the CPD mainly cares about macro-level administration and overall social trends. Joseph Y. S. Cheng (1998, 655), however, maintains that the CPD exercises influence over a much broader scope of the media from researching and drafting laws related to the media, to producing guidelines and policies, to checking over fifty mainstream official newspapers and journals in details. The control of information by the Party-state is realized by the combination of self-censorship and top-down surveillance (Latham 2007, 37). The censorship orders from the CPD largely deal with what the media should do or refrain from doing

(W. Tang 2005, 80). Apart from following these orders, the media apply self-censorship according to their own interpretation of the general guidelines from the CPD. How self-censorship works, however, varies vastly among different media and remains undisclosed without exception. The list of censorship stories in post-Mao China goes on, ranging from preventive filtering and prohibition to coercive clampdown.

Most China-based major websites, for example, practice filtering of "sensitive words" [*mingan cihui*] to prevent messages containing those words from being posted on the BBS, blogs, micro-blogs, and other public interfaces. Users of these words will be requested to take out the sensitive words or have part of the message automatically altered or replaced by a reminder phrase "filtered as sensitive words." Considering the possibility that the CCP and its leaders might be mocked or humiliated in the cyber world, some websites include the names of the Chinese leaders, "*zhengfu*" [the government] and "*gongchandang*" [the CCP] in their filtering grid. An advertisement recruiting doctoral students of the Beijing Normal University was posted or pasted in March 2009 at kaoyan.studyez.com/news/18185.htm. The advertisement included a perfunctory clause related to moral standards, requiring the applicants to "uphold the leadership of the filtered sensitive words [*yonghu zhongguo minganci guolu de lingdao*]" (Hujiang English 2009). Clearly, yet amusing, it should have read "the Chinese Communist Party" instead of the phrase "filtered sensitive words" to which the candidates are required to submit themselves wholeheartedly! Thanks to the automatic filtering mechanism, probably with the help of some software, the moral requirement clause in the advertisement turned out to be so unusual that it immediately became as well known as the Beijing Normal University itself. It is not clear whether the filtering had been done by the University before the message was copied and pasted to other websites, or in the posting or pasting process by the studyez.com, a small website that otherwise might remain unnoticed.[2] Nevertheless, the story and its effect still linger in online commentaries and memories. Given that different websites filter various vocabularies, no portals based in China, which practice filtering sensitive words, have explicitly disclosed their filtering criteria or providing any related explanations in their management policies. The Beijing Normal University advertisement is but a demonstration of online self-censorship.

## META-CENSORSHIP IN CONTEMPORARY CHINA

Meta-censorship, or censorship being censored, means anything that leads to knowledge, discussion, exemplification, and explication of censorship is rigorously censored or denied. It is an institutionalized or individual system that censors open production, discussion, and documentation of censorship rules and practice as result of an awareness of the derogative connotations of the term *censorship* being against the well-received concepts of freedom and democracy. Censorship rules are kept unwritten, secret, or so generalized that it is difficult to associate certain censorship practices with any written provisions. Censors rely on oral messages and usually refrain from producing written justifications for censoring decisions or even signing official statements of approval or rejection (R. J. Goldstein 1989, 14). Censorship authority is institutionalized in the ruling power instead of by the rule of law. The harsher the censorship reality, the more intangible the censorship rules may turn out to be as censorship of censorship permits the censors to operate under assumed names (Jansen 1988, 203). Where censorship is censored, information control is practiced without open and explicit rules but at the discretion of the censoring authority or the management of an outlet.

The boundary between transparency and the tolerance of censorship is deliberately left blurred so that the censors, who can simultaneously be promoting transparency rhetoric, can tighten controls according to the needs of the moment. More importantly, it becomes increasingly difficult to justify censorship when the voices of the vast poor and victimized are stifled in the waves of capitalist economic development led by the Party which keeps calling itself representative of the fundamental interests of the people. These justification difficulties have resulted in prevention of public awareness of censorship, hence censorship of censorship.

In general, meta-censorship rejects inquiries, commentaries, and criticism that lead to any critical discussion of the censorship apparatus, policies, practice, and their implications for the administration and management of journalism. While promoting transparency rhetoric in public, government agencies and officials blatantly rebuke any claims of a lack of transparency and press freedom. Media outlets, on the other hand, tend to seek flexibility in their reportage as much as possible and, to a point, even exhibit some degree of dissatisfaction with government information control while refraining from discussing or acknowledging self-censorship in their own management.

In practice, meta-censorship involves various strategies to downplay the negative connotations of censorship. It takes various forms to deny the existence of censorship reality, namely positive self-presentation, countering accusations, toning down, moral blackmail, and denial of legal construction.[3] These strategies share a common purpose: to gloss over the censorship reality and sustain the censorship apparatus. The dilemma, however, is that these strategies do not comply with the official transparency rhetoric nor do they help building the Party's image. Instead, meta-censorship epitomizes the Party-state's difficulties in justifying its censorship apparatus because this apparatus has nothing to do with communist political values but aims to defend the rule of the Party-state as a mere mechanism of power.

## Positive Self-Presentation

The Party-state's positive self-presentation involves the apparent promotion of official transparency rhetoric and denial of any censorship reality. Commenting on the regulation of the Internet services in China, Cai Wu, director of the State Council Information Office, maintained that Chinese netizens enjoy the greatest freedom of information and expression in the world (H. Fan 2006). Liu Jianchao, the spokesman of the Ministry of Foreign Affairs, denied at a press conference in October 2008 the existence of any harassment against free speech or of "internal rules" formulated by local governments restricting foreign journalists from carrying out journalistic activities in China (Z. Yu 2008). Zhang Fuhai, director of the Department of International Exchanges and Cooperation of the GAPP, explicitly denied the existence of any censorship system in China at a press conference at the book fair in Frankfurt in October 2009 (Miaozi 2009). To echo such denials, the editorial of the October 25, 2010 edition of the *People's Daily* declared that it highly values the Chinese public's freedom of speech and publication and defined the accusation of lack of freedom and transparency to be part of the Western anti-CCP and anti-China conspiracy (W. Ren 2010). Meanwhile, adoption of e-government and the promulgation of the Decree of Government Information Openness are well celebrated as demonstration of the Party-state's move towards transparency.[4]

The denial of existence of censorship rules and the self-promotion of a censorship-free image reflect the fact that censorship reality itself is censored and kept from public knowledge. Walter Lippmann argued in 1922 that propaganda work was impossible without some form of censorship, but China has never established an identifiable central censorship office, unlike the former Soviet Union and other authoritarian regimes (Brady 2008, 93). In order to be able to ensure that censorship is out of public awareness, all censorship policies, rules, and orders are kept undisclosed. Censorship orders are given by informal pressure such as oral orders by phone (Brady 2008, 94). Recording such phone calls is of course strictly prohibited (Brady 2008, 94).

Media outlets, on the other hand, are willing to present themselves positively as popular sources of information and, therefore, worthy destinations of marketing investment. *Huaxi Metropolis Daily*, for example, appears in the market as a fully commercialized and reader-oriented outlet with a corporate slogan of "*zeren Huaxi* [Responsible Huaxi]." The secret to HMD's market success without breaking any censorship taboo, at least in part, lies in its carefully managed positive self-presentation to both the readers and the authorities. The daily content emphasizes entertainment and leisure to cater to the popular culture while the possibility of irritating the authorities is minimized.

Liu Weimin, former chief editor of the HMD, divulged that the content of the HMD's investigative journalism must be strictly limited to 2 to 3 percent while the journalists and editors are required "to be good at transforming the elements of 'negative stories' into positive ones" (W. Liu 2003, 28).[5] The editorial rationale of the HMD, according to Liu, is to "share the government's cares and relieve the people's burdens," and above all, "to satisfy both the Party and the government" (W. Liu 2006).[6] But how much openness and accountability can one expect from a profit-seeking media that practically restricts investigative journalism? How much credibility and relevance can one expect from a news outlet that aims at pleasing the Party and the government? How much transparency can one expect from a media when its editorial policies and rules are kept distant from public knowledge? What internal censorship does it have to apply in order to transform negative stories into positive ones? These are questions to which answers are avoided in positive self-presentation.

Positive self-presentation can also be achieved by misleading public opinions in interpreting controversial media events. *Southern Weekend* is an outlet that enjoys global reputation for its investigative journalism and liberal editorial style (Rodan 2004, 184; J. Tong 2011, 62). It attracted attention both at home and abroad for its November 19, 2009 edition that carried two blank spaces on the front page (A1) and page A2 where the weekly published its exclusive interview with the U.S. President Barack Obama.[7] These blank spaces were interpreted by some observers to be a combative response to official censorship (Dean 2009; LaFraniere and Ansfield 2009). Xiang Xi, the interviewer, was demoted from de facto number-one leader to number two (Buckley 2009). However, the demotion of Xiang Xi was denied by the news outlet to have anything to do with the blank spaces but was "normal personnel adjustment" (R. Feng 2009). In fact, there is no evidence that the interview with Obama was censored because the Chinese version published on the weekly was identical to the English version from White House sources.[8] Therefore, some argue that these blank spaces have nothing to do with protest against censorship but are the result of self-promotion [*ziwo chaozuo*] and presentation of fake contradictory opinions (Wennuanyangguang 2009).

Indeed, there is no evidence that the propaganda authority had been involved in formulating the questions to be used in the Obama interview, and there is no evidence that Xiang Xi was using blank pages to protest censorship. Further, there is no official document to support the allegation that the demotion of Xiang Xi was the consequence of his editorial decision on the particular edition.

An atmosphere of speculation surrounding the silence seems to be agreeable to all parties involved. The Party's publicity authority does not want to talk about its censoring power in broad daylight and subject it to public discussion. The consistency between the Chinese and English versions seems to be enough to clear its reputation of censorship. It appears that the more the authority is accused of being responsible for the blank pages, the more innocent it turns out to be. On the other hand, the *Southern Weekend* seems to have exhibited a rebellious banner against censorship, mimicking the rebellious press which left blank pages to utter protests against the GMD censorship apparatus before 1949.[9] The *Southern Weekend* has borrowed this particular legacy without having to openly clash with the authority. Consequently, Xiang Xi, by default, has also had his name attached to the fight against censorship. Xiang, a bureau-level official within the CCP officialdom, together with probably many others in his position who pose to be pushing the boundary of censorship, has had nothing to lose but much to gain as long as he refrains from explicitly declaring disobedience.

There seems to be an unspoken understanding that silence must be kept about the blank pages. The propaganda authority, the press, and the demoted official have all refrained from making any comments thereafter. What had happened behind the scenes of the blank pages is anybody's guess. Although silence may confuse and mislead the public and give rise to ill-informed speculation and debate, it creates room, at least in part, for interpretation in favor of each party.

## Countering Accusations

Refuting against accusations is a strategy of offense as defence when the accused seeks self-justification and self-defence by attacking the credibility of the accusers. Chinese government officials and media outlets tend to defend the image created through positive self-presentation by counter-attacking against those who hold critical views of them. Bias and lack of objectivity in Western reports of China, are often used in both academic and official discourses to reject criticism from outside. Domestic protest, on the other hand, can easily be put down by simple but harsh clampdowns.

Listing the flaws in the reports by the Western media, such as using wrong pictures and biased comments on the Tibetan riot in March 2008, Wang Lili (L. Wang 2008) maintains that the Western concept of press freedom does not exist in reality in the West while the Chinese public actually enjoys it in considerable measure. Wang posits her argument on the observation that the news industry in the West is controlled by either the government or the capital, or both; therefore, press freedom is highly restricted. The problems in the Western media that Wang Lili refers to are largely in existence. However, she never explains how the Western media's wrong can be used to defend or justify the censorship reality in China. Indeed, the pitfalls of Western journalism have demonstrated the fallacies in the Western media system and free market myth. But, these pitfalls are no justification for offense-as-defence purposes.

Similarly, with the stumble of Murdoch's News Corporation over its 2011–2012 *News of the World* phone-hacking and bribery scandal, Chinese official outlets such as Xinhua and *People's Daily* whipped "the hypocrisy and empty sloganeering of the Western media and political elite" who "hopped on their favourite soapbox to lecture China on the virtues of press freedom and human rights" (Ewing 2011). In response to the publicly articulated concern about China's restrictions on press freedom by Barack Obama on the World Press Freedom Day on May 3, 2010, Jiang Yu, the spokesperson of the Ministry of Foreign Affairs, commented that the United States should "respect the truth, hold correct view on China's press freedom status, and stop finding groundless fault with China" (Z. Luo 2010).

Such a countering strategy is set in the logic of defensive counterattack. Firstly, the purpose of counterattack seems to be projecting a positive image. Media boom and unprecedented information accessibility have added considerable credit to the positive image that the Party-state and the media have built up.[10] Therefore, critical views that may lead to damage of such an image are regarded as part of the Western anti-CCP and anti-China conspiracy, Western hypocrisy, and bias (W. Ren 2010; L. Wang 2008). Secondly, it seems that the Chinese government and academia seldom judge press freedom in the West unless China is criticized. This defending position has actually enabled the accused to find flaws in the accuser so that the accuser can be denied credibility. Subsequently, the accuser's critique against censorship in China is defined to be "groundless fault-finding" and without credibility. To challenge critical reports of China by Western media, some commentators, such as Xie Rongzhen (2008), would point to how the U.S. government manipulated the media to mislead the public in the report of the 2003 Iraqi War, suggesting that the Western media is running out of credibility and, therefore, not qualified to criticize China. Wang Lili (2008), in the same vein, asserts that in the West the people have no press freedom as they think, and it is in Western discourse that the press freedom of the Chinese media and people is excluded. The take-home message is that Chinese media administration becomes the victim of prejudiced accusations and, therefore, counterattack to such accusations is no more than self-defence.

Moreover, the countering strategy aims at more than defensive strategy. This strategy distracts attention from the cause of censorship to the conflict between China and the West as two de facto hostile camps. It tries to draw on criticism of the Western media to justify or at least provide some leverage for the censorship reality in China. Still, such a strategy does not hold water because it avoids the fact that what happens in the West, manipulation of the media by politics and commercial interests at its simplest, happens in China in a similar fashion.

The problems that plague Western media can be attributed to the marriage between politics and the media (Louw 2010, 1). This relationship is analyzed in depth by Mobo Gao (2004a), for example, in the case study of the promotion of patriotism in support of the Iraqi War by the private media in the United States despite the public opinion being apparently opposed. But Gao's analysis is drastically different from Xie Rongzhen's argument in terms of research purpose and methodology. The latter counters criticisms by setting up the Western media as a "straw man" for his attack so as to find some justification by making the West look bad. Gao, however, sets out to explain why private ownership and free market do not necessarily lead to press freedom in the West and discusses how press freedom can be influenced by politics and commercial interests. Gao's research pinpoints the problems in the West and can be used as a precaution in the ongoing capitalization in China.

This influence, or the collusive relationship between politics, commercial interests, and the media, is at least against media ethics because it flagrantly defies the principle of editorial independence and media's public nature. This is why the Murdoch's ties to the British government can be defined as a scandal and destructive menace to healthy journalism according to both journalistic values and common sense. Therefore, the state–media collusion is condemned in both the West and China.

However, not only does the counterattack strategy avoid addressing the collusion between politics and the media in China, it also tries to justify and defend a relationship in which the Party-state and the media management have largely reached a consensus on political control of editorial content and pursuit of profit. Since the marriage between politics, commercial interests, and the media is unjustifiable in the West, how can the intimacy between the Party-state and the media in China, leaving behind their supposed representational relationship with the public, find its own justification and defence in the same logic?

**Toning Down**

Establishment of a system of content review to monitor the press and publication industry using the term "*shendu* [review reading]" instead of "*shencha* [censorship]" is a typical form of toning down which features using discursive reasons to justify an act, minimize its negative effect, redistribute responsibilities, or redirect the blame.[11] It is another discursive strategy of meta-censorship because it aims to mitigate, upon full awareness of, the derogative connotations of censorship.

The definition of *shendu,* as vaguely stated in the Provisional Measure on Review Reading of Newspapers and Periodicals,[12] does not clearly explain its purpose and how it works. Its purpose, according to the official document, is to "strengthen the administration of, maintain the order of, and improve the quality of the press and publication" by reviewing and evaluating newspapers and periodicals on a regular basis after their publication. In practice, under the leadership and guidance of the GAPP, publication administration authorities at provincial level and the central government agencies will urge the newspapers and publications within their jurisdiction to adhere to laws and regulations and, most importantly, to direct public opinion *correctly*. Reports are to be made on a regular basis to the GAPP, which will study and select major issues found therein to report to the State Council and the CCP Central Committee. The GAPP will present annual awards to the outstanding reviewing units, reviewers, and reports.

Wang Shoucheng, awarded the honor of "Excellent Reviewer" by the GAPP in 2009, further elaborated the purpose of the *shendu* system in his 2008 book. He maintains that the danger of lack of supervision by public opinion, to quote Deng Xiaoping's warning that "It is most dangerous to a society where no voice is heard" and "It is most dangerous to a party when there is no different voice," is no longer the case (S. Wang 2008). He claims that the news media today tends to be "freer than appropriate" and consequently more and more engaged in various kinds of scandal and misconduct. He also maintains that the power of the news media should be checked because "unchecked power, even that of the news media, is dangerous" (S. Wang 2008, 33). The more tolerant the environment, the more the news media needs to be contained. Therefore, the fundamental purpose of *shendu* system is to "supervise and check the news media to ensure the healthy development of the news and publication industry" (S. Wang 2008, 250). According to Wang, unlike the *shencha* system of the nationalist GMD regime before 1949, the current *shendu* system is "the servant of the public interests and a friend of the press" (S. Wang 2008, 250).

It is clear that Wang is trying to use the toning down strategy to minimize antipathy and objections. This way, public opinions are guided to the belief that the news media is dangerous and should not be set free. According to Wang (2008), bribery, paid, fabricated, and misleading news are certain results of media freedom; it is not the government that wants to limit press freedom—the evil nature of the media and their sins have invited it. He denies the coercive and clampdown nature of censorship, portraying *shendu*, "as a friend" that is helping the media to avoid professional errors and misconduct and is guiding them in the right direction. The premise of this friendship is that the media must meet the quality standards ambiguously prescribed in the 2009 Provisional Measure. Failure to do so, according to clause 11 (3) of Method of Annual Review of Newspapers and Periodicals, will lead to suspension or termination of publication. Therefore, there is a price to be paid for having a "freer media environment." The freer the environment, the more limit is imposed. According to this *shendu* system, the news media is unable to develop healthily without having its power curbed by the Party-state and its administrative authorities. Hence, limit of editorial activities is rhetorically legitimized to be necessary and inevitable.

However, the *shendu* system functions as an extension of elite politics and the power mechanism as the weak and poor do not have a place in such a review system. The reviewers are carefully selected experts who construct, or at least comply with the Party line and official discourses. Such a system does not support effective supervision by public opinion and does not aim to hold the government and elite politics accountable. The accused "evil" of press freedom is no more than another straw man borrowed from the state-versus-media dichotomy to justify the meta-censorship regime. It is factual that the media has pandemic corruption problems. However, as Wang and Hu (2006, 248) points out, unprofessionalism not only incurs but also invites interference by the state power and constitutes the social base for state control. That said, the corruption problem cannot be conveniently assigned to press freedom per se, but to the media system plagued by political and market control which has practically destroyed the ethical beliefs and professional integrity.[13] This corruption problem, in turn, has lent the Party-state a glittering justification for further interference and control. This way, not only does the *shendu* system reinforce control, it also serves to justify such control.

## Moral Blackmail

Control, however, is not limited to the application of *shendu,* which mainly governs the post-publication inspection. Real-time scrutiny is also a common practice. Moral blackmail, usually by taking advantage of others' moral weakness to justify one's immoral actions (McConnell 1981), is more often than not adopted for justifying this type of scrutiny. This strategy transforms negative connotations of censorship such as control and loss of freedom into morally acceptable reasons such as protection and precautions. It is considered to be a discursive strategy of censorship because it creates a moral obligation so that objection to censorship is suppressed.

Moral blackmail here means to integrate a policy or act with a publicly recognized moral consensus or common sense when the intended consequences are not necessarily in conformity with the actual obligation. For example, to increase taxes to cover government deficit from extravagant spending may incur objections and criticism whereas to do so in the name of improving social welfare, such as building a modern, public hospital, generates a morally binding effect because it offers a lofty reason for a bulging government budget. Objections to increasing tax rates will be regarded as against the interest of public welfare. Therefore, the ransom we are obliged to pay is to support or follow the government decision in order to avoid being morally condemned. In the case of censorship, it is not desirable to restrict or interfere in accessibility to information. However, prevention of pornography and violence, particularly in order to protect minors, suits social values in most cultures and therefore constitutes a morally binding effect when policies and initiatives for the purpose of much more extensive and intensive information control are made in the name of protecting the children.

Motherhood is perhaps one of the warmest terms, and it can be employed in upholding the censorship legitimacy. The Mothers Reviewing Group [*mama pingshentuan*] is a group of volunteer mothers recruited by the Beijing Hotline for Reporting Illegal and Unhealthy Internet Information, supposedly targeting pornographic, violent, and other information considered inappropriate. With the help of these mothers using parental perspectives, the Hotline was able to report to the authority ten websites that had disseminated "profane" information within a single day on December 9, 2010 alone (L. An 2010). China Mobile Shanxi Branch, following the Beijing Hotline, took a further step. According to the report on Shanxi Television on December 25, 2011, a group of mother technicians was organized to monitor websites that provide unhealthy information. Besides filtering 30,983 pieces of information defined as "inappropriate" in 2011, the group remotely tested 110 terminals online and disabled the menus on some of the terminals that allegedly had access to inappropriate information.[14]

However, the moral blackmail that may lead to justification for unchecked censorship is worrying. What makes the mother reviewers in Shanxi powerful is their capabilities and authority to scan, control, and disable terminals online without having to disclose to the public the legal ground of their intrusion in the name of parental care. Although it is obvious that what is on the censorship list is not always confined to such, justification usually, if not always, rests on prevention of pornography and violence. The neutralization effect is prominent through parental outrage toward harms that may be done to the children. Thereby, censorship is seeking justification as a protective measure rather than a blocking apparatus.

The failed compulsory promotion of the Green Dam Youth Escort software has a similar justification problem. The content-control software, according to a directive from China's Ministry of Industry and Information Technology (MIIT) that came into effect on July 1, 2009, was meant to keep the minors safe from pornography and violence online and, therefore, to be pre-installed in all new personal computers that were sold in the Mainland (Bristow 2009). The purpose of the software, according to the MIIT directive nevertheless, was to "respond to the request of the massive teachers, students and parents" (Bao 2009) and to "build a healthy and harmonious online environment" (Bristow 2009). As many would understand, this means more than just to prevent pornography and violence and includes politically sensitive content. Consequently, overwhelming objections from computer manufacturers, and more importantly, public concerns about privacy, information accessibility, and data safety, forced the MIIT to change the pre-installation plan from compulsory requirement into one of voluntary choice.[15] Wary of the software's ability to block websites at the discretion of the authorities, record and report users' online activities, and the fact that sensitive content and websites such as youtube.com and facebook.com have been blocked, the users have every reason to object to installation and application of any software of this kind promoted by the government. Soon after the withdrawal of the government financial and policy support, the Green Dam project went bankrupt and was terminated in July 2010 (B. Li and Niu 2010). Its poor market performance has revealed the moral blackmail embedded in the officially alleged demand from the masses.

**Denying Legal Construction**

The censorship reality develops in the absence of transparent and relevant rules. Despite numerous government rules and regulations governing various sectors of the media industry, there has been no specific law for journalism to date. As indicated in a statement elaborating the achievements of China's legislature disclosed by the portal website of Central Government of China (F. Chen 2009a), 231 draft laws and 1,133 executive rules have been proposed to the National People's Congress over the past thirty years (F. Chen 2009b).[16] However, the draft Press Law [*xinwenfa*] is among the few that have been shelved since it was first proposed in the mid-1980s. Some believe that the suspension is all for the prior consideration of social stability because the lawmakers have been deterred by a superstitious analogy that the former Soviet Union fell apart right after the enforcement of its law of journalism.[17] On the other hand, the four freedoms, having existed for twenty-three years in Mao's era and guaranteed by the 1978 Constitution, namely "to speak out freely, air their views fully, hold great debates and write *dazibao* [big character posters]," were removed from the amended Constitution in the same year of the restoration of the CPD authority in 1980 (Tsou 1986, 322). Denial of the Maoist freedoms in the post-Mao legal framework, according to Gerry Groot (2004, 113), is rooted in the Party-state's fear of potential threats from these rights, *dazibao* in particular.

Putting journalism and censorship in the legal framework does not seem to be a welcome idea among the Party leadership. Chen Yun, former chief editor of the fortnightly *Jingji Xiaoxi* [*Economic Information*] in 1945 in Yan'an and later member of the top Chinese leadership in the 1980s and early 1990s, delivered his concerns about the press law not long after the CCP took over state power:

> The GMD regime forged a *Press Law* during their reign. We communists took advantage of its loopholes by carefully studying its stipulation and finding its flaws. Now that we are in power, I think we'd better not have any press law in case others may take advantage of our loopholes. In the absence of the law, we can take the initiative and control the way we want. (Zhong 2003) [18]

To avoid the bridle of the legal framework, authority over the media was assigned to the Party framework. As a result, the power was shifted from the government to the Party although the administrative work is carried out through government institutions. The Central Publicity Department was restored in October 1977 after being dismissed in the Cultural Revolution. According to the *Report on Establishing the Central Publicity Department* approved by the CCPCC on October 31, the CPD is responsible for making the guidelines, strategies, and policies of the propaganda, cultural, and publication work (L. Chen 2008, 347). In the early 1980s, though, the Ministry of Education had most factual authority over ideological work. This status quo, however, was changed by the Notice on Matters Relating to the Joint Management of Education System Cadres by the Central Committee Propaganda Department issued in July 1982.[19] The Notice granted the CPD the power to co-decide the positioning of the cadres of the Ministry of Education above the bureau (*si, ju*) level by taking charge of "investigating, understanding, transferring, appointing, removing, nurturing, training, and political screening of cadres who are under the jurisdiction of the Central Committee and work in the education system" (Burns 1989, 34). By taking over the authority over the career ladders of high-ranking cadres of the media administration authorities as well as those managing the media, the CPD has more influence over ideological work than ever before. This systemic arrangement has not only ensured the Party's control over critical positions regarding administration and management of the media, it has also defined administration and management of the media as a Party business within the Party framework rather than a mere public service under the jurisdiction of legal framework.

The Party-state loathes having its controlling power subject to statutory laws. As a result, the official promises of transparency and supervision by public opinion are unable to be substantively realized within a legal framework. One such example is the pledge that Premier Wen Jiabao, on behalf of the Central Government, made in March 2010 that "the government should create conditions for the people to criticize and supervise the government, and let news media fully play their oversight role so as to put the authorities under sunlight" (Milligan-Whyte and Min 2010).

But tellingly, Wen's pledge is subject to government discretion, which resents ideas, concepts, and rules with any substance against the Party-state. First, it is through government efforts instead of a legal framework that conditions in favor of the people's criticism are to be created. Administration of journalism remains a matter of Party guidelines, government regulations, decrees, and documents. Therefore, the extent to which the people are able to criticize the government is limited to what the government and, more realistically, its powerful officials can tolerate. Second, Wen's pledge does not define what conditions should be made to enable the people's criticism. Third, the substance of *full playing their oversight role* is ambiguous. What does "fully" mean? How full can it be? Who can decide the boundary of such "fullness"? This ambiguity leads to no answer to questions like: To what extent can the government and the Party be checked by the media? What if the people want to fully play their supervisory role while the Party does not want to give in? These questions are also closely related to the intrinsic conflict between journalistic values and Party logic. As a result, legal construction that may lead to substantive progress of transparency through supervision by public opinion tends to be delayed and, more often than not, replaced by government pledges which usually do not carry any substance.

The lack of substance in Party-state pledges explains why the 2004 tentative efforts to create "legal conditions" to grant journalism more rights in Shenzhen were frustrated. The draft of "The Regulation of Shenzhen Municipality on Preventing the Crime by Taking Advantage of Duty," a bill to join social political efforts including that of the news media against abuse of state power, proposed "journalists' rights to know and rights to reasonable no-fault suspicion" (G. Zhang 2003). The proposal was made in the awareness of the flexible and fragile nature of investigative journalism against crimes that may involve powerful government officials. It is believed to have borrowed the Western "actual malice principle" that significantly limits government officials' ability to lay charges against journalists for reports against governments and officials (Kang 2004). The proposal excited discussion in the media and academia, most of which valued the initiative as a breakthrough. Yin Yungong, director of the Institute of Journalism of China Academy of Social Sciences, quoted the proposal in an interview and maintained that government should work under public supervision (T. Yang 2004, 12). Some from the judicial system also supported the draft. An article released on the website of the Yunnan Provincial People's Court states that such rights are crucial to the news media in helping prevent crime committed by public servants (L. Yang 2009).

However, the stipulation of "rights to know and to no-fault suspicion" was deleted in the final version of the bill before it was passed by the Guangdong People's Congress in 2005.[20] The reasons for the deletion, as given by the drafting committee, included "lack of legal support of upper-level law such as the Law of Journalism" (G. Li 2005). Such a reason is not convincing enough. The rights to know and the rights to freedom of speech are enshrined by article 35 of the Constitution. These rights need to be specified in laws that substantiate enforceable provisions. Except for the overwhelmingly positive feedback in public opinion, there has been no open debate over the proposal. The real reason why the well-received proposal was deleted remains unknown. Still, the frustration of the attempt to adopt the actual malice principle to enhance muckraking journalism is another demonstration of the difficulty in embracing protective rather than restrictive stipulation in the legal framework.

Without proper and specific protections, the news media find themselves under constant pressure from the coercive authority of state power. The "double action theory [*Shuangqi Lun*]" forged by Wang Lijun, former head of Chongqing Public Security Bureau, in October 2010, is a telling example.[21] Wang threatened to sue any media or journalist who dared to attack the reputation of Chongqing law enforcement. He declared that

> If individual civil police officers were singled out for attack, said Wang, the officers would bring a suit against the journalist responsible in the courts, and the Public Security Bureau would sue the media organization. (Bandurski 2010)

Such a hard-line attitude has demonstrated the mentality that the media must be at the service of the Party-state and that there is no such a thing as journalism holding the Party and the government accountable. In contrast, Wang's threat of exercising judicial power against the media is coercive because his *Shuangqi Lun* is rooted in fact that the current legal framework is unable to provide legal support for effective supervision by public opinion. Interestingly, there has been not much protest or counteraction, apart from a few grudges, from the media against the *Shuangqi Lun*.

The weaker and emptier the legal framework is, the more discretion the Party-state has. With this discretion, the Party state is able to apply censorship without having to be held open and accountable by statutory legal framework. I'm not trying to present a legalistic perspective of any kind here. In fact, legalism has been well adopted in the Party-state governmentality in the reform era, which prefixes every government decision and action with "according to the law [*yifa*]." Although pledges to more transparency and favorable media environment for the populace are heard on various occasions, these pledges are made without substance and therefore not practical for the construction of a substantiated legal system, which may otherwise bestow some realistic legal rights upon the media, the professionals and the populace. From a meta-censorship point of view, the denial of substantive legal construction aims to keep censorship covert and powerful in practice at the same time.

## Changing Party, Changing Censorship

The meta-censorship reality reveals the justification problem of not only the censorship regime but also the disjuncture of the Party-state and the media from the people and manifested the collapse of the Party principle of journalism [*xinwen dangxing yuanze*] and the "throat and tongue for both the Party and the people" discourse from within. First appearing in the CCP publication in 1929, this discourse has been reinforced in the reform era to define how journalism is to be administrated and managed (Y. Zhao 1998, 26). Deng Xiaoping (1983, 236) reiterated that "Party newspapers and publications must propagate the Party's propositions." Jiang Zemin, former president of China, also declared that "Our country's newspapers, radio and television broadcast are the throat and tongue of the Party, the government and the people" (G. Xu 2004, 4). Wang Weiping, deputy director of the Bureau of Television Administration of GARFT, proclaimed that "Television is the tongue and throat of the Party and the people," and those who do not follow this primary rule are "lack of IQ" and "unable to play the game" (Y. Zhang 2007). The "throat and tongue of the Party and the people" discourse, stipulated as the number-one Party principle of journalism, was re-emphasized by former president Hu Jintao during his visit to the People's Daily Press on June 20, 2008 (C. Feng and Dong 2008). To follow this Party line, Guo Chaoren (1997), former director of the Xinhua News Agency, made a clear cut division between the news media being a Party instrument and being a means of social justice [*shehui gongqi*], arguing that the nature of news media as the throat and tongue of the Party and the people must never be changed by the reform.

The semantic basis of the throat and tongue discourse implies a representation relationship between the Party and the people, and therefore legitimacy of the Party-state's control over the media. This basis, however, is from time to time shaken by censorship's justification problems because it is the weak and poor's voices that are largely stifled. Hence, the Party's implied representation rhetoric, as Gao (2004a, 2103) points out, cannot explain why the Party and the media have strangled their own "throat and tongue" by censorship and self-censorship.

A workable explanation is that the Party has changed so much that it has drifted away from its original communist philosophy and commitment to its present representation that harnesses what McNally (2008a, 122) called "capitalism without democracy." The Party has remained in power for more than sixty years since 1949 without having its supreme authority being substantially challenged. However, the CCP today is vastly different from what it used to be due to "considerable changes in its composition, its attributes and its role" (Béja 2007, 209) over post-Mao years. Powerful Party elites have joined the new rich, either by reaping the success of the capitalist economy, forming what Jonathan Unger (1991, 20) called the "red capitalist class," or recruiting the capital elites to the party membership (Dickson 2003, 32) and central leadership (Rein 2012, 15), not to mention the "grey income" (Ngo 2009, 15) the few powerful have harvested through rent seeking.

According to Marxist materialism, which is supposed to be the CCP's fundamental philosophy, the superstructure is determined by and at the service of its economic base, and definitely not the other way around (M. Gao 2004a, 2103). The CCP, which proclaims itself as a communist party of the people and represents their fundamental interests, is no exception. The role of the news media, which is also part of the superstructure, is mandated to follow the nature of the Party which changes along with its economic base. While the Party holds on to its throat-and-tongue parlance and rests its pragmatic political legitimacy on the continued capitalist economic growth, a gap opens between the proclaimed communist representation and the capitalist economic base (McNally 2008a, 122). This gap has given rise to the dilemma in the Party's publicity business mentioned at the beginning of this chapter. As a result, the present censorship machinery is not necessarily concerned with communist values but the interests of elite politics and capitalism that the Party actually represents.

In reality, the growing societal imbalance and disputes between the beneficiaries and the victimized have given rise to the need for the elite politics to reinforce the censorship system, particularly when conflicts arise between the powerful and the weak in media events that are defined as "negative news." As the censorship apparatus makes everyday efforts to put a lid on "negative news," the wealthy and powerful are provided with a shelter while the weak and victimized, in land seizures and forced relocation cases, for example, are restrained from seeking help from the media and hence public support. The "good news" for the poor, on the other hand, is sometimes on the censors' list. According to Chen Guidi and Chun Tao (2004), the approval of a reform program that relieved the rural households from heavy taxes was ordered by the former Chinese premier Li Peng not to be released publicly because "if it were known that Li approved it, everyone everywhere would get on the bandwagon before the consequences of the program were known" (M. Gao 2004b, 115). The way that "bad news" for the powerful and "good news" for the weak are censored has demonstrated that censorship in modern China has considerably hampered the interests of the disenfranchised groups although the latter, according to the CCP charter, is supposedly represented and pioneered by the Party.

Moreover, the political elites and capital elites have forged an alliance of common interests. While the policy settings are made to support the development of the new entrepreneurs, the economic elites have to find themselves fully incorporated in the activities of the Party-state (Goodman 2008, 33). Many of the political elites are themselves entrepreneurs or part of the network of the economic elites, such as the family of Li Peng.[22] The trading between power and money [*quanqian jiaoyi*] cannot happen in the absence of the interest-based relationship between these two parties (C. Li 2000, 148). Both elite groups, as pointed out by Yu-ming Shaw (1988, 50), "grab illegal wealth." The political elites use their power to step into and benefit from the market activities while the market elites harvest much more than what they have invested in the political-economic elites relationship both in terms of monetary profits and policy patronage. Both the elite groups make money in the reciprocal preferential treatment (Tubilewicz 2006, 70).

Wary of the power and potential of the news media, the last thing that the political elites would like to see is public discussion of the intimacy between the elite politics and capital, including local government officials and property developers, for example. The media is censored and obliged to apply self-censorship on behalf of the Party-state which actually patronizes the elite politics and capital. Such a censorship system, of course, cannot find justification in this contradictory commitment. The disconnection between the Party and the people, in return, has created a side-taking question for the media: "Are you going to speak for the Party or the people?!"

This is a question that Lu Jun, former deputy director of the Planning Bureau of Zhengzhou City, asked in retort to a journalist in an interview. Apparently, blundering on the disparate relationship between the Party and the people, Lu revealed the censorship taboo that the media should, without saying, be censored or self-censored for the Party and against the people when the two run into dispute. Lu was immediately suspended from his position for his taboo-breaking slip of tongue.

The Planning Bureau plays a decisive role in determining what a piece of land is to be used for. According to sections three and five of the Regulations for the Implementation of the Land Administration Law of the PRC and article 17 of the Law of Urban Real Estate Management, the planning authority is responsible for defining the purpose of land in general plans. Any changes to the use of land must be submitted to the planning authority for review and approval. It was reported that a piece of land in Xigang village of Zhengzhou was allocated for affordable housing for low-income people.[23] Instead, twelve expensive townhouses and two detached houses were built and sold underhand. The developer's profit was estimated over fifty million yuan (equivalent to about 7,700,000 Australian dollars). When questioned by a reporter from China National Radio, Mr. Lu apparently lost his temper, unmasking the meta-censorship taboo.

Lu's blunder was his anger with the reporter's attempt to disclose the relationship between the elite politics and capital. By declaring the CCP and the people as mutually incompatible, Lu, a typical high-ranking local political elite, implicitly rejects communist ideology. To Lu and many others, the Party is a ruling power instead of a congregation sharing the proclaimed ideology. As Wang Hui (2009, 6) maintains, "The party is no longer an organization with specific political values, but a mechanism of power." Censorship is intensified to reinforce such a mechanism. Consequently, censorship is censored because of its justification problem in the Party-versus-the-people reality. In effect, Lu's question epitomizes the disjuncture between the Party and the masses.

## CONCLUSION

This chapter describes how censorship is censored to explain the justification problem of the post-Mao censorship apparatus. This problem arises when the CCP endorses capitalist developmentalism and censors the voices of the poor and victimized by the "capitalization of the Party and the marketization of the state."[24]

The justification problem epitomizes the discrepancy between what the Party is and what it claims itself to be. The legitimacy, or the raison d'être, of the Party is supposed to be based on its commitment to "equality in human society" and "privileges of the working class" (M. Gao 2005, 20). However, Chinese politics has undergone "a dynamic and changing process" (M. Gao 2003, 391). The orthodox Marxist ideology and Maoist practice of "big democracy" have given way to capitalist pragmatism at all costs in the reform era (M. Gao 2008). The communist principles have gradually ceased to exist in practice and retreated to pure ideology in an ideological dilemma (Shaoquan Zhang 2006, 61). The reduction of legitimacy comes along with dilution of the communist nature of the CCP, which has seen China develop into one of the most exploitative and unequal nations on the earth (M. Gao 2005, 20).

This justification problem and discrepancy have also demonstrated what Wang Hui (2009, 79) points out as "the structural contradictions" because the post-Mao China is full of "internal tensions and contradictions." These internal tensions and contradictions are reflected in the difficulties in reconciling communist ideology and capitalist economic base. These difficulties, in turn, have complicated the justification problem and deepened the transparency illusion.

Therefore, given its justification problems, censorship is intensified yet censored and denied. Discussion of the censorship reality becomes a taboo. Not only has the justification problem engendered a sophisticated censorship and self-censorship system in the post-Mao era but it has also rendered the official transparency rhetoric hollow and self-defeating. The disjuncture of the representation relationship between the Party-state and the victimized workers and peasantry has created the social political base for this complex censorship system and therefore needs to be addressed when discussing problems related to media transparency.

## NOTES

1. The *Frankfurter Zeitung* was one of the few democratic papers in the early twentieth-century Germany, in which works of most of the great minds of the Weimar Republic were published.
2. The content of the web page that the ad was posted or pasted on the studyez.com has been replaced by some irrelevant English learning material at the time of writing this chapter in April 2012. The article that gave first comment on this issue on the website *xinyusi* [the new threads] on March 28, 2008, has also been removed from the original web page This advertisement is still retrievable up to November 2013 from hjenglish.com, a Shanghai-based commercial website that is specialized in education of English language, at www.hjenglish.com/kouyu/p343000/.
3. In 1992, Van Dijk deconstructed the connections between the press and racism by examining several discursive strategies that the press usually employ to defend their racism. These strategies include positive self-presentation, denial and counter-attack, moral blackmail, subtle denials, mitigation, defence, and offence. Critical discourse analysis was adopted as Van Dijk's research methodology. However, Van Dijk did not define these strategies in his 1992 article but used them as examples for his discourse analysis (Van Dijk 1992).
4. The e-government framework was initiated by the Central Government in 2001. National E-government Standardization Working Group was created in January 2002 to supervise and steer the construction of the framework. Since 2003, local governments have played a major role in building the e-government system. See (F. Yang 2009, 91). The Decree of Government Information Openness came into force in May 2008.
5. Translation by author.
6. Translation by author.
7. Please refer to the appendix for the pages A1 and A2 that carry blank spaces.
8. The English version of the interview is available from the website of the White House at www.whitehouse.gov/the-press-office/interview-president-obama-xiang-xi-southern-weekly.
9. Please refer to chapter 6 on how the press, including communist outlets, openly uttered against the GMD censorship before 1949.
10. See The CCP Central Committee Decision on Propaganda Policies of the Newspapers, Publications, News, and Radio Broadcasting issued on January 29, 1981.
11. There are various English translations to the term "shendu." The term "control reading" is used in: (Fischer 2009, 191) Another term is "reading inspection" in: (Gu 2004, 37). Also, "media monitoring" is used in: (Y. Zhao 1998, 21) (Quick 2003, 190). The literal version of "review reading" is adopted in this chapter in order to reflect its downtoning effect.
12. The Provisional Measure on Review Reading of Newspapers and Periodicals [*baozhiqikanshenduzanxingbanfa*] was issued by the GAPP on February 9, 2009.
13. The corruption problems will be discussed in chapter 4.
14. The text of the TV report is also available from www.sx.xinhuanet.com/jryw/2011-12/25/content_24404736.htm.
15. An online survey shows that 80 percent of the netizens hold suspicious attitude toward the software and worry about their privacy. See S. Liu and Li 2009 and Chao 2009.
16. NPC, the National People's Congress, is China's legislative branch of the state power.
17. Zhan Jiang is a professor of journalism from China Youth University of Political Sciences.CYUPS, located in Beijing, was established in 1985 under the direct leadership of the Central Committee of the Communist Youth League, designed to produce future leaders of the Communist Party of China.Viewed on Jan 10th, 2010 from media.people.com.cn/GB/22114/42328/145310/8792516.html.
18. Translation by author.

19. Zhonggong Zhongyang Zuzhibu, Zhonggong Zhongyang Xuanchuanbu, "Guanyu Zhongyang Xuanchuanbu Fenguan Jiaoyu Xitong Ganbu Youguan Shixiang de Tongzhi." (82) Zutong 27 (July 23, 1982), BD, 366–67. See Burns 1989, 33.

20. The final version of the bill is available from www.asianlii.org/cn/legis/gd/laws/rosmoptcbtaod814/.

21. Wang Lijun was removed from his office of Deputy Mayor of Chongqing and placed under investigation soon after he visited the U.S. consulate in Chengdu on February 6, 2012. Viewed on March 29, 2012 from www.bbc.co.uk/news/world-asia-china-17539232.

22. Li Peng is former Chinese premier (1988–1998) and NPC chairman (1998–2003). His son, Li Xiaopeng, and daughter, Li Xiaolin, are dominant figures of China's energy industry. Li Xiaopeng, former head of Huaneng Corporation, now assumes the position of governor of Shanxi Province, the biggest producer of coal and electricity in China. Li Xiaolin is vice-president of China Power Investment Corporation and president of the Hong Kong-listed China Power International Development Corporation. See Oakes 167.

23. Zhengzhou is the capital city of Henan Province. Mr. Lu is an official of deputy bureau (*si, ting*) level. See Xinhua 2009.

24. Please see the preface by Mobo Gao.

*Chapter Four*

# Pandemic Media Corruption

*An Ownership Problem?*

Despite its rapid growth in financial terms at a double-digit rate over the years since the late 1970s, the media industry has experienced a considerable loss of ethical integrity and consequently an increase of corruption and malpractice (B. Xie and Gao 2013). Among all the symptoms of the ailing media system, the most ostensive ones are the managerial officials blatantly abusing their power (Y. Zhao 2008a) and malpractice among editorial professionals who thrive on journalism on bribery, blackmail, paid news, and sensationalism (Bandurski and Hala 2010; Z. He 2000; Y. Zhao 1998, 2000). The increase of fake and false news (B. Xie and Gao 2013), in particular, has become an eyebrow-raising malpractice issue over the last two decades crossing the threshold of the new century.

Malpractice is usually referred to in legal terms as "negligence committed by a professional that causes a recipient of his or her services to suffer an injury, loss or damage" (Goldman and Sigismond 2010, 84). Professional malpractice features "breach of commonly recognized professional standards" (S. L. Davis, Weisgal, and Neggers 2001, 789). Media or press malpractice consists of three fundamental elements, namely duty, breach, and damage. This chapter uses "malpractice" instead of "corruption" because the latter implies intentional breach of duty while the former includes both intentional breach and unintentional negligence. It involves various journalistic misconducts that go against ethical principles, including but not limited to inaccuracy, sensationalism, and press harassment (V. Howarth 1991, 118). As a result, the professional principles of truth and objectivity are considerably impaired and ethical standards compromised when media credibility is undermined. This chapter aims to explain the causal connections between malpractices and the political and market impact on the professionals. Discussion will show that such media malpractice derives from at least two sources: the pursuit of profits at the corporate management level and political control at the administrative level, the former more likely in a capitalist market economy and the latter in authoritarian or semi-authoritarian politics (Ho 2008, 20). Both scenarios are unmistakably the case of China today.

Figure 4.1 shows the top-ten fabricated and misleading news items produced by official and non-official outlets from 2001 to 2010. The irony is that sensationalism, a strategy that Lagerkvist calls "breaking social taboo for profits" (Lagerkvist 2008, 197), produced by official media has been steadily on the rise since 2006. It is ostensible that both official and commercialized outlets have been involved, showing that both are experiencing the problem of malpractice in a similar way. From 2010 to October 2011 alone, 160 fake and false news items were placed under investigation, 22.9 percent of the total corruption cases investigated by the GAPP (Qu 2011). This can, at least in part, demonstrate that information control, education of politically engineered journalistic values and the market have failed to keep such misconducts as sensationalism under control (B. Xie and Gao 2013).

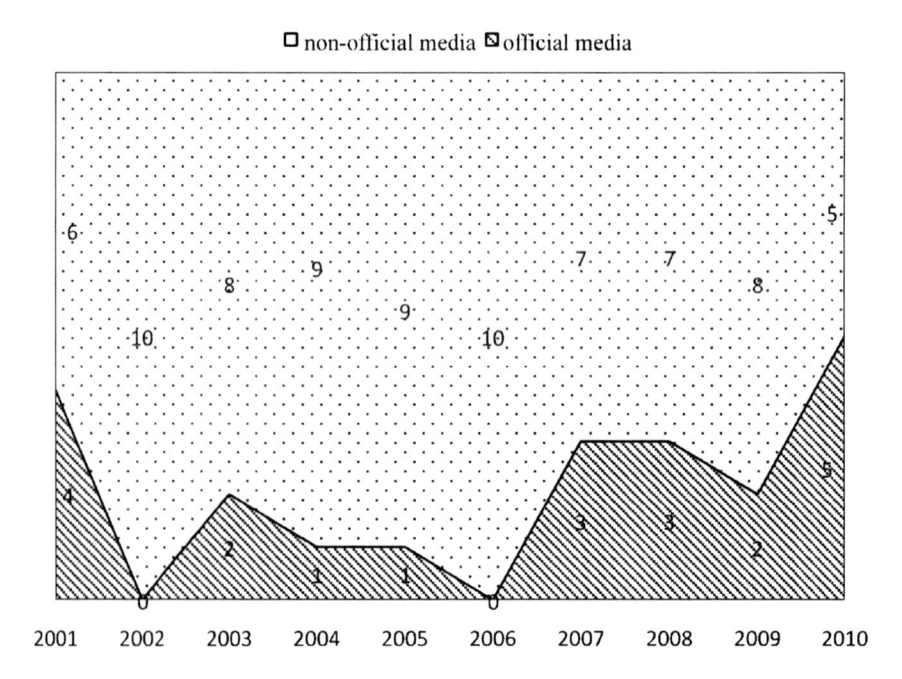

**Figure 4.1.** Top-ten fake and false news items in China from 2001 to 2010. Compiled by author from *Journalism Review* 2002, 2003, 2004, 2005, 2006, 2007, 2008, 2009, 2010, 2011.

One of the high-profile fake reports in recent memories appeared on November 17, 2012 on *Jinri Zaobao* [*Morning Post Today*], a commercialized subsidiary of the Zhejiang Daily Press Group.[1] The front-page story, titled in bold characters, "Women Sentries Learning the Spirit of the 18th CCP National Congress," carries a picture of seven young women in reserve force uniforms at a township post in Zhejiang Province reading *The People's Daily*, *Zhejiang Daily*, and *Taizhou Daily*, which are Party-state mouthpieces at the central, provincial, and city level, respectively. Within a few hours after the paper was released, some readers found out that, in the picture, three ladies were actually reading a report on Zhuhai Airshow on page four of *the People's Daily* and the other four *Taizhou Daily* readers were happily reviewing a full-page smart phone advertisement on page twelve (Fake News Research Project Team 2012, 50). This finding traveled instantly throughout the Chinese blogosphere and became a subject of cynicism and criticism. To tackle the simmering credibility crisis, the Photo Centre of Zhejiang Daily Press Group released an apology statement immediately later on the same day, confessing that the picture was but an orchestrated [*baipai*] charade. As an autopunition, the responsible photo editor of the Photo Centre had his one-month bonus withheld and the responsible photojournalists were suspended for six months (Su 2012).

That the picture was identified as "faulty" so quickly and the press group responded in such a unprecedentedly timely manner aside, the fact that photographers working for a highly commercialized newspaper today still have to set up a scene for a propagandistic picture is thought-provoking. Actually, it has long been long practiced convention that the media follow up major political events such as the Two National Conferences [*lianghui*] with reports carrying propagandistic pictures unfailingly showing workers, students, soldiers, and people from all walks of life studying official documents or reading official newspapers together. It would be no surprise if these pictures should be taken in a carefully orchestrated way. Yet, the *Jinri Zaobao* picture was not only considered a serious offense to journalistic values, but was also counted as one of the top-ten fake news 2012 (Fake News Research Project Team 2012).

Although the photo saga started with a picture related to a political event, the following online commentaries and academic discussions were curiously depoliticized. Most of the domestic public opinion as well as official reports have interpreted this event as a problem of professionalism among journalist practitioners. Condemnation was bombarded on the journalists for their lack of professional awareness and quality while praises were generously given to the press group for its timely response to the problem. Some commented that the punishment of the photojournalists was of "epoch-making significance" (P. a. Zhou 2012). A follow-up report by the *Xinjing Bao* [*The Beijing News*] calls for honesty and self-discipline among the professionals (Jing 2012).

Another commentary on the *Jiancha Daily,* quoting famous journalism scholars such as Chen Lidan, states that "the Zhejiang Daily Press Group's apology statement is a historical progress" especially for its courage to confess its technical mistake made in an attempt to positively report one of the most high-profile Party events (S. Wang and Wang 2012).[2]

Beneath all kinds of unprofessional practices like the *Jinri Zaobao* photojournalism saga are the ongoing trend of depoliticized content (Z. He 2000; K. X. Zhou 2009), profit-making marketization (Z. Pan 2005; Jing Wang 2010), and dynamic corporate restructuring (Fischer 2009; Guoguang Wu 2000). While this trend is not something unique or particularly of Chinese characteristics, that it has been happening in a highly liberalized and capitalized economy proclaiming pragmatic communist ideology and one-party rule yet yielding prosperity and rising power has made any black-and-white judgment overtly simplistic and bigoted. Thence, how this particular context is related to the rampant loss of professional integrity has become a profitable hotspot for debates. Whereas there has been a common recognition of the corruption and malfeasance problems, paradigms for observation, and subsequent proposals for solution vary drastically. Still, we want an answer to such a question as: With market logic and its libertarian implication of accountability prevailing today, why would journalists and photographers still tend to choose what is false yet more acceptable to chief editors rather than simply hanging on to what is true and objective?

Along the lines of the debates, state ownership, along with their propagandistic role as a Party organ, has become a much targeted blame for the media's fallen ethical standards. Given that the dominating conglomerates and especially the news production sector remain exclusively state-owned under close Party supervision on the one hand and a range of media ownership options exist outside the news room on the other, ownership discourses are more often argued in dichotomous terms (Picard 2007, 111). Confined to state-private dualist frameworks, the ownership narratives usually focus on state-media or media-market relationships and finishes with a privatization prospect, shunning investigating journalism as a conviction of public representation and journalists as individual workers in the public sphere. Yet, I will argue that corruption and professional malpractice in the media industry, like those in other Party-state systems, is not simply caused by state ownership but the result of a mixture of dilemmas caused by political and market control funnelled through the profit-driven management and elite politics, which have alienated the journalists from their representation relationship with the public.[3] This disjuncture of representation relationship has engendered considerable ideological confusion and loss of public conviction, leading to the collapse of the politically and commercially inflated ethical rhetoric.

## STATE-OWNERSHIP AS A PRINCIPLE-AGENT PROBLEM?

Likening the state as a principal or the owner and the media as its agent or manager, Peng Hwa Ang and Guozhen Wang (2010) have argued that it is the state ownership and the role of party organ that have subjected the mainstream media in China to an inevitable principal-agent problem causing corruption and malfeasance. This problem, as Ang and Wang have claimed, arises when the agent has failed to work for the best interest of its principal due to the irreconcilable conflicts of self-interests between the state and the media, which is unavoidable once the principal employs the agent. They believe that, in a context where commercialization and industrialization have to be maintained within the orbit of the party-state, the long-existing party journalism (Z. Pan and Chan 2003; Y. Zhao 1998) and burgeoning professional journalism (Hugo de Burgh 2003a, 2003b) have become incompatible with each other due to the fact that the Party has political control over the media and that the managers and journalists, particularly those senior in hierarchy, are torn between the belief in social responsibilities and a realistic urge to make money for themselves. Thereby, Ang and Wang define the plague of corruption and malfeasance to be a "principal-agent problem" rooted in the combination of state-ownership and the Party organ role, and propose to alter such principal-agent relationship by privatizing state-owned media and allowing private ownership.

This solution is based on the rationale, as David Croteau and William Hoynes (2006) have insightfully critiqued, that private media is conceptualized as businesses selling products to the market rather than providing utility services to the state and therefore are accountable to the market or the buyers. Such expectation on private ownership has implied its full market effects in threefold. One is that management following the free market regulation by demand and supply will assure private media of their financial well-being and editorial integrity. Second, private ownership and market logic will be able to extricate the media from government intervention and leave official ideological orchestration obsolete. Third, the market is where the subjectivity of journalists can be acknowledged and their ideal of professionalism materialized. In the same vein, others such as Milton Mueller and Tan Zixiang (1997, 120), Milton Friedman (2002), and John Whale (1977) have also argued in favor of privatization and marketization as an effective pathway towards less information control and more freedom and transparency.

Ang and Wang might be right about the phenomena side, when citing others' observations, that the corruption and malpractice problem is systemic and institutional, and that "opportunistic journalism" is about making quick and easy money. The case of the *Jinri Zaobao* photo orchestration saga is only one of the many demonstrations that journalists have little choice but to cater for political mandates and consumerism simultaneously even at the cost of professional ethical standards. Propagandistic messages are usually carefully conveyed in a way that readers may not object to them as sheer formula propaganda. The *Jinri Zaobao* photojournalists chose to set up the scene, by using images of good-looking young ladies instead of that of local politicians, to deliver a much more relaxed and amiable atmosphere yet with strong propagandistic effect. Yet, according to the market logic of the principal-agent argument, *Jinri Zaobao*, should it be privatized, would not have had to report Party-state events the way it did, and the journalists then would not have had to fake photos for soft propaganda but simply allow the market to decide what to report and what photos to take. However, the promise of political-commitment-free premise by private ownership to eradicate faulty journalism has neglected the fact that even the freest media in the post-communist Europe (Curry 2005, 157) and the capitalist West (Chomsky 2002; M. Gao 2004a) as well as the Asian democracies and autocracies (George 2008) are still subject to various forms of government control. It is not how the media is owned but how it is managed has directly led to the malpractice problem.

Some of the unobserved missing links, between these factual elements and the ownership conundrum as a boiled-down explanation as well as between the corruption and malfeasance as a problem and privatization as a solution have rendered the principal-agent argument vulnerable to closer scrutiny. If the state is considered opposite to the private as the public to the private,[4] how can the relationship between the Party-state and the media be simplified as a "principal-agent" one when both the Party-state and the state-owned media are public apparatus at least nominally serving the best interest of the public, especially the workers and peasants who are the nominal ruling class? Is it not, then, a fractured relationship of the public with the state and the state-owned media caused by the Party and state bureaucracy coming between and misappropriating the media for its private use? Whereas the state is no more than a nominal owner while the Party has seized the real mastership and encouraged full-fledged marketization, how can the crooked state-media relationship be attributed to public ownership rather than to public ownership being plagued by Party politics and the profit-seeking market that actually do not represent the public but, as Herman and Chomsky have opined (1994), the political supremacy and capitalist interests? Should the state-media relationship be a principal-agent one and causing the existing problems, must not the agent do whatever it can to put things right instead of finding fault with its owner's equity structure? While privatization means the state voting itself out of the board of directors, this voluntary resignation does not seem to fit in usual principal-agent logic as the principal is apparently harvesting in a good season. How about firing the agent and finding a better one? This happens in the business world only when the agent has failed to meet the financial or functional goals set by the principal. However, why should the state fire its profit making and obedient agent while the agent does not pose any substantial threat to the interests of the principal? Should private media be a better agent and thus state-owned media be privatized, where is the assurance that private media will do a better job speaking for public interests rather than for its private principal in the marketplace? Is not the media a niche market where most profits are generated from advertising while advertising is about appealing to the urban middle class and high end patrons? Otherwise, if a normative principal-agent relationship is about the agent working for the best interest of its owner, a privatized media outlet is bound to serve its private owner. Is this not what has been causing problems in the West? How many News International phone-hacking scandals (BBC 2012) do we need before coming to the sense that a capitalized media outlet or conglomerate is bound to seek interests and make profits, as an obligatory priority, for its investors and stake holders? As for privatizing the state-owned media, who but the powerful and rich have the resources and power to take over the business? It can be any established political and capitalist elites and their family businesses, and probably media tycoons with transnational backgrounds, but not the populace and definitely not the vast majority of the weak and poor who are struggling at the bottom of the polarized social-class pyramid. Would this be not just what Herbert Schiller (2013, 44) and Nickesia S. Gordon (2008, 72) have elucidated as a shift of threat to free expression from the government to private corporate power? What has made it a taken-for-granted assumption that private ownership favors openness and accountability any more than public ownership does? What reassures more transparency from private ownership than from public ownership so as to ensure more credibility and less corruption and professional malpractice? None of these questions have been addressed or can hardly be answered by the principal-agent analogy and its privatization paradigm because they do not investigate beyond the state-media dichotomy into relationships inside the system such as labor relations, working conditions and their implications for the journalists and journalism, a critical question regarding journalism by whom and for whom.

The principal-agent argument does not attach much importance to what have turned journalists into mere wage earners working for survival and social status and their labor into a source for surplus. Is this not what has been justified in libertarian democracies and capitalism in the West? In China, commercialized journalism has already been managed as a profit-generating business and reports as consumer products, a situation which the shift to private ownership will not change but more likely intensify. What difference would a privatized principal-agent relationship make to journalists and editors, such as those working for the *Jinri Zaobao*, whose livelihood, value, and subjectivity have already been fixed on the orbit of the profit-driven and capitalized market logic? Instead of considering the *Jinri Zaobao* photo saga to be just another isolated incident of fallen ethical standards concerning individual journalists as the official commentaries and elite professionalism tend to lead us to believe,[5] this chapter attempts to seek the answers by looking into the dilemmas that characterize the current market-oriented media environment.

## THE SURVIVAL DILEMMA

The survival dilemma, or market dilemma (B. Xie and Gao 2013), refers to the situation in which media professionals are torn between difficulties in surviving exploitative management in a highly competitive market and fulfilling their professional commitment at the same time. Journalists and editors have to face on daily basis inadequate pay, excessive workloads, aggressive evaluation systems, and a real potential of losing their tenure. As a result, the majority choose to follow the Party logic and the market logic (Y. Zhao 1998) funnelled through everyday editorial management and stay on the safe side and take only calculated risk (Bandurski and Hala 2010, 57). Such a situation is called survival dilemma because, to many journalist professionals, their profession is no more than a means for making a living. This dilemma results from the changing of working relations and conditions within the media system characterized by commoditization of the professional labor (W. Wang 2011) under a profit-seeking management catering to consumerism and propaganda commitment (B. Xie and Gao 2013). Alongside this dilemma is the development of a media market where journalists and editors are transformed from revolutionary cadres (Cheek 1997, 220) to mere wage-earning employees, as well as journalism from public service to consumer products. However, this is not only a change of employment status from lifetime tenure to term contracts but also a transformation of purpose, commitment, and process of journalist profession as "a form of labor" (W. Wang 2011).

Most commercialized outlets such as *Jinri Zaobao* have adopted a cost-sensitive management in response to the increasingly competitive market. Newspapers and broadcasting services are still physically confined to locality despite that trans-local connections and networks have been established as a result of technological advance (Sun 2012, 26). As there are usually quite a number of outlets in the same city or prefecture, competition between these outlets is getting increasingly intensive, especially in larger cities such as the capital cities and more populated ones in relatively developed regions. For example, there were sixty-eight newspapers and 217 magazines in Zhejiang Province in 2005. Of the four major press groups in the province, two are located in the capital city of Hangzhou where Zhejiang Daily Press Group has sixteen newspapers and three magazines; and Hangzhou Daily Press

Group has seven newspapers and three magazines (B. Zhang 2005, 60). Established as a fully commercialized outlet in 2000, *Jinri Zaobao* maintains a steady daily circulation of about 600,000 copies. Like other local commercialized papers such as *Dushi Kuaibao* [*Metropolitan Express News*],[6] *Jinri Zaobao* targets its niche market among business leaders, senior white-collars, and private business owners. The competition between these papers in Hangzhou, dubbed as a "white hot war zone filled with the smoke of gunpowder" (S. Huang and Zhou 2003, 255), is getting progressively fierce not only due to being geographically confined but more importantly to being self-limited to narrowed elite urban readership and content similarity. This is so because the relatively wealthier readers are the target of advertising clients who are the major "sponsors" (Y. Zhao 1998, 63) and sources of profits, and therefore urban elite taste for pleasure and even sensationalism becomes a major benchmark for producing marketable content.

To cope with the intensified competition, it becomes essential to cut down cost and secure market share. In doing so, these outlets have exhausted all strategies that one can find in the no-holds-barred free market including, but not limited to, abolishing lifetime tenure and replacing it with term or casual contracts, outsourcing news collection and editing, paying by word count and on reimbursement basis, prescribing advertising assignments, and using various kinds of monetary incentives (B. Xie and Gao 2013).

Since the start of the reform era in late 1978, the labor relationships within the state-owned media system has experienced fundamental changes with the personnel management scheme shifting from government system to corporate governance. From the *chengbao* system and hierarchical contractual arrangements in the early 1980s, to the personnel agent system [*renshi daili*] and labor dispatching [*laowu paiqian*] arrangements since the late 1990s, journalists and their editorial labor have gradually become "an important factor of production" (W. Wang 2011, 91). The relationships of editorial staff with their outlets have changed from that between state-owners [*zhurenweng*] and state-owned institutions to that between employees and employers, and then to that between labor and capital.

The *chengbao* system involves rearrangement of responsibility, authority, and interests, allowing the management to subcontract with lower-level departments and branches to delegate responsibility and profit assignments as well as accountability in a downward direction. The subcontractors, including departments specializing in news collection, editing, printing, advertising, and distribution, were allowed to retain some of the profits as long as they fulfill, or exceed their contract commitment. With the promise of profit retainment also came punitive measures. *Shaanxi Daily*, the mouthpiece of the CCP Shaanxi Provincial Committee, initiated a complex *chengbao* system in 1983 in which the printing branch was assigned a profit goal while the editorial department was allocated a line for cost control. The contract and subcontracts were broken up into units and assigned to individual staff members until each was responsible for a certain fraction of the general target. Once the target was reached, 60 percent of the profit could be retained as development fund, 20 percent for collective welfare, and 20 percent for staff bonus. Those who failed the assignments will have their salary withdrawn by 1 percent to 15 percent (W. Wang 2011, 91–92). In some more vigorous schemes such as that of *HuashangBao*, an urban daily in Xi'an, those who fail to fulfill their tasks will be fired (W. Wang 2011, 98). Considered an effective way to boost efficiency, *chengbao* system in various forms began to be adopted across the country, and, as a result, many outlets have managed to turn loss into gain.

Within the *chengbao* framework, the personnel system was reformed so that most of the staff members, except for the top executives who remained Party-state officials, became employees under term or casual contracts. Since 1992, in particular, the media reform has seen most commercialized outlets adopt "all-staff appointment contract system [*quanyuan pingyongzhi*]" and "labor agency dispatching system [*laowu paiqianzhi*]." In some commercialized outlets, even chief editors could be recruited from outside under term contracts. In an appointment contract system, outlets recruit editorial staff from within or outside and appoint them to vacant positions. The labor relations remain between the outlets and the employees. However, in a labor-dispatching system, the outlets only contract with Talent Exchange Centers (TEC), which are commissioned by the outlets for recruitment services. As virtual employers, the TECs offer positions to job applicants and sign contracts with them, and then "dispatch" the recruited staff to the outlets. The TECs were initially designed in the 1980s to archive the personnel profiles [*renshi dang'an*] and provide employment information for job seekers who are not within the state personnel system such as freelance writers and workers in the private sector. But the TECs have now become major labor contractors on behalf of both public and private employers.

However, this labor agent dispatching system has created an awkward situation. There is no contractual relationship between the outlets as employers and the recruited staff as employees; nor is there labor relationship between the TECs as the offering party of labor contracts and the recruited staff as the other party. This system has now become the most widely adopted personnel management scheme in the reformed media system because, at least in part, it circumvents the employer's legal obligation under the article 14 of the Labor Contract Law (2007) to offer open-ended tenure to those who have worked consecutively for it for ten years.[7] Commenting on an article on media personnel reform by Wei Wenbin, former president of Hunan Radio, Film and Television Group, Wang Weijia (2011, 97) is careful to note that:

The complete (official) logic of using journalist labor in a commoditized environment has been revealed in brief: First, labor is the most important factor of production in producing journalist commodities; Second, the exchange of value under the law of value and market demand, rather than people-centered social relationships, must be observed in using the labor; Third, efforts are to be made to break any traditional personnel system that may impose limits on businesses in recruiting free labor, distort price relationships, and hinder efficiency maximization.[8]

Wang's critique uncovers the rationale, conditions, and nature of the labor relationships in the reformed media system. When the media businesses, like other market-oriented and profit-seeking businesses in the private or public sector, can find cheap and "free" labor and easy ways to bring the labor and its cost under control, they would certainly prefer such a surplus-based labor relationship that defines the value of journalism in financial terms. Such a relationship is largely regulated by the demand and supply in the labor market in which the market logic apparently has the upper hand, and journalists and editors are practically selling their labor to the outlets.

It is within such a reformed labor framework that the media outlets started to outsource some of their businesses that are time-consuming, labor intensive, and cost sensitive, but with low direct profit prospects, including news collection that often requires journalists to travel for field investigation. One of the strategies, apart from using the dispatching system, is to recruit "special" [*teyue*] journalists and editors or casual correspondents [*tongxunyuan*]. Opposite to the proud and sweet childhood memory of many who wrote in the 1970s and 1980s as "special correspondents" for school magazines, the prefix title of "special" here means no more than disposable and cheap labor, and the outlets do not have to provide basic salaries, welfare, health care, and, above all, managerial accountability and responsibility for them (B. Xie and Gao 2013). There are usually no formal service contracts between the outlets and the "special" correspondents. Sometimes, an oral agreement can just get things going, and they can be fired at any time at the discretion of their supervisors (W. Wang 2011, 157). The informal employees are paid only by word count (Melton and Pillsbury 2005, 586). In most cases, writers will not get paid or their cost reimbursed unless their work is accepted and then published (Bandurski and Hala 2010, 106).

Such labor relationships and working conditions can be well illustrated in Wang's (2011, 160) account of a journalist who had been working on casual employment basis for almost ten years for a magazine in Henan Province. This journalist found himself in a difficult situation when he was informed that he could only renew his employment by signing a contract with a labor dispatching TEC service instead of with the magazine that had employed him over the years. This is the dilemma: either he should sign the contract with the TEC in order to continue his career but lose his legally sanctioned opportunity to request a permanent contract with the magazine, or he should seek renewal of his employment with the magazine in order to be able to lodge his request of a permanent contract but could instantly get fired and lose his TEC contract as well. Similarly, CCTV, China's largest and richest state-level broadcasting giant, started to use an informal employment scheme in the early 1990s and switched to a labor-dispatching system in 2005. Among its 9,620 staff cohort in 2003, 7,142 were informal employees. On the eve of the enforcement of Labor Contract Law in July 2007, CCTV shed 1,800 informal jobs, a record cutback yet officially trumpeted as an achievement of the reform of personnel system in state-owned enterprises (W. Wang 2011, 106). The change of the employment system and labor relationships as such clearly and simply demonstrates a ruthless market-driven management rationale: professional labor is nothing but a factor of production, of which the cost should be kept as low as possible according to the market logic. If outsourcing and casual employment can extract the surplus out of the labor, there will be no point offering continuing contracts and a *zhurenweng* status.

Dai Guoliang and Zhao Hongliang, two photojournalists working for *Jinri Zaobao* and responsible for the abovementioned orchestrated photo, are two of the many "special" professionals. Their official title appearing on the newspaper is "*tongxunyuan*." Although the official apology statement declared that they were suspended for six months, there has been no photo under their names being published up to date[9] either on *Jinri Zaobao* or any other local newspapers since the photo saga, suggesting a possible indefinite suspension or even boycott. The public opinions, from *Xinhua* and *the People's Daily* commentaries to common bloggers to scholarly discussions, have been curiously using one voice either morally or cynically condemning the "unprofessionalism" of these photojournalists. However, none of the higher-level managers or chief editors was held responsible, punished, or even condemned. This chapter is not trying to defend this "unprofessionalism," but to question the way that accountability was delegated to the lowest level so that the management can get away with their exploitative management, which is not the least answerable to the labor relations whatever the form they take.

To ensure and sustain the "labor control" (W. Wang 2011) established through the salary and tenure system, media outlets are keen to implement quantitative evaluation system that keep the editorial efforts under managerial supervision (B. Xie and Gao 2013). Such systems are usually used as incentive as well as coercive and punitive measures. For example, *China Youth Daily* (CYD) uses a credit point system, under which journalists are awarded cash bonuses according to the frequency with which their stories are favorably mentioned by high-level party and government officials (Baum 2008, 177). That the CYD's evaluation system is smarmy to the bureaucracy reflects the paper's determined collaboration with the Party-state's political control agenda. As this political control is increasingly legitimized by portraying the disenfranchised groups as sources of danger and social instability, the media plays an indispensible role in rationalizing and popularizing this portraying. Accordingly, the media subscribes to class containment and displaces class antagonism (Y. Zhao 2008a, 274). When addressing crime and social injustice involving transgressors from the disenfranchised groups background, the CYD and many other outlets do not seem to hesitate, as Yuezhi Zhao (2008a, 274) illuminates, to produce editorials banging on presumably universal values of journalistic professionalism and judicial justice "to negate class divisions and conflicts." In a CYD editorial commenting on a murder case, Wang Binyu, a migrant worker who committed the murder, was described as "psychologically distorted" and "extremist" so that not only people like him are perceived dangerous, any sympathy for these people is also "a signal of danger" (Yuhen Xiao 2005).[10] While clearly constructing the weak, victimized, and desperate transgressors as the internal "other" of the society, the CYD "was blunt in its hegemonic mission to displace class politics and defuse class conflict" (Y. Zhao 2008a, 275). Not only has the gulf between the rich and the poor and between the powerful and the weak been depoliticized and translated into bloody, exciting, and sensational stories of sex and violence, as one could easily found in newspapers, TV reports and portal front pages, such depiction also serves to justify the urban elite and societal contempt on those who are less educated, less articulate and underrepresented social groups as "low *suzhi* people," to whom many like Sun Wanning (2009, 2013), and Yuezhi Zhao (2005, 2008a) have dedicated genuine concern. Embracing the class containment dimension, the CYD's evaluation system characterized by direct money incentive, and many others alike (B. Xie and Gao 2013), encourage reportage and editorials to follow the media's blatant de-politicization of public opinion, collaboration with the political control agenda, and its market strategy to meet the urban craving for sensationalism.

The survival dilemma does not mean that journalism has been dumped into one of the poorest profession categories in financial terms. On the contrary, under the stress imposed by the ever-increasing consumerism created by journalism and on the journalists in return, they may find it easy to turn their professional skills into a lucrative tool for making "grey income" and alleviating their social status from heavily exploited labor to "reconstituted middle-class social strata" (Y. Zhao 2004b, 47). Market logic works with coercive as well as incentive effects particularly when it is associated with employment contracts and income prospects, and therefore, has direct implications for the journalists" attitude toward the information control reality, changing from frustration in the 1980s (Lee 2004, 15; Scotton 2010, 123; X. Zhang 2007, 2) to impotence in the early 1990s (Lee 2003, 17) and to complacency in the new millennium (Lee 2004, 15). As Chin-Chuan Lee (2004, 15) puts it well, "Material gains provide a key explanation to this psychological role transformation; the wealthier journalists become, the less politically engaged they are." Following a mixed sense of slavery, loss of public conviction, and gain of materialist complacency, journalists tend to adapt themselves to the profit-driven market logic, including what Ang and Wang (2010) called the "opportunistic journalism," not only on part of the outlets but more realistically for themselves. This way, the freer the market is, the easier it will be for the employers to control the labor by cutting the costs on one hand and stimulating workers incentive with financial gain on the other. However, this can hardly be defined as an ownership issue but a problem engendered from sheer market logic.

## THE SUBJECTIVITY DILEMMA

The subjectivity dilemma, or identity dilemma (B. Xie and Gao 2013), in this chapter refers to a situation in which media professionals are lost between who they are in journalistic belief and whom they are shaped into in the highly controlled reality, an identity confusion caused by the discrepancy between subjectivity ideals and experiences. Externally, it is the professional image of journalist practitioners. Inwardly, it is how they reconcile themselves to the confusion in the inner world. It becomes a dilemma particularly when the journalist's subjectivity is suppressed and they become instrumentalist objects under the political and market control.

Subjectivity refers to the total of different dimensions of a certain subject. The understanding and definition evolve over time from Rene Descartes' continental rationalism departing from humanist ontology (Caton 1973) to Freudian schema of unconscious, preconscious and conscious mind (Elliott 2004, 26) to Lacan's shift to the language aspect of gender, power, and identity (Mansfield 2000, 48), and to Foucault's power analysis and his notion of "instituted models of self-knowledge and their history" (Foucault 2000). Contemporary understanding of subjectivity has been much abused in libertarian justification of private ownership and free market logic as much as it can be suppressed in an authoritarian context. An individual's subjectivity can be considered as the existing being of a person, a sum of knowledge that builds up the content and defines from inside out the private ego identity (Davidson 2005). From a socio-political perspective, subjectivity, rather than a static being, is subject to temporary shifts (Ishihara and Tarone 2009, 103) as well as permanent evolution constantly shaped by the social, political, historical, and cultural contexts (Fulga 2005; McLaren 2013, 222), and an individual, acting as a social actor with political subjectivity, can have a number of different subject dimensions and positions (D. R. Howarth and Stavrakakis 2000).

As much as subjectivity is an internalized process, an individual's ethical system starts with an internal recognition of the other that is not merely the object for cognition or comprehension but that beyond one's grasp and powers (Critchley 1999, 14). This means that no code of ethics has any practical meaning and efficacy without being internalized by individual practitioners into their subjectivity. Ethical values, therefore, do not exist as a static framework of moral standards but stand for an internalized value-laden system of relationships of the subject with other parties in the same group. In this regard, ethics is not only the reflection of external institutions but, as Foucault (2000, 300) has opined, a self-reflexive and historical process of subjectiviation, which characterizes "the relationship of the self to itself, and . . . [covers] the range of practices that constitute, define, organize and instrumentalise the strategies which individuals in their freedom can use in dealing with each other."

With the above understanding, the journalist's subjectivity can be considered here to be an internalized relationship, state of existing being, and nature of reflexive representation. Firstly, journalistic subjectivity is an ongoing construction of self-identification and perceptions that engage the journalists as the subject processing the surrounding world as the objects. It involves not only the individual dimensions of the practitioners but also the relationships among the parties in the process of news production cycle including journalists and editors, chief editors, media outlets, audience and readers, the state and the market, and the citizenship. Journalist's subjectivity presupposes editorial subjective initiative as a relative, if not an opposite, term to ration as a way of thinking and responding to the external factors. Both their transcendental ration and empirical experience can be influenced by other parties of the journalism cycle.

It is worth noting that journalism is a result of subjective human labor involving a complex process of observation, synthesizing, interpretation, and critique of the objective world. This process, characterized by the labor relations described previously, stands right in the middle of the predicament of journalism as both an objective observer and a subjective participant, of journalistic roles as both neutral and participant, of the professional values as both social responsibility and self-responsibility, and of the conflict of interests between the self, the management, and the state (Burd 1978), rendering the much-celebrated principle of truth and objectivity to the realm of relativism. As each of these parties may exert impact on both the form and content, their relationships can be both cooperative in attaining a common ideal (not necessarily the truth and objectivity per se) and competitive in vying for editorial power in their own interests. In such an intertwined nexus of relationships, the journalists' subjectivity remains critical because news production can be seen as the result of the negotiation between the journalist's subjectivity and the factors that may influence it. That said, journalists and editors are the major party whose transcendental ration and empirical experience are the direct descriptive and interpretive mechanism underpinning the reportage. Thus, the bid for editorial power among all these parties ultimately becomes internalized competing pressures shaping this dimension of the journalist's subjectivity. To a great extent, a suppressed subjectivity under such shaping pressure tends to seek relief by shifting its committed efforts from the forbidden zone where things are difficult, provoking and prohibited to a comfort zone where things are allowed, easy, and entertaining.

Secondly, apart from its distinctive individualistic self-reflexive feature, there is a public facet of the journalist's subjectivity in its intricate relationship with the citizenship. Journalist's subjectivity represents not only the ego being as an individual citizen and its own interests but also stands in the forefront of the public sphere that requires professional skills as well as political conviction and engagement. In the public domain, as much as it is an internalized process of individuation, subjectivity is equally a process of politicization or de-politicization in the opposite direction at both conscious and subconscious levels, affecting how the objectives are perceived through the filter of subjectivity and reproduced in journalism as supposedly subjectivity-free objectivity. In this sense, the empowerment of journalists' subjectivity lies not only in its skilled capacity to describe and interpret the reality and produce quality reportage but more significantly in its public representation and responsibility to reflect the objective world with a genuine concern of the represented instead of a mere detached party.

However, as mentioned earlier, the Chinese media has experienced a trend toward de-politicization over the reform era (Z. He 2000; Latham 2007; Lu ; Y. Zhao 2003, 2008a; K. X. Zhou 2009). Beneath this trend lies the neoliberalization of the Enlightenment concept of universality of moral values centring on humanity as the end and individualism as the means, which traces back to Immanuel Kant in his late-eighteenth-century publications (Kant 2006; Korsgaard 1996; Louden 2011). The Kantian ethics, a major philosophical source for the modern idealism in the West, presupposes a good will committed to the duty to the moral law, which is categorized into "perfect duty" and "imperfect duty" (Louden 2011). The former duty, such as refraining from telling a lie, is a constant truth and absolute principle while the latter, such as doing good deeds, is a flexible and relative one. The division of the duties has made it possible for human beings to formulate autonomy on a rationalized basis so as to promote their own perfection by their own will (Louden 2011). Within the Kantian idealism framework, subjectivity evolves as a process of self-positing subjectiviation that justifies the notions of "What does not exist is not a subject" and "The subject exists only for itself" (Neuhouser 1990, 154).

This Kantian conception of morality is defended by J. Habermas (1974, 1990, 1991, 2005) with the latter's discourse ethics framed into his communicative theories rationalized as "Kantian pragmatism" (Baynes 2004, 194). Leaving the intrinsic moral worth of rational agents a matter out of question, it becomes a primary task for an individual to authenticate one's subjective existence and justify the purpose of the existence by his or her own maxim of good will. Simply put, for example, one must not and does not have to tell a lie while it is up to the individual's own subjective principle of volition how to do so. Alternatively, as long as one does not tell a lie, which is very often considered as a relative term, he or she can tell anything, or at least, does not have to speak the truth or the whole truth. Even when supposedly speaking the truth, one can choose perspectives, methods, and stance according to his or her own maxim of good will. Applied in the journalistic profession in the public sphere, the perfect duty of "representing the truth and objectivity" and its public commitment ceased to be as absolute and comprehensive as one may conceive by its literal meaning. Rather, journalists are propelled, either by political coercion, financial incentives, or personal interests, to claim their own maxim in authenticating their existence by materializing the face value of their title of "uncrowned king" and thus justifying their self-interests and professional behavior in realizing these interests.

Jogging along the trend of de-politicization is the self-reflexive subjectiviation in de-politicization of the golden principle of truth and objectivity. Journalists may regard themselves as the pre-ordained incarnation of this principle and, more often, tend to believe that de-politicization is the best way to avoid ideological bias and facilitate objective journalism. This way, they are not only able to draw a line between their subjectivity and the objective world but to follow their own instinct to make their own judgment of media events. The likelihood is that journalists, as rational agents and subjective humans, tend to resort to the imperfect duties as long as their activities do not constitute direct conflict with their perfect duties according to their internalized moral standards. After all, making money is not such a bad thing. Balancing political risks and financial reward, therefore, popular culture becomes a commonly agreeable category of profitable and morally justifiable public consumption that absorbs almost all aspects of social life. Hence, consumerism and sensation easily found their way in the "environment of depoliticized capitalism" (A. Fung 2003, 253).

In China, despite the journalist's professional role and social identity as working class defined by their labor relations with the employers and the Party-state, few of them would recognize themselves as part of, or associated at any level with, the "disenfranchised groups." Those who do so will be called "activists" and their number is small. Even the reformist impulse of the small cohort of investigative journalists who claim to speak for the people is consciously limited to their selective incorporation of the voices of particular disenfranchised and dispossessed groups (Y. Zhao 2004b, 44). Instead, the majority of them perceive themselves as part of the "reconstituted new urban middle class" and "beneficiaries of the economic reform of the 1990s" (Y. Zhao 2004b, 44). This relatively well-off financial status has become an effective compensation for the loss of the editorial freedom as well as for their submission to state orchestration.

Thirdly, subjectivity has an inescapable impact on how journalists perceive their own existence, which in turn affects how they judge news events and how they produce stories. As David Randall (2000, 23) maintains, subjectivity "pervades the whole process of journalism and no reporter or news editor, try as they might professionally to suppress their prejudices, will ever be able to do so completely." Antonio Cimino (2012) argues that the determination of existence does not necessarily require the determination of "what" of the existence but only its "how." However, the complexity in constructing a fair and just perception of one's own subjectivity is as much as its apparent difficulty. According to Thomas Metzinger's "transparent self-model" (2004), there are no such things as "selves" existing in this world but an ongoing process of phenomenal existence in conscious experience. In other words, no one should be certain about his or her existence unless the pre-reflexive property of "selfhood" leads to the certainty of one's existence (Metzinger 2004, 398). Such a self-affirming process requires a substantial amount of proof of epistemic experiences that constantly provides reassuring, highly invariant source of body-related "nowness" leading to the phenomenal quality of self-certainty (Metzinger 2004, 295).This way, it can easily slide into a self-justified destruction of journalistic integrity and loss of public conviction when their subjectivity is limited, or forced to be limited, to a matter of self-interest based means of ego-identification and pursuit. Given such unavoidable relationship between the "how" and "what" of its existence, it becomes an essential question where the journalists' subjectivity is rooted and how it determines its interactions with the objective world.

The subjectivity of journalists does not exist by itself, and there is hardly any justification for innate professional value or integrity. Being individual subjects who make a living by selling their labor, the journalist practitioners are guided to the belief that their existence can best be authenticated and evaluated by the contribution they are able to make to the industrial prosperity and by the financial reward they subsequently receive from their employers. This is a more realistic version of subjectivization as their sense of "nowness" is framed into a set of materialist identity criteria and identification process. However, when the conscious experience of financial incentives and political risks becomes prominent and the subconscious knowledge and impulse of public commitment is heavily suppressed, the inevitable confusion diffused within the self-evaluation system and deepened by material compensations takes up much of the content of the subjectivity, reducing the practitioners' self to mere controlled surplus producers and wage earners no other than anyone else in the private sector. Their existence as skilled professionals who are capable of processing information as well as generating entertainment in the public domain, therefore, is perfectly shaped into a submissive yet lucrative role designed by the Party logic and the market logic.

Therefore, nothing else, even in sheer realistic sense, can better provide a subjective affirmation than a middle-class status as a form of both social and financial recognition externally and reassuring comfort internally. Mr. Summer, a Chinese financial reporter located in the Pearl River Delta (PRD), perhaps is a living example of those many journalists who not only comfortably position themselves in the middle-class zone but also observe and comment on the society starting from a higher than the lowest and lower than the highest social ladder. In a Globalpost report (Carlson 2013), Summer, a former village boy and now Shenzhen resident, seems to have secured everything that benchmarks a middle-classer: dresses and gadgets in an upper-middle-class American style, good education, stable job, increasing salary, mortgaged property, a foreign-brand car, Western religion, a fine taste for Hollywood movies, and an English nickname. Being proud of himself as a white-collar professional, he calls himself and his friends "true middle class" and recognizes China's economic miracle by happily listing his own new rich belongings. As for the deteriorating social inequality, he offers two solutions: reforming the residential registration [*hukou*] system and political transformation. These solutions, however, are predicated upon two premises: the rising market and American-style democracy, both of which he adores and believes to be advantageous to the middle class.

It would sound utterly insulting and unacceptable to Summer and his middle-class friends if they should be branded as "exploited labor" like the hundreds of thousands of migrant workers who are struggling in the PRD where glamorous prosperity and dire poverty co-exist. It would be even harder for these Western-minded journalists to step in the shoes of their fellow migrant workers and attune themselves to their voice. Like many others in his position, Summer believes in the market and Western democracy without giving a second thought to how exploitative the private-dominated market in the PRD has advanced into over the Reform era and how liberal the local media claim themselves to be. Curiously, the belief in class containment in Summer's interview is as patent as commonly seen in any other middle-class oriented media reportages. Proudly proclaiming his personal metamorphosis as something "hardly exceptional," he actually has rejected any notion of class antagonism, implying that anyone, like his friends from the same village, can make it to the club of middle class as the same pathway is fairly available to all. In other words, those who have sunk to the bottom of the society were not working hard enough or smart or "lucky" enough to change their fate. Narratives as such are typical political manifesto of the new middle-class journalists who have much to gain from the political and market status quo (Y. Zhao 2004b, 66), which has not only offered them an opportunity to cooperate with the Party-state and the market by a win-win approach toward stability, prosperity, and sustainability (Robison and Goodman 1996; Y. Zhao 2004b, 66), but more significantly an entrenching romantic notion that the "gap between journalist aspirations and reality" (Chin-Chuan Lee 2000; Lee 2001), as well as that between the rich and the poor, can be filled by the expansion of the middle-class cohort and the Party-state's increasing accommodation to their middle-class materialism and idealism.

To these relatively well-off journalists, there seems to be nothing fundamentally wrong with the market in which the capital always has the upper hand, or with the idea of expansion of urbanization costing the peasants their land, or with the American democracy and Hollywood products which have exerted blatant ideological impacts on the developing countries and their social political transitions that usually happen with heavy property and human costs, or with their own middle-class perspectives which always start from where they are, rather than where their objects (the disenfranchised groups, for example) are. Tragically, even if people like Summer can hardly be enlisted in the "elite" category according to, for instance, C. Wright Mills's (2000) definition of "elite" in terms of their role and power in the "ruling group" or "higher circles," they tend to elitize themselves by comparing their present with the past as well as their subjectivity with that of the disadvantageous groups by "*suzhi*" criteria judging by education level, income status, and material possessions. Despite the fact that journalists like Summer have to unconditionally submit themselves to the Party-state orchestration and management on a daily basis, their middle-class stance manifests in such an explicit manner that one can hardly tell whether this could be called loss of true subjectivity or gain of a false one. Hence, I call it a subjectivity dilemma.

## Discussion: Disjuncture of the Relationships between the Journalists, the Party-State, and the Media Management

This chapter describes how journalism has been plagued by professional malpractice and questions the predication of a clean and clear media environment on private ownership, contending that the relationships between the journalist practitioners, the Party-state, and the state-owned media have little to do with the principal-agent analogy or state ownership but are disconnected by the dilemmas in the trend of de-politicization propelled by the Party logic and market logic through everyday management. Following what Foucault (2000, 74) has analyzed as "the internal rule of maximum economy," the Party-state escorts the market logic by silencing anyone that might get in its way such as leftist outlets and websites that are keen to question the Party-state's ongoing capitalization and socio-political problems engendered thereby. Subsequently, left-wing outlets such as the journal *The Search for Truth* was shut down in 2001 (Y. Zhao 2004b, 69); websites such as www.maoflag.net [*maozedong qizhiwang*] and www.wyzxsx.com [*wuyouzhixiang*] were ordered indefinite closure for "technical maintenance" in 2007 and 2012, respectively. As a result, although both the Party-state and the state-owned media are supposed to represent the public in politics and the public sphere, respectively, such representation relationships virtually do not exist in the reformed media system, whatever model it may be named.

While the cause of media corruption and professional malpractice remains an open question (Hugo de Burgh 2003a, 118), this chapter has argued that, instead of focusing on the state-media dichotomy, we should look further into the intertwined relationships involving journalists and editors. These relationships are vital to the media's public nature within the public sphere because consideration as such touches upon the question of whose public sphere we are talking about. If the public sphere is a space or distance free of political intervention as Habermas (1974) has claimed, journalism should be responsible and transparent enough to promote the freedom of information and expression in the interest of the disenfranchised groups. However, this has not been the case in the reformed China. The principal-agent argument pivoted on private ownership takes no count of the tendency that private ownership in a "free market culture" can be just as restrictive and anti-democratic as state ownership (Philo and Miller 2001). The assignment of a privatized principal-agent relationship in a free market to the Habermasian idealism is dubious because such a relationship but justifies the agent's commitment to its private owner of seeking best political and financial interests, or simply put, profits and power. In reality, it is within the no-holds-barred market media economy where journalists may find political accommodation and maximize financial gain. Journalism is sold out for power and profits, neither of which can be offered by the weak and the poor. As Hugo de Burgh (2005, 11) has commented on Chin-Chuan Lee (2005), journalists have seen themselves over the Reform era as instruments to the Party-state's mission to wealth and power, to which any ethic and practice must be subjected. Hence, corruption and malpractice is not a state-ownership problem but rather a problem of twisted societal and political relationships within the media system where neither the media nor the professionals represent the best interests of the weak and the poor. Therefore, this chapter has concentrated on the causes of the dilemmatic situations in order to provide an explanation to the disillusionment and collapse of the ethical belief system and to examine how the public nature of media representation has been undermined by political and market control.

The survival dilemma addresses how the professionals are alienated from their journalistic idealism due to their having to struggle for a living rather than for a public conviction in a niche-market-oriented media system. The labor relations within this system have been restructured that the journalists have lost their nominal title of "owners" [*zhurenweng*] of the state-owned media and the state that are supposed to represent their fellow citizens who are equally nominal owners of the state and the state-owned media. As mere wage earners, the professionals are no more than representatives of corporate interests (Hugo de Burgh 2003a, 188) and subject of personal benefits with the labor of the journalists being commoditized and their value reduced to the surplus productivity on the balance sheet. Their middle-class social status (Y. Zhao 2004b, 48) is destined by the labor control through market-oriented human resources management including but not limited to tenure, evaluation, workload, incentives, and restructured working relations (W. Wang 2011). The extent to which they are able and willing to promote openness, accountability, credibility, and information relevance, to a considerable extent, is subjected to the boundary-driven shear at the discretion of the editorial dictatorship within the corporate system.

The subjectivity dilemma was engendered in the transformation of the role of journalists from "revolutionary" intellectuals (Cheek 1997, 68) responsible for producing cultural products for the masses (Ip 2005, 155) in Mao's era to a mixed subject of a comfortable situated middle-class phantom (Y. Zhao 2004b, 47) and "controlled labor" (W. Wang 2011, 167) struggling for a living at the "McDonalised and trivialized" (Lee 2003, 8) assembly lines in the consumerized media industry. The boundaries within the repertoire of the subjectivity are blurred as journalists can be heavily exploited wage labor and well-off middle class at the same time, as well as private interest seekers and public intellectuals. This dilemma translates into the difficulty for journalists to locate their subjectivity in the midst of a heavy mist of political and ethical confusion.

As skilled professionals who are supposed to seethe over the public sphere to voice for the unvoiced and represent the underrepresented, the professionals have no operative ethical ground to accommodate the journalistic ideal of truth and objectivity. This is not only an ethical problem but also a transparency failure because there is no openness, accountability, credibility, and information relevance in the confusion surrounding the so-called socialist journalistic value intertwined with Party-state indoctrination and market-oriented priorities. The official ethical standards are no other than Party doctrines, which are not subject to interpretation and public debate. It is so because, as Yuezhi Zhao (1998, 187) has warned, "although there is plenty of room to get rich and get corrupt, there is little space for political imagination. The Party has sunk into ideological and moral bankruptcy." In such circumstances, contradictions embedded in the promulgated professional ethics, such as the conflict between the promotion of supervision by public opinion over corruption and the compulsory commitment to "correct direction of public opinion," have not only rendered the idea of openness through journalism null and void but also have bestowed much discretion on the administrative authorities and the management to deal with outlets and professionals on case-by-case basis. As corruption and professional malpractice become epidemic, neither the administrative authorities nor high-profile management are held accountable by these doctrines. Rather, corrupt officials are usually found guilty merely as a result of internal power struggle within the officialdom (Dillon 2009, 145) while the yoke of accountability is laden upon the professionals who are punished as the substantial bearer of the wrongdoings. Lack of openness allows discretion for Party-state orchestration and exploitative management and hinders the policies and processes from public scrutiny, leaving management behavior and editorial decision-making behind the door. Absence of accountability, particularly in high managerial hierarchy, reduces the belief in social responsibilities to an empty slogan.

Neither the Party-state-orchestrated, market-oriented media, nor the vast majority of the journalist practitioners have a clear and firm public conviction based on strong representation relationships with the citizenship and particularly with the vast majority of the disenfranchised groups. Even the occasional and short-lived activism can be just a form of commoditization of politics based on the pursuit of self-interest. As Daniela Stockmann (2013, 7) argues, "When media face competing demands of propaganda authorities and audiences, they tend to reflect the position of the state, and when interests converge, they tend to be representative of both state and society." This can even hardly be called a representation relationship but an opportunist alignment strategy balancing the imperative of maximizing financial gain and political security with that of diffusing social tension in the "state-sanctioned watchdog journalism," both proven to be profitable (Y. Zhao 2004b, 70; Y. Zhao and Gu 2010, 534). And, it is within the boundary-blurred scopes of these imperatives the dilemmas have arisen and ethical standards fallen.

## NOTES

1. *Zhejiang Daily* is the mouthpiece of the CCP Zhejiang Provincial Committee.
2. *Jiancha Daily* is an official newspaper fully sponsored by the Supreme People's Procuratorate of the people's Republic of China.
3. Please see (B. Xie and Gao 2013) for detailed discussion of the ethical dilemma.
4. It must be pointed out that the state is not the same as "the public," whether the government is a result of free election or dictatorship. However, it should not be too difficult to recognize that, in a modern nation-state which proclaims democracy and republicanism, the state as a political power mechanism is supposed to represent its public, whether nominally or relatively substantively.
5. The official *weibo*, a twitter style microblog in China, of *The People's Daily* commented on November 18, 2012 that "no doubt that the professional standards of the journalists are problematic, but the craving and eulogizing mentality for greatness and success [*haodaxigong, gegongsongde*] needs more rethinking" (Fake News Research Project Team 2012). Dong Tiance and Feng Fan (2004, 37) discussed orchestrated photography in Chinese journalism

from an academic point of view, and concluded that professional ethical education must be reinforced, and institutional build-up must be strengthened, and wrong-doers should be punished and even fired.

6. Established in January 1999, the *Metropolitan Express News (MEN)* is a commercialized subsidiary of Hangzhou Daily Press Group. *Hangzhou Daily* is the mouthpiece of the CCP Hangzhou Municipal Committee. Huang and Zhou (2003, 256) pointed out that *Jinri Zaobao* copied the entire page design from the *MEN* in its early years following the latter's success in the market.

7. The article 14 (1–3) of the Labor Contract Law (2007) stipulates that "an open-ended labor contract may be concluded between an employer and an employee upon consultation. If an employee proposes or agrees to renew and conclude a labor contract in any of the following circumstances, an open-ended labor contract shall be concluded, unless the employee requests the conclusion of a fixed-term labor contract instead:

1. The employee has been working for the Employer for ten consecutive years;
2. When the Employer first introduces the labor contract system or the state-owned enterprise that employs him re-concludes its labor contracts as of restructuring, the employee has been working for the Employer for ten consecutive years and is less than ten years away from his legal retirement age; or
3. Where a labor contract was concluded as a fixed-term labor contract on two consecutive occasions and the employee, in the absence of any of the circumstances stipulated in Article 39 and items (1) and (2) of Article 40 of this law, renews such contract.

8. Translation by author.
9. To the best knowledge of the author, no photos from these two photojournalists have been adopted by *Jinri Zaobao* up to October 2013 when this chapter is written.
10. See Y. Zhao 2008a, 275.

*Chapter Five*

# Marketization and Conglomeration of State-Owned Media

*A Market-Oriented Corporate Governance Myth?*

According to the official *Theory of Socialism with Chinese Characteristics* and the Scientific Perspective of Development, "problems existing in the process of development" can only be solved by "further development."[1] In a macro sense then, the ongoing economic reform will eventually lead to a solution to existing socio-political problems including those related to the superstructure. This language has been translated into the reform of the news media system [*xinwen tizhi gaige*] based on the rationale pertaining to commercialization, corporatization, and conglomeration. That the media have changed from rigid government-subsidized soviet-style propagandistic apparatus to flexible and prosperous market-oriented modern businesses has led to expectations that the official promise of transparency and supervision by public opinion would eventually be fulfilled.

Apart from the public listing of *Beijing Youth Daily* on the Hong Kong Stock Exchange in December 2004 (Y. Zhao 2008a, 116) as a milestone of internationalization and introduction of foreign capital, a recent move toward further marketization and corporatization is the initial public offerings (IPO) and public listing in April 2012 of the people.com.cn [*renminwang*], the online branch of the *People's Daily* and the mouthpiece of the CCP Central Committee. This move, being the new high point of reform of the state-owned news media outlets over the past three decades, implies the introduction of non-state capital to more official, semi-official, and commercialized media.

Centering the trend of going public is a myth that all businesses listed in the stock markets, especially the major overseas exchanges, must be operated by internationally recognized standards of corporate governance that upholds independent management, transparent decision-making processes, full accountability to stakeholders, and above all, answerability to the market. The relatively high standards and stringent review and approval processes have, in turn, lent much credibility to the successful IPO applicants and even to those that claim to follow the same standards of corporate governance. The market-oriented corporate governance gives hope of a new tiding against the old, as many have rightfully noticed, that state control remains unabated (Lee 2003, 24; Shirk 2007, 42). In light of this new hope and yet the complexity of reality, there have been beliefs that the censorship regime will lose its effectiveness due to the fragmentation of authority resulting from the rapid expansion of the media in both size and content (Keane 2001, 793) and introduction of new market-oriented programs (Pei 1998, 165). It is widely recognized that news media with less official identity and more market drive tend to be more flexible, freer in their reportage, and, therefore, more credible and transparent (Shirk 2011, 5). Even Party media and their affiliates are impelled to adopt more or less market-oriented strategies and have exhibited more flexibility than ever before (Shirk 2011, 5). Some scholars, Xiao Yuanlin (2004, 46) for example, attribute the trend of market-oriented reform to the inspiration of Western management, compelling competition in the marketplace, and the need to establish market order. The introduction of private and foreign capital, limited as it is, has led some like Kate Xiao Zhou (2009, 165) to believe that marketization and ongoing conglomeration will result in liberalization sooner or later. Some have claimed that conglomeration of the flourishing media outlets will weaken the Party-state's control over it and the media as the market is playing a prominent role in the newly established corporate governance (Park and Curran 2000, 22; X. Zhu 1998; 2006, 344). In the same vein, Liu Junning (1998, 362) asserts that press freedom is predicated on the "invisible hand of the market."[2]

These beliefs in the magic of the market have set the tone of market discourses and portrayed a phantom of press freedom. As Chin-Chuan Lee (2003, 19) has critiqued, many would believe that, by following the current trend of marketization, the realization of substantive freedom and transparency is just a matter of time. However, neither profit-driven nor Party-state-steered media have so far lived up such expectations. Lee (2003, 19) also points out that the market advocates are curiously silent on issues of fairness, power and domination and largely ignorant of the plight of Chinese peasants and workers. Therefore, to discuss the possibility of media transparency today, one must understand whether the reform, which has been successful by all financial means, is meant to generate and improve transparency in the public interest or to encourage pursuit of profit and enhance state control.

The media reform has basically taken two steps in terms of organizational restructuring. Firstly, the transition from the media as public institutions to market-oriented businesses has seen the adoption of enterprise management [*qiyehua guanli*] revitalizing the outlets. Secondly, the establishment of a prosperous niche market and organization restructuring have re-aligned the state-media relationship in modern corporate governance commonly applied in conglomerates and their subsidiaries. Tracing these steps, this chapter examines why increased financial autonomy and market-oriented management has failed to generate substantive media transparency. It is argued that the institutional restructuring and installation of new corporate governance have re-aligned the state-media relationship by enabling and facilitating profit-seeking management and reinforcing effective state control over journalism rather than substantiating transparency and supervision by public opinion as promised by enlightened politics and liberalized market.

## BUSINESS MANAGEMENT AND MARKETIZATION

Business management refers to the management system in which the media, although still regarded as political and cultural institutions, are managed as business enterprises (Y. Zhao 1998, 53). Since the late 1970s, media outlets have been gradually transformed from government bureaucracies to business enterprises, and their financial sources shifted from government subsidy to the market. This transformation made it necessary for outlets to start to streamline their operations and take costs, profit targets, and government taxation into consideration (Y. Zhao 1998, 53). The decision to reform was made when the media industry was facing financial difficulties and shrinking readership by the late-1970s while the government was unable to sustain its full state sponsorship (Di 2011, 92). As Yuezhi Zhao (1998, 53) has observed, the government investment priorities then were in such areas as science and education rather than in the media.

The first financial challenge the news media had to face at the threshold of the reform era was the soaring operational costs which constituted a direct threat to their survival. The price of newsprint, for example, rose from 760 yuan per ton in 1979 to 1,900 yuan within the planned allocation system and 3,400 yuan per ton on the market in 1988 (Compiling Committee of the *Annals of Harbin* 1994, 227). Given the shortage of centrally allocated supply, a large proportion had to be purchased on the market at a much higher cost, a common scenario of the double-track system of resource allocation.[3] The situation for radio and television stations was even worse because the programs were delivered on free-to-air basis. Outlets relied heavily on government subsidies, and the modest incomes generated by subscription and distribution sources became increasingly insufficient to sustain everyday operations, not to mention further development to accommodate the public's increasing demand for more media services (Y. Zhao 1998, 53). As subsidies declined, more than two-thirds of the media could hardly make ends meet (Lai 2005, 53).

In a joint report to the Ministry of Treasury, eight newspapers at central level including the *People's Daily* proposed application of "public institutions, business management [*shiye danwei, qiyehua guanli*]" at the end of 1978, pleading for permission to try "independent accounting and retainable surpluses" (X. Wu and Jin 2004, 17; Y. Zhao 1998, 53). The proposal was quickly approved, and the media started to transform gradually from total government institutions into market-oriented businesses. Consequently, while government subsidies were gradually pruned, market forces were reintroduced and commercialized financing encouraged (McNally 2008a, 134; Y. Zhao 1998, 53).

The first step toward financial autonomy was to allow paid commercial services. *Tianjin Daily* took the lead to produce advertisements on its January 4, 1979 issue. *Wenhui Bao* placed an advertisement for Swiss-made Radar watches on January 23, 1979, the first of its kind for foreign products (Zhi 2005, 5). Shanghai People's Radio Station aired the first audio advertisement on March 15, 1979 (Yun Liu and Cai 2010, 177). The first TV commercial since the start of the reform era was introduced on January 28, 1979 by Shanghai TV (Yuhong Zhang 2010, 175).

For newspapers, the limitation on the number of pages per issue stood in the way of expanding advertising services. Early in the reform era when various aspects of the national economy were given access to market and eager to promote themselves, there was no shortage of advertising clients. Yet, it was common in cities like Guangzhou, Beijing, and Shanghai that an advertisement request had to wait for one or two months before being visible to their clients (Cao 1999, 166; Lan 1995, 33). The *People's Daily* was the only daily nationwide that had the luxury of printing eight pages per issue. Municipal dailies were only allowed four and had too much obligations for official news and editorials to spare any room for advertising.

In 1987, *Guangzhou Daily* was the first municipal newspaper to be allowed to enlarge its size to eight pages, and much of the expansion was used to meet advertising demand. Not surprisingly, the limit that advertisement should not exceed one-eighth of total pages was soon broken (Lai 2005, 72). Supported by this new source of revenue and expanded pages, *Guangzhou Daily* was also able to cater its journalism more to the market demand. As a result, its daily circulation increased from 200,000 copies per issue in 1981 to 337,000 in 1988 and 610,000 in 1995 (S. Huang and Zhou 2003, 189; Lai 2005, 68). In light of the obvious financial benefits, the CPD reduced restrictions even further after Deng Xiaoping's southern tour in 1992 (H. Yu and Deng 2000, 127). As a result, advertising sales turnover via newspapers, television, and radio surged from 0.23 billion yuan in 1983 to 174.1 billion yuan in 2007 (X. Wu and Gao 2010, 404). The media was able to develop financial autonomy at various levels and survive the withdrawal of government subsidies.

The other step was to unleash the market potential by moving from *youfaheyi* to self-reliant distribution. The financial situation of newspapers deteriorated under *youfaheyi,* a circulation system in which subscription and distribution were taken over, monopolized by the state postal service, and treated as a political obligation (Bai 1998, 454).[4] Subscriptions and distribution were guaranteed by being assigned to the postal network on the one hand, and the outlets had no autonomy in related decision-making processes on the other. Both the press and the postal service obviously lacked incentives to expand subscriptions because they were not allowed to take initiative to broaden distribution channels, expand the size of issues, and adjust prices without prior permission by the administrative authorities (Zhiyong Wu 2006, 124).The postal service did not like the idea of allowing the newspapers to take control of subscriptions and distribution. And, these two systems usually did not consult each other before making any changes to their practice, and poor coordination often led to disputes and low efficiency.

The *youfaheyi* system was blamed for considerably slowing down the cash flows of the press. It usually took a long time for subscriptions collected by post offices to be transferred to the newspapers. Annual or quarterly subscription fees were collected from the subscribers in advance before a new distribution season started. Newspapers, however, were only reimbursed by monthly installment. Even the *People's Daily* was in serious financial trouble because millions of its subscription fees were misappropriated and delayed by the postal service to such an extent that the former hardly had sufficient funds for purchasing newsprint (Institution of Journalism of China Academy of Social Sciences 1989, 131). As a result, at least in part, the media lost incentives and ability to fund new technologies and to improve services.

In 1984, given the heavy distribution costs and insufficient government subsidies, *Luoyang Daily*, a local official newspaper located in Luoyang, Henan province, pleaded to *Luoyang People's Post* to lower the commission rate from 25 percent to 20 percent. The proposal was instantly rejected. In 1985, the Henan Administration of Post and Telecommunication decided to raise the commission rate chargeable to newly established newspapers and magazines to 35 percent. Official newspapers and periodicals continued to be charged 35 percent within the *youfaheyi* system in 1987 (Shao 1994, 227). This decision was made when the local papers and magazines had been struggling keeping their operational costs under control at the verge of bankruptcy. *Luoyang Daily*, for example, had a financial deficit of 240,000 yuan in 1983. In response to the rejection of its price deduction appeal and the subsequent postal service price rise, it became the first newspaper nationwide to announce its divorce from the *youfaheyi* system and establish its own distribution network [*ziban faxing*] in 1985. Subsequently, its daily circulation volume almost doubled from 62,000 copies to 110,000 copies in the following year (Zhi 2005, 11).

More and more newspapers then began to practice self-reliant distribution and found it a good way not only for cutting back costs but also for expanding their market. Six other outlets in other provinces followed suit in 1986, eleven in 1987, and more in later years (P. Sun 2004, 197). *Guangzhou Daily* started self-reliant distribution in 1990 and elevated it to the height of "a matter of life or death" in 1991. Its own delivery system guaranteed that readers received their newspapers before 7:30 a.m., catering to the Cantonese custom of "morning tea with newspapers" (Zhi 2005, 16). *Huaxi Metropolis Daily* initiated its door-to-door sales model in 1996, aiming to generate personal ties between the paper and its readers (Zhi 2005, 28).

Self-reliant distribution system trashed the *youfaheyi* restraints on printing volumes, delivery times, subscription channels, and cost management. To maintain distribution income, post offices started to give up their monopoly mindset and sought cooperation with newspapers by lowering commission rates and tolerating the co-existence of postal and self-reliant distribution. By the mid-1990s, the *youfaheyi* system ceased to exist (Yuan 2000, 213).

Having obtained financial and distributional autonomy, the media industry began to boom. The number of newspapers, and radio and television stations experienced a dramatic rise between 1979 to the mid-1990s. The number of newspapers with national serial numbers [*quanguo kanhao*] increased from 186 in 1978 to 2,089 in 1995 (Cui and Zhang 2010, 41).[5] Local serial number [*difang kanhao*] papers surged to 6,453 (B. Tong and Lin 2001, 19). With this rise came increases in information volume. Total printed pages per year rose from 11.4 billion in 1978 to 170.1 billion in 2007 (Cui and Zhang 2010, 41). Radio and television broadcasting services underwent a similar growth. The number of television stations rose from 47 in 1982 to 923 in 1997 (H. Li and Shen 2010, 208), and radio stations from 99 in 1979 to 298 in 1999 (Fang 2000, 45; NSB 1980). Notably, the boom followed the Document No. 37 of the CCP Central Committee in 1983 which lifted restrictions on establishment of radio and television stations at city and county levels (Zhiyue Wu 2005).

Public access to the media also increased considerably. In the mid-1990s, "television villages"—where every household has a television set—no longer hit the headlines (Y. Zhao 1998, 53). Many non-Party and semi-official newspapers adopted flexible editorial styles in reporting social events, and increasing content diversity attracted an unprecedented number of private subscriptions. Household subscription rates rose from 48.48 to 92.69 copies per one hundred persons per year (H. Xie and Wen 2000), demonstrating the popularity of non-Party newspapers amongst private subscribers. At the same time, the subscriptions for official newspapers kept falling in both urban and rural areas (H. Lin 2004, 142).

There has been structural reform of the media since the adoption of business management in 1979. The former exclusively public outlets have been generally divided into Party [*dangbao dangkan*] and non-Party media [*fei dangbao dangkan*]. This division, however, was made in terms of organizational sponsorship and management models, with the former being regarded as official mouthpieces and the latter as marketized outlets. The Party news media outlets consist of the government and CCP mouthpieces from central to local levels including official newspapers, TV, and radio channels. Non-Party media include subsidiaries of media groups, financially autonomous radio and television channels, and outlets sponsored by but not managed by state-owned enterprises, institutions, and organizations. Private ownership is seen in some new media businesses as well. Portals such as Sohu, Sina, and Netease were set up using private investment and are listed on overseas stock exchanges.[6]

## CONGLOMERATION AND NEW CORPORATE GOVERNANCE

As the media industry has grown into a vibrant and diversified new phase, it became increasingly hard for the state to control it effectively through direct discipline the way it used to. The implications of this change are twofold:

1. given the content diversification, the Party media is losing audience to the market-oriented outlets that adopt more flexible editorial styles; and
2. given the quickly enlarging size of the industry, direct control of editorial decisions by the Party-state has become increasingly difficult.

It was obvious that the Party newspapers and journals saw their readership shrinking and central and provincial-level broadcasters were losing audience to lower-level outlets that were more flexible and more entertaining (Guping Wu 2008). While the Party media are perceived by the state as the most important instrument for guiding public opinion, their popularity is relatively lower than non-Party media (Stockmann 2011, 180). The emergence of local urban newspapers in the mid-1990s accelerated the marginalization of the official ones (H. Lin 2004, 140). In result, it became harder and harder for the Party-state to implement direct supervision and control. The Party media, on the other hand, could not afford to lose its dominance in shaping public opinion, and therefore, the focus of their reform has shifted from surviving financial difficulty to reinforcing political control.

## Conglomeration

Conglomeration offers an ample solution for the above two problems in post-Mao China by restructuring and reorganizing single outlets into multi-functional and multi-platform conglomerates each headed by a Party media. There are hardly any exception models or alternatives. The head media of each group has ultimate power over the subsidiary outlets. Press groups are led by a Party newspaper and comprise periodicals, magazines, Internet portals, publishing houses, and other profit-making branches unrelated to publication business such as real estate branches.[7] There were forty-one such press groups at the end of 2009, two of which are at the central level, twenty-five at provincial level, and fourteen at municipal level (Cui and Zhang 2010, 44). Radio and television groups, under the governance of the SARFT, were also restructured in similar way. Wuxi Broadcasting and Television Group, the first of its kind, was established in June 1999 (Y. Zhao 2004a, 195). The number of these groups rose to eighteen at the end of 2004 (Y. Luo, Zhang, and Shan 2005, 21).[8] Provincial and local media groups have also been established by conglomerating profit-generating businesses that are not directly related to journalism.[9]

Guangzhou, capital city of Guangdong Province, had eighty-nine newspapers with national serial numbers at the end of 1998, sixty-five of which were established after 1979 (Compiling Committee of the Annals of Guangzhou 1999, 946). The Guangzhou Daily Press Group was the first of its kind, conglomerated on January 15, 1996. The Group is flagshipped by *Guangzhou Daily*, the mouthpiece of the CCP Guangzhou Municipal Committee, and consists of fifteen local newspapers, five magazines, and two portals. The supportive branches of its industry chain such as printing, distribution and advertising have been corporatized and marketized. Its full subsidiary, Guangzhou Dayang Industrial Company Limited, owns 90 percent share of the public-listed Guangdong China Sunshine Media Company Limited, which runs advertising, printing, and press retailing businesses. Guangzhou Daily Printing Centre, with a production capacity of 4.7 million double-sided standard newsprint pages per hour, provides printing service not only for the newspapers and magazines within the group but also for those from other parts of Guangdong province. The revenue of the group reached 3.96 billion yuan in 2008 and supported an average circulation of 1.85 million copies per day.[10]

## Restructured Corporate Governance

However, the Party media has been situated in the dilemmatic backdrop of increasingly tightened content control since the 1989 Tiananmen Square crackdown and the thriving niche market that breeds content diversity, blatant consumerism and political apathism. Although some Party media, such as *Guangzhou Daily,* are behemoths within the conglomerates under their leadership, it is not uncommon for leading official outlets to be much smaller than the commercialized subsidiaries. While the official media kept losing individual readers and audience, much of their distribution had to be allotted to institutional subscribers by force [*qiangxing tanpai*]. In 2000, for example, the average circulation volume of Party newspapers was no more than 60 percent of that in the mid-1980s (Jun Wang and Wang 2006, 259).

As the "public institutions, enterprise management" model, which did not make structural alterations to the strategic part of the system such as personnel administration and internal labor relationships, was considered incapable of coping with the new situation, a new set of corporate governance was introduced to realign the state-media relationships as well as the relationships within the restructured organizations. Corporate governance is "the system by which companies are directed and controlled" (Hicks and Goo 2008, 239), which involves "a set of processes, customs, policies, laws, and institutions" (Baker and Powell 2009, 84). It deals with a set of relationships between a company's management, its board, its shareholders, and other stakeholders, and provides structure through which corporate objectives are set (OECD 1999, 159). The reform of China's media, by shifting the management of outlets from the state bureaucracy to business management and then into new Party-dominated corporate governance, has seen the establishment of a system that allows marketization for profit purposes on the one hand and maintains effective editorial control over the other.

The new Party-dominated and market-led corporate governance adopted in conglomerated media groups shares the following features:

1. flagship status of a Party media;
2. *Sheweihui* system;
3. the separation of news production and *jingyingxing yewu* [operational businesses, meaning non-editorial business];
4. capital-labor relationships.

First of all, the relationship between the state and the reformed news outlets is manifested by the flagship status of the Party mouthpieces. Flagship status is not only a demonstration but also a function of political significance. The new corporate governance has enabled incorporation of media businesses into a group of market entities and put the non-Party outlets under the direction and supervision of the leading Party mouthpieces. The primary goal of conglomeration is not only to prevent them from being marginalized but to ensure their dominance in the ideological and political domain. The integration of the weakening official outlets and the flourishing non-Party media within one organization assures the leadership of the official outlets despite their inability to compete in either domestic or overseas marketplaces. Hence, market competition, as Yuezhi Zhao (2005, 66) elucidates, provides a perfect excuse for the Party-state to consolidate its power over the media by merging existing outlets or establishing conglomerates. Endorsed by its leadership authority, the head Party media is able to reallocate resources within the group including financial and human resources as well as hold coercive power over the subsidiaries and their professionals. Meanwhile, conglomeration has not necessarily been the result of voluntary unions but usually arranged by the Party-state through administrative orders (Lee, He, and Huang 2008, 15; F. Lin 2008, 55). By taking over non-Party outlets, a small number of media groups are able to bring many more non-Party outlets under close surveillance.

The Wenhui-Xinmin Press Group is a telling example of takeover of a much more affluent and influential marketized semi-official outlet.[11] *Xinmin Wanbao* was a more commercialized media while *Wenhui Bao* remained a Party mouthpiece chaired by the head of the Shanghai Propaganda Authority. In the 1990s, *Xinmin Wanbao* was known for its flexible editorial style and aggressive marketing strategies that were quite different from Party newspapers. Its *Summer Hotline,* initiated in 1994, for example, listened to the readers and helped common people to contact the government for help with everyday difficulties. Not only was *Xinmin Wanbao* distributed nationwide, in 1994, it became the first news outlet to establish overseas branches including an office in Los Angeles to promote the newspaper among the overseas Chinese. It also set up a special subsidiary in charge of international distribution and advertising business. *Xinmin Wanbao*'s circulation volume surged to 1.85 million per issue in 1990 and had remained around 1.7 million until the conglomeration took place in 1998 (J. Xu 2006, 248). Its advertising revenue kept mounting and reached 720 million yuan in 1998, an increase of 13 percent from 1997 (Institution of Journalism of China Academy of Social Sciences 1999, 118). In contrast, *Wenhui Bao*'s advertising revenue was 106 million yuan in 1998, only 14.72 percent of the *Xinmin Wanbao*'s (Institution of Journalism of China Academy of Social Sciences 1999, 118). At the time of the conglomeration, *Wenhui Bao*'s circulation had fallen from 1.71 million in 1983 to less than 0.5 million in 1997 (H. Hu and Chen 2009, 154; Xiong 1999, 256).

The marriage between the two was ordered by the Shanghai Municipal Government and CCP Shanghai Publicity Department (Cao 1999, 220). Although *Xinmin Wanbao* was financially stronger and more influential, its non-Party mouthpiece status has defined it inferiority. *Wenhui Bao* took the flagship status, and its former party chief, Wang Zhongwei, became the head of the new Wenhui–Xinmin Press Group.[12] Not only was *Xinmin Wanbao* subordinated, it had to surrender its advertising business to the group. Losing its financial advantage and autonomy, *Xinmin* was unable to improve its competitiveness by upgrading its equipment, printing quality, and raising salaries, suffering a major blow to its management and editorial incentives (Zhi 2005, 168). Subsequently, its circulation dropped to one million copies in 2002, a dramatic 41.18 percent decrease.[13] The conglomeration did not boost the *Wenhui Bao*. Its distribution volume remained at around 400,000 up to 2007 (Shanghai Culture Yearbook Compiling Committee 2007). Nevertheless, *Wenhui Bao* has successfully taken control of the financial resources and senior personnel administration within the group and, therefore, is able to effectively constrain all subsidiaries. Subsidiaries cannot preclude the commitment to deliver official messages while the head outlets are able to strengthen the official voice through their non-Party subsidiaries.

This form of corporate governance has also enabled the co-existence of marketization of the business operation and enveloped control over editorial content by establishing a corporate governance of *Sheweihui* [Publishing House Committee], for example, board of directors under the leadership of the Party committee [*dangwei lingdaoxia de Sheweihui fuzezhi*]. Although the application of this governance varies from one outlet to another, dominance by the Party-state through *Sheweihui* is out of question.

In July 2004, the CPD and GAPP jointly issued the Notification on Division of Administration and Management and Strengthening Administration of Transferred Newspapers and Periodicals, reiterating that the Party and the government should refrain from participating in the management of newspapers and periodicals.[14] By withdrawing from management, all Party and government officials are precluded from holding concurrent posts in administration authorities and media outlets. Party and government agencies should not have financial connection with media outlets nor get involved in advertising and distribution businesses. Such an official document gives the impression that the Party and the government are willing to step away from interfering in the management of the news outlets so that the journalism is less influenced by politics.

However, according to the same notification, the administration and management systems [*zhuguan zhuban zhidu*] must be retained and observed, meaning that media outlets remain administered by government supervisory agencies and subjected to the leadership of the head media within each conglomerate. The mandatory structural arrangement of the senior management of the media groups has not only reinforced Party leadership but also enabled its influence in a less noticeable manner. By adhering to the administration and management system within the group, the subsidiary outlets have to subject themselves to the administrative authority and the guidance of the sponsoring or responsible government agencies.

Structurally, the senior management of media groups is composed of a Party committee and a *Sheweihui*. Both are subject to the Party leadership. As stated in a GAPP document, a press group must have a Party committee to which the *Sheweihui* reports.[15] *Sheweihui* is equivalent to a board of directors and is the senior executive body of a media group. The head of *Sheweihui* usually chairs the Party committee concurrently. *Sheweihui* undertakes responsibility for everyday management while critical decisions must be approved by the Party committee. *Sheweihui* is usually divided into two divisions. The editorial board [*Bianweihui*], headed by a chief editor, consists of a number of deputy chief editors who are in charge of the editorial content and responsible for editorial work of subsidiary outlets (Fischer 2009, 184). The management board [*Jingweihui*] is usually made up of a number of deputy presidents in charge of the profit-generation section (Fischer 2009, 184). The *Sheweihui* is generally headed by a president [*shezhang*], who usually simultaneously assumes the position of the head of the Party committee (C. Cai 2008, 110). Within such a corporate structure, the chief editor, unlike the popular organizational arrangement before conglomeration, has ceased to be the highest ranking leader of senior management and instead become subject to the president and Party committee, both of which represent the ultimate leadership of the Party-state. Such new structural arrangement has made it possible that chief editors of subsidiaries be recruited from outside the Party-state officialdom. The subsidiary news outlets usually resemble the parent group in terms of their organizational structure in which editorial staff at all levels are subject to the leadership of the Party committee of corresponding level as well as that of the parent media group.

Before 1996, the management of *Guangzhou Daily* used to be headed by a chief editor responsible to the editorial board [*Bianweihui lingdaoxia de zongbianji fuzezhi*] (Y. Sun 2002, 314). The ten-people senior management was made up of nine senior editors and only one non-editor (Y. Sun 2002, 315). Since conglomeration, the Guangzhou Daily Press Group has been under a president who chairs the collective leadership of the *Sheweihui* [*Sheweihui lingdaoxia de shezhang fuzezhi*]. The number of non-editors increased to five. Chief Editor ranks number two instead of number one. This arrangement effectively places the chief editor in a less senior position. The president does not have to step into everyday editorial work. Even so, the supreme position of the presidency over the chief editorship has practically drawn the editorial free range within the Party's orbit.

After conglomeration, the ten-people *Sheweihui* of Guangzhou Daily Press Group is composed of one president, one chief editor, three deputy presidents, four deputy chief editors, and a consultant. The deputy presidents are members of the management board while the chief editor and the deputy

```
┌─────────────────────────┐
│  President/ Party Chief │
└───────────┬─────────────┘
            ▼
┌─────────────────────────┐
│      Chief Editor       │
└───────────┬─────────────┘
   ┌────────┼────────┐
   ▼        ▼        ▼
┌──────┐ ┌──────┐ ┌──────────┐
│Deputy│ │Deputy│ │Sheweihui │
│Pres. │ │Chief │ │Consultant│
│ x 3  │ │Ed.x4 │ │   x1     │
└──────┘ └──────┘ └──────────┘
```

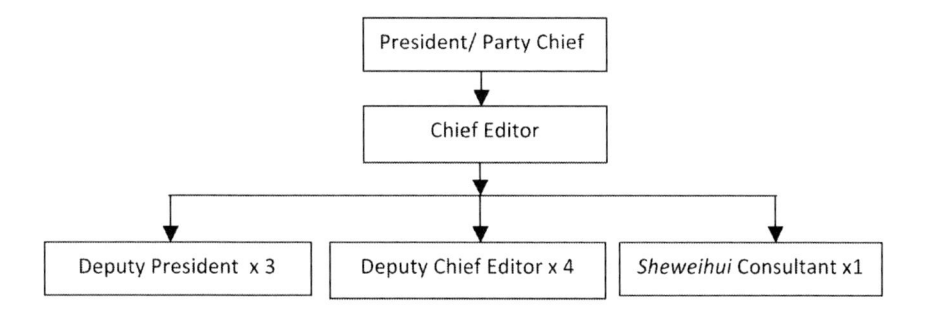

**Figure 5.1.** Organizational structure of the senior management *Sheweihui* of Guangzhou Daily Press Group. Source: co.gzdaily.com/201106/10/62345.shtml.

chief editors make up the editorial board. The number of senior editors in the senior management is significantly reduced in the new corporate governance, and so is the power of the chief editor who now has to report to the Party committee and *Sheweihui* headed by the president.

The Wenhui-Xinmin Press Group has a similar organizational structure. The Party committee and the president of the press group constitute the top layer of management, overseeing six major executive leaderships and departments, namely chief editor of *Wenhui Daily*, chief editor of *Xinmin Evening Post*, general manager and Business Management Office, deputy president and Publicity Office, deputy Party chief and Party Affairs Office, secretary of Discipline and Organizational Personnel Office (Y. Sun 2002, 315). The Party Committee and the president took over control of the supreme authority from the editorial boards of the former individual outlets and have ultimate power regarding both editorial and market operations, although they do not necessarily have to interfere in the everyday operation of the subsidiary outlets. Not only has the senior management of the press group taken the power to reallocate all editorial, financial, and personnel resources within the group including taking over the lifeline advertising business of the *Xinmin Wanbao*, it also has maintained effective influence over the subsidiary editorial and management boards. The leadership model featuring senior management chaired by a president accountable to the *Sheweihui* prevails in the current conglomerated media groups. The chair of *Sheweihui* overlaps with the Party committee chief, integrating in effect Party leadership with management decision-making process. This way, Party-state control has been significantly consolidated through the *Sheweihui* governance.

As the everyday management of the news outlets is divided into editorial work and market operations, much flexibility has been given to the latter while the Party is able to concentrate on the former to keep the editorial decision-making process under immediate Party surveillance. By separating the editorial section from the market section, the new corporate governance has strategically lifted sanctions on marketable operations while deliberately leaving the editorial sector untouched. In practice, all media outlets are encouraged to follow the principle of "clear division of editorial management and market operations [*caibian yu jingying fenli*]," meaning editorial functions should by no means be treated the same way as the profit-seeking sector. Advertising, printing, distribution, and other profit-generating branches can be fully commercialized and open to non-state capital to maximize financial success without much interference from the administrative authorities. Meanwhile, the market performance is more often evaluated by profit rather than quality of reportage (Y. Zhou 2008, 16).

Financially, the separation of editorial and market management enables private and foreign capital investment. Media marketing sections were officially opened to non-state capital with the 2003 promulgation of Administration Measures for Foreign Investment in Distribution of Books, Newspapers and Periodicals. In 2004, $133 million U.S. dollars poured in to establish fifty-five foreign-owned printing businesses, and the GAPP approved the entry of eleven foreign-owned businesses with paid-up capital of 570 million yuan to explore the distribution market (Cui 2005, 206).

Structurally, the Party-state-media partnership has been considerably reinforced with influx of private and foreign capital as they now have more to share on the ground of common financial prosperity. Meanwhile, editorial control remains a no-go area for non-state capital. However, this does not seem to have bothered the capital very much because both the Party-state and the capital understand that news production, although vitally important to the media's raison d'être, is a labor intensive and costly business with low direct-profit prospects. It is the most lucrative part of the non-editorial business, which is advertising, distribution, and entertainment, all pointing to the niche market that is open to foreign and private capital. The three-year road map that the GAPP set in 2008 for the reform of the press serves to realign the Party-state-media infrastructure in such a way in order to facilitate the new state-media-capital relationships, leaving the reform largely irrelevant to the news production division. Liu Binjie, director of the GAPP, presented the plan as follows:

> The first step is to complete reform of the non-public sphere newspapers and publications sponsored by state-owned units and public institutions; the second step involves the non-public sphere newspapers and publications sponsored by social organizations such as industrial associations; the third step is to complete reform of the newspapers and publications sponsored by ministries at central government level. (X. Tang and Zhuo 2009, 64)[16]

According to Liu, such reform is focused on marketizing the profit-generating sector, particularly by transforming the non-editorial branches from public institutions to full-fledged businesses, establishing multi-layer corporate organizations with diversified business scope and allowing multi-ownership corporate infrastructure within conglomerates. The organizational restructuring aims to ensure the application of corporate governance that mutually accommodates the political and capitalist interests. In order to clarify questions regarding the subjects and purposes of the reform, Document No. 114 issued by the State Council in 2008 reiterated that it is the market sector of the former public cultural institutions and units that are to be transformed into enterprises.[17] What was tellingly omitted was the editorial sector as it is apparently not a subject that the Party-state and the capital would spend resources to negotiate over.

Apart from re-aligning the state-media relationship, the new corporate governance can be boiled down to a restructured capital-labor relationship within the media system between the journalist professionals as employees and the outlets as the employers. It has been described in chapter 4 how the labor relationships have been altered by the reform of the personnel administration and management system. This chapter further argues that the restructured labor relationship is vital to the functionality of the corporate governance because it ensures the profitability of the information industry as well as the Party-state mission to wealth and power, both requiring the journalists to be available, capable, manageable, and dispensable.

When the financial objective of the corporate governance is to foster a cost-efficient management that aims to be able to optimize their human resources to better supports the performing media economy, there will have to be a vast labor market where available labor is a commodity exchangeable at value for money as well as a considerable free labor force that compete for job opportunities. However, this would require a significant change to the pre-Reform public institutions [*shiye danwei*] personnel system in which all journalists were employed as cultural workers and propaganda cadres. Editorial practitioners were employed as formal public institutional employees with *bianzhi* status. They were cadres at various administrative levels within the Party's propaganda system [*xuanchuan xitong ganbu*] (J. Ren and Liang 1999, 229). Their employment was not only dependent on government budget but more importantly included in the *bianzhi* system. As Kjeld Erik Brodsgaard (2006, 104) explains, *bianzhi* [establishment] refers to the authorized number of personnel in a unit, office, or organization and categorized into administrative *bianzhi*, enterprise *bianzhi*, and service organizations *bianzhi*, a system that is used by the Party-state to exercise power over administrative apparatus from central to local level.[18] While *bianzhi* is a prerequisite for job opportunities in public or state-owned institutions, one has to go through a lot to secure a *bianzhi* vacancy in order to apply for a new job or transfer to somewhere else. Before the reform of personnel system, there was not much liberty in choosing employers or positions for college graduates and others who are entitled to a *bianzhi* status. Those who were entitled to *bianzhi* status were assigned to various positions, and they were not required to sign any contract with the employers because a secured *bianzhi* status did not only mean a continuous tenure, but also meant the identity of workers of the state. Declining an assigned job or position, on the other hand, means willfully giving up one's *bianzhi* entitlement.

The *bianzhi* system has undergone changes since the media reform took off in the 1980s, and the labor relationships within the system were fundamentally capitalized in the 1990s when the media industry continued to grow rapidly particularly after 1992 and the media economy kept boosted by domestic investment, and particularly by the influx of private and foreign capital across the twenty-first century. While the mobility of existing human resources was confined by the *bianzhi* system before the mid-1990s, college graduates found it increasingly hard to find job opportunities within the system due to government budget cutbacks. Thence, the idea of "free labor" in a free marketplace was packaged and promoted in the early 1990s in such a conceptual background that *bianzhi*, limited in number and limiting in practiceas a public institutional personnel system, could no longer keep up with the rapid development of the service industry, and therefore, a new employment system is needed to provide more options for both the employers and the employees.

That said, with more options for job opportunities, higher mobility, and pay promised by the new market mechanism supported by the rapid expansion of the media industry, the reform of personnel system within the media system initiated in the 1980s and deepened in the 1990s did not experience much resistance. The great demand of professional practitioners had mutually accommodated the human resources supply. The media industry experienced two remarkable rounds of rapid growth in size in the 1980s and 1990s, respectively. For example, the total number of newsprints increased from 186 in 1978 to 1,445 in 1985; and further surged from 1,444 in 1990 to 2,089 in 1995 (Cui 2009, 41). An Gang, former head of the Institute of Journalism of the Chinese Academy of Social Sciences, pointed out in his preface to China's first *Journalism Year Book* that approximately 200,000 people were employed in the media industry at the threshold of the 1980s (G. An 1982, 10), and this number grew fast. The survey conducted by the Bureau of Journalism of the CCP Central Propaganda Department in 1983 shows that about 300,000 people were working in newsprint, television, and radio broadcasting stations, including specifically 48,500 editors, reporters, journalists, and translators in the outlets (Zhong 1997, 417). The number of professional editors and journalists, in newsprints alone, reached 41,900 in 1985. The total journalism work force increased to 420,000 in 1990, to 550,000 in 1991, and further to 750,000 in 1992 (China Radio and TV Year Book Compiling Committee 2002, 510).

The concept of free labor in free labor market, drawing heavily on neoliberal knowledge of freedom and market, has been posited on consensual contractual agreements that define the restructured relationship between the employers and the employees to be one of market demand and supply. Therefore, given the limitations of *bianzhi* status, it became a primary urge to make the supply available by reforming the *bianzhi* system and transforming the practitioners from the Leninist "cogs and screws" of the "revolutionary machinery" (Cheek 1997, 69) to a commoditized "factor of production" (W. Wang 2011). The *pinyongzhi* [employment under appointment contract] was introduced to the media management system in the second half of the 1980s (Zhong 1997, 460). In 1991, the CCP Central Organization Department and the Ministry of Personnel jointly issued an official document titled *Quanmin Suoyouzhi Qiye Pinyong Ganbu Guanli Zanxing Guiding*,[19] stipulating that "this regulation can also be applied to the administration of the personnel work in public institutions." In 1992, *Shenyang Daily* became one of the first official media that applied *pinyongzhi* to its entire editorial staff, which was considered to be a huge success and widely celebrated within the official academic discussions and the media system. About 165 outlets nationwide flocked to Shenyang to learn from its experience (Institution of Journalism of Chinese Academy of Social Sciences 1994, 467). However, *pinyongzhi*, apart from facilitating various financial incentives, did not yet fundamentally alter the labor relations and cadre status of the journalists and editors (W. Wang 2011, 96) but prepared for a more radical phase of the capitalization and commoditization of the journalistic labor.

Wang Weijia (2011, 98) points out that the commercialized urban newspapers which mushroomed in the second half of the 1990s became the pioneers of a more radical *pinyongzhi* versions. These newly established outlets adopted various sophisticated recruiting standards characterized by high pay, high level of work target, and high attrition rate. Most of their employees are recruited from the labor market outside the existing cadre system and are clearly categorized as "free labor" (W. Wang 2011, 99). The recruiting mechanism quickly evolved from *pinyongzhi* to *laowu paiqianzhi* in late 1990s, as previously discussed in chapter 4.

The implications to the labor relationships are threefold. One, the employees no longer share the same political commitment as it used to in the old cadre system, regardless of how distant their commitment is from its nominal significance. While the journalism remains state-owned and nominally represent the state and ultimately the populace, the journalist employees are no longer state cadres and thus no longer represent the state in the least but only stand on behalf of the interest of their employers and responsible for the financial and editorial tasks assigned by the management. Second, the communist ideology, regardless of how it has been experimented, re-interpreted, and emptied over the People's Republic's socialist practice over the years, is no longer relevant in the least to the journalist practitioners today. Instead, professionalism has taken over and practically detached the practitioners from their political being and representation. As the mainstream practical ethical standards, professionalism absolutizes the principle of truth and objective while ignoring the reality that the so-called "truth" is no less relative than what Tom Goldstein (2007) has critiqued as the eyewitness to history in Shakespeare's historical dramas. However, such a principle is not only where the media market and practice claim credibility from but also a sanctuary for selective reportage of social life and de-politicization in blatant consumerism which practically commoditize all aspects of socio-political life framed into the themes of sex, violence, psychological perversion and all sorts of entertainment and materialism. Thirdly, the impressive cost-efficiency in the labor-capital (both state and private capital) relationship under the new corporate governance has been achieved at the costs of the journalists in the most exploitative manner. Such a labor relationship, from the capital perspective, aims to maximize the value for money by extracting every bit of energy, talent, and time from the employees. A telling example is from CCTV, the largest and richest broadcasting service in China. According to Wang Weijia (2011, 104), the Department of News and Commentaries of CCTV, the major production unit of journalism, has to be self-reliant in seeking financial sources to fill up the gap between its operational costs and the limited allocation of fund within the corporation. Although the employees are highly qualified, their number is small. A three-person team will be responsible for everything that needs to be done for a ten- to twenty-minute news program. It is not uncommon that the employees of this department have to work day and night over the week to get the job done before the deadline and feed themselves with instant noodles just to save some time for the work. This is not an exception, but a common story everywhere and justified by the market discourse and professionalism. As one of the CCTV informal employees said about her situation:

> We work every day under the eyes of the producer, who has absolute power over appointment. Reporters are jealous with each other for relations with him. Everybody has to work hard and be cautious lest you will lose your job the very next day if he is pissed off or suspicious of your ability. (W. Wang 2011, 157)

A sampling survey in 2000 among journalist practitioners in Shanghai shows that, among the deceased professionals in the ten investigated outlets, the average mortality age was 45.7 and 72.7 percent of the mortality resulted from cancer (Jia 2000).[20] In such intensive working environment, there is practically no political and social relations but sheer labor-capital relationship between the journalists and the management (W. Wang 2011, 158). The highly celebrated market jargon that "to widen the differences in income is the key to high efficiency" epitomizes not only the hierarchical working relations and financial incentives quantifiable in monetary terms but also the labor-control mechanism causing and widening the gap between journalists as a mere factor of production and their commitment to public representation in the public sphere, as well as that between journalism as a cause of public services and journalistic profession as a means of making personal living or fame and materializing maximum interest for the corporate stakeholders.

## DEMYTHOLOGIZING MARKETIZATION AND CONGLOMERATION

By introducing full-fledged market forces and establishing new corporate governance, the Party-state has actually strengthened its ties with media management from the top layer leadership to the journalists and editors at the lowest level. Contrary to the expectation that marketization and release from government subsidies would lead to a freer and more transparent journalism, what has been effectively enhanced is a re-aligned win-win state-media relationship and the control over editorial content and professionals. Meanwhile, the new governance has reinforced and assured the dominance of the Party media. The boom has not only vindicated the profit-seeking market logic but also in effect camouflaged the media's commitment to Party logic by affirming the flagship status of the Party media and consolidating Party-state leadership.

The new corporate governance rules have also effectively divided the profit-generating market sector from editorial content production. The former has been given an almost no-holds-barred access to the market and is open to private and foreign investment while the latter is managed with the same cost-efficiency logic placing the journalist labor under control. Such labor control has provided an assurance for content control. Media outlets are allowed to reap benefits from commercializing the printing, distribution, and advertising businesses. The journalistic content production, however, has not been included either in GAPP's 2008 three-year road map or in the current media reform agenda. The win-win collusion between the state and the media management as well as the effective labor control within the media system has diminished the demand and hope for the political engagement of journalism with the socio-political reality.

Through the conglomerated organizational structure and the new corporate governance, the Party-state is able to maintain political control and keep commercialized outlets and their employees in line. Pivoted on the leadership of the Party media within each group, the loyal conveyance of official messages through non-Party media is guaranteed. In this way, the new Party-dominated corporate governance suppresses substantive expansion and empowerment of the underrepresented voices, and therefore, stands in the way of media transparency.

More significantly, the mixture of Party-state control and market discourse has resulted in consensus among the Party-state media authorities and media management that the CCP leadership should be safeguarded by all means (Lee et al. 2008, 29). This consensus is summarized in the media administration's cardinal principles that the news media must be "led by statesman (the Party bureaucrats), managed as enterprises, operated in market and serving society" (Lang 2003, 135). Among these doctrines, the Party's leadership and market logic have become the leading and kernel principle. This chapter argues that this consensus is the premise and goal of business management and conglomeration. Following this line, this chapter demythologizes the "further development" illusion created by the market-oriented corporate governance and restructured labor relationship, which promotes professionalism that suits all market demand but in favor of the weak and poor. As many Chinese elite politicians and intellectuals fancy various models and pathways toward liberal democracy such as those in Korea, Taiwan, Russia, East Europe, Japan, and Singapore and look down upon India's democracy, they tend to ignore the fact that both India and China have a population of workers and peasants much larger both in number and proportion than that in any aforementioned liberal democracies that have benefited either from the Cold War–conditioned economic development or direct patronage from the United States (Y. Zhao 2001, 42). What is often made light of is the fact that the weak and the poor in China have little place in the so-called public sphere dominated by the elites either through depoliticized content or consumerized professionalism or through both. As Yuezhi Zhao (2001, 42) maintains, the role of Chinese workers and peasants and their voices remain a key problematic for media and democratization in the post-Mao China. Journalism remains a depoliticized political tool as "a mechanism of power" (H. Wang 2009, 6). Just because the media have grown richer, bigger, and stronger does not mean effective expansion of the public sphere proportionally (H. Wang 2011b, 68). Therefore, this discussion finds it hard not to concur with Mobo Gao (2008; 2011, 163) that the media reform featuring state-conditioned commercialization and conglomeration is part of the Party-state's capitalist market agenda. This agenda leads media credibility and accountability to nowhere but rhetoric and illusion.

## NOTES

1. Former president Hu Jintao reiterated in his speech at the APEC CEO Summit 2010 in Yokohama that the problems that China is facing can only be solved by further development. Viewed on April 1, 2011 from money.163.com/10/1113/11/6LC7Q5K400254JQQ.html.

2. Also see a critical review from Lee 2003, 19.

3. Before the double-track system of goods supply was abolished, limited amount of materials for production was supplied within the planned economy at fixed rate while the unfulfilled part of the need had to be met by resorting to the opening-up market at the rate determined by the demand and supply.

4. *Youfaheyi* literally means integrating newspaper circulation with postal service.

5. Each openly circulated newspaper must obtain a publication licence from the administration authorities. The licence bears a serial number indicating whether a publication is nationally or locally distributed.

6. Sohu, Sina, and Netease went public on NASDAQ in 2000 and Tecent in Hong Kong in June 2004.

7. See the appendix which shows the levels and numbers of press groups approved by the GAPP as of end of 2009.

8. There was no clear division between the editorial and market sectors within these conglomerates. Since late 2004, the SARFT has ceased to accept application for establishment of new radio and television conglomerates that are public institutions and managed as business enterprises. However, conglomeration of mere market divisions [*jingyingxingyewu*] including advertising and distribution businesses is not prohibited.

9. A recent example is the establishment of Anhui Radio and Television Media Group in February 2010. The business scope of this group focuses on profit-generating businesses such as advertising and TV shopping channels that are not directly related to journalism. See Yuebo Li and Song 2010.

10. The information about Guangzhou Daily Press Group is available from its official website, viewed on June 19, 2011 from co.gzdaily.com/201106/10/62881.shtml.

11. Both *Xinmin Wanbao* and *Wenhui Bao* are located in Shanghai.

12. Wang Zhongwei had been the deputy Party chief of Shanghai Administration of Press and Publication (1993–1995), Party chief and deputy editor-in-chief of *WenhuiBao* (1995–1997), deputy director of the secretariat of the CCP Shanghai Committee (1997–1998), director of the Information Office of the Shanghai Municipal Government (1997–1998). Given the level and nature of a news outlet in China is reflected by the official level of its party chief, *WenhuiBao* ranks the second official newsprint in Shanghai next to *Jiefang Daily*.

13. The circulation volume of *Xinmin Wanbao* remained 1.03 million copies per issue in 2010, ranking 46 among the top 100 bestselling dailies worldwide (Z. Chen 2010, 13). This shows that the new corporate governance does not necessarily strangle the commercialized subsidiaries but to some extent allows their prosperity in a contained manner. Nevertheless, *Xinmin* cannot go any further than what is allowed by the group administration as its financial resources and senior personnel administration are subject to the senior management of the press group.

14. According to the *Guanyuguanbanfenli he huazhuanbaokanjiaqiangguanli de tongzhi*, government department and administrative authorities should draw a line between administration and management of the media outlets under their jurisdiction. Some county and district-level Party newspapers will be transformed into non-Party papers or merged into higher-level Party newspapers or conglomerates. The former administrative [*zhuguan*] and sponsoring [*zhuban*] institutions are no longer responsible for the personnel management, finance, and distribution of the transformed outlets. See Xinhua 2004.

15. The *Basic Conditions and Reviewing Procedures regarding Establishing Press Groups*, GAPP Document No. 914, was issued on August 2, 2002 and remains in effect as of the end of 2011.

According to Fischer, a typical newspaper publishing house is headed by *Sheweihui*, which is supervising everyday management of the news outlet including both editorial and market operation. See Fischer 2009, 184.

16. Translation by author.

17. The State Council No. 114 document in 2008 is an update of the SC document No. 105 issued in 2003. The new document is titled *Regulations on Transformation of the Market-based Public Cultural Institutions into Enterprises in the Reform of the Cultural System*.

18. The *bianzhi* system can be divided more roughly into two categories, which are public institutional establishment [*xingzhengshiyebianzhi*] and enterprise establishment [*qiyebianzhi*]. Exchange of positions and status across these two divisions has been every difficult, especially to those lower-level employees. As the state-owned media outlets were entirely public institutions, the journalists and editors were employed in the pubic institutional establishment system.

19. *The Provisional Regulations on Cadres Employment under Appointment Contract in Fully State-owned Enterprises*, Ministry of Personnel official document No. 1991 [5]. The first official document of this kind was issued by Shandong Provincial Government on May 30, 1988, titled *The Provisional Regulations on Recruiting Cadres in Fully State-owned Enterprises and Public Institutions under Appointment Contract*. Both official documents extended the regulations to public institutions which included the state-owned media.

20. The research findings of this article were reported to be exaggerated by some media in 2004. Some claimed that the mortality age was applied to the whole journalist cohort nationwide. Such claim was spread with sensational debate and discussions to the extent that it was finally defined as one of the top-ten high-profile "fake news in 2004" by *Journalism Review* in 2005. See B. Chen and Jia 2005.

*Chapter Six*

# "Opening a Skylight"

*Media Activism Revived?*

"Opening a skylight [*kaitianchuang*]," a metaphor of blank space left on publications, dates back to the media protests against the heavy censorship imposed by the Nationalist Guomindang (GMD) government before 1949. It seems to be reviving today as a form of media activism against the CCP censorship apparatus. Since the start of the reform era, China's media industry has from time to time been spurred by complaints about intensified information control. One of the most frequently mentioned examples was the blank spaces left on a number of newspapers on July 30, 2011, suggesting simmering grievance against censorship orders banning reporting and commentaries on the tragic Wen-Yong high-speed train collision on July 23. It is considered to be a "new high point for China's developing and professionalizing media" (Bandurski 2011a). Implying to readers that there is something to be said but forbidden so, these blank spaces are interpreted by some to be a collective protest against today's CCP Party-state and its publicity authority (F. Wu 2011; X. Zhou 2011).

Such comments have not only revived memories of media activism before 1949 but have also built up expectations of similar media movements as the media today are increasingly financially prosperous, technologically equipped, and market-oriented. Disobedience is celebrated as commercialized outlets' "one-dimensional" efforts to break away from state control (Pei 1998, 14). Some would believe that the reformed outlets, by fighting a costly battle against the government control, tend to render the government censorship useless (Pei 1998, 165). In the midst of the media's martyrized sensation rises an activism myth that predicates the revival of the pre-1949 media activism on the commercialized, marketized, and liberalized outlets in the reform era. Such predication projects its rationale on the ostensible similarities of the media environments: heavy censorship imposed by the government and blank spaces on the media in response. Much less noted, yet significant nevertheless, is that the so-called media activism today is drastically different in purpose, process, and practice from that before 1949 and therefore has different political implications and prospects.

Media activism obtains its name because it always goes against the will of state hegemony, as termed by Tim Jordan (2002, 61) as acts of "civil disobedience." According to Henry Yuhuai He, opening a skylight means "leaving a blank in a publication to show that something has been censored" (H. Y. He 2001, 221). It was a media response to the scrutiny system of the GMD regime (Liang 1984, 350), which condemned its information control and injustice and prescribed its doomed destiny. By this definition, a space left blank on publications can be called a skylight when:

- the space is left blank as an intentional editorial decision;
- the purpose is to reveal and protest against the censorship apparatus.

The pre-1949 skylights had openly challenged and embarrassed the ruling GMD government and overtly represented and encouraged the political groups that had been fighting for freedom and democracy. Not only did the blank spaces serve as a protest tactic, they also escalated into direct confrontation between the media and the GMD's censorship regime in 1945 when numerous progressive and left-wing media outlets across the country openly refused to subject themselves to the censorship apparatus. That was an age when non-compliant outlets could be suspended or forced to close down at any time while editors and writers had to from time to time risk their personal freedom and even their lives. Some journalists were actually assassinated (Song and Zhu 1988, 407).

However, the media activism today seems to sit in a different and dilemmatic situation. On the one hand, it can be immediately interpreted as a protest against the state censorship apparatus and information control. On the other, despite grievances emerging here and there from time to time, few outlets have maintained a consistent and constant standpoint with a clear and loud voice against the censorship apparatus. As information control has been tightened and censorship prevails in the reform era, few media outlets have openly declared non-compliance or even exposed censorship orders. What usually happens is that newspapers and journals follow the orders and replace the censored content with something acceptable to the authorities. Even when part of a newspaper page or book was left blank and interpreted by commentators as an unuttered protest, the outlet would usually downplay any rebellious implications or compensate with positive and less critical reportage immediately. Although it is not uncommon that activist journalists and editors are suspended, fired, or persecuted for their outspoken journalism, few outlets constantly and consistently follow the bold line. Soon after a skylight fades from public attention, most involved outlets will carry on their profit-making stories and positive publicity obligations: business as usual.

While leaving blank spaces on newsprints today may inspire the memory of skylights in the past, its rationale and content should not be simply interpreted as equal to that of the pre-1949 period. Given the heavy censorship both before 1949 and in the reform era, a question arises: Why are the media today, although much more prosperous and better equipped, unable to wage a real war against information control or even promise so? By answering this question, this chapter aims to challenge the popular sentiment that the re-emergence of skylights suggests a rising media activism parallel to that before 1949 as a result of the media commercialization and marketization. I will argue that:

- The rising media activism is not an institutional behavior powered by any political conviction for public interests. Rather, the most prominent activist elements have been few individual professionals who not only dare to stick their necks out but are willing to risk their career and freedom for outspoken journalism.
- While the pre-1949 activism had resulted from nationalist movements striving for freedom and democracy and, therefore, had been highly political, the skylights in the reform era have been largely rooted in the burgeoning professionalism characterized by consumerism and niche-market orientation and, therefore, had been much de-politicized.
- The intention and process of the so-called media activism in the reform era, unlike that in the pre-1949 period, has been kept out of public discussion. There is practically no transparency in the tacit state-media agreement on keeping silence and secrecy regarding censorship, self-censorship, and counter-censorship.

To substantiate these arguments, a historical comparative perspective is adopted in this chapter. Firstly, some pages will be spent on the pre-1949 counter-censorship movement to exemplify the revolutionary legacy on which today's activist sentiment draws and thrives. Secondly, three skylights in the reform era will be examined to show how the media activism re-emerged with heavy professionalism sentiment but little political significance. Thirdly, a notion is put forth that the new consensus reached between the party-state and the profit-seeking media on political and market control favors lack of transparency, which has provided infinite space for speculation and imagination from which professionalism keeps reaping sympathy and profits. Through the discussion, the disjuncture of the media's political representation is demonstrated.

## Chapter 6

## PRE-1949 MEDIA ACTIVISM

### Opening a Skylight

The origin of the skylights dates back to the republican movement before the Xinhai Revolution. *Guofeng Daily* [*National Wind Daily*], first published in Beijing in early 1911, was one of the progressive newspapers that targeted monarchism, warlords, and those who attempted to restore monarchism (Y. Chen, Jiang, and Wang 2003, 62). Today, *Guofeng Daily* is remembered for its two skylights. One was on October 11, 1911, the day after the Wuchang Uprising that marked the start of the republic revolution. Prohibited by the censors of Qing court from carrying any report on the Wuchang Uprising, *Guofeng Daily* titled its front page with a protesting remark that "This newspaper has a lot of information about Wuchang. However, due to interference by the police, all relevant information has to be withheld. Forgiveness by the readers is appreciated" (Y. Chen et al. 2003, 62).[1] The rest of the page was left blank. The skylight humiliated the ruling Qing court because it revealed that the latter was too weak to afford any bad publicity. The blank page actually forecasted the impending doom of the royal reign. The other skylight took place four years later. Protesting against Yuan Shikai's attempt to restore the monarchy,[2] the front page of December 12, 1915 edition was left entirely blank. Jing Dingjun, the chief editor, was immediately arrested and locked up behind the bars until Yuan died in 1916 (M. Zhang 2009, 147).

After Jiang Jieshi took power in 1925 and ordered the purge of many thousands of communists, leftists, and labor union organizers in 1927,[3] the Nationalist GMD government suppressed all news media that were perceived to be threatening its one-party rule. In response, newsprints left blank spaces on their publications to protest censorship orders. *Wenhui Bao*, *Shen Bao* and many other democratic newspapers opened skylights after their editorials had been banned by GMD censorship orders (R. Zhuang 1993, 75). The CCP *Xinhua Daily* also opened one on its January 6, 1940 edition. Its front page carried a headline in bold letter "Anti-Japanese War First! Victory First!" and left its upper-half front page blank. At the bottom of the blank space, there was a brief comment: Two editorials of today's issue, namely *On Victories of Attacks Launched in the Winter*, and *Rise Up! Put Down the Traitors*, are withheld as per ordered. Readers' understanding is highly appreciated (Jialin Liu 2005, 507).[4]

Skylights on publications before 1949 explicitly exposed and protested against censorship. Publishers refused to replace censored content with something else acceptable to the censors. The editorial decisions were made to reveal, embarrass, challenge, and protest against the censorship apparatus and the GMD regime at the risk of the newsprints being forced to close down and journalists being persecuted. Both the activist newsprints and journalists were willing to pay any price for their ideals of press freedom and democracy.

## *Jujian Yundong* [The Rejecting Censorship Campaign]

In the afterglow of the Anti-Japanese War, Jiang Jieshi and the GMD regime seemed to have a better chance than ever to win over the liberal elements of the intelligentsia and the media. In his speech on August 15, 1945 to celebrate victory in the war against the Japanese invasion, Jiang uttered his belief in perpetual peace based on equality and freedom of mankind, and promised democracy and cooperation through "letting the bygones be bygones [*bunian jiu'e*]" and "being nice to others [*yuren weishan*]" (X. Zhang 1996, 584).

But the GMD regime never gave up its attempt to silence critical and dissident voices. Jiang's failure to generate or at least bring hope to democracy and economic recovery, accompanied by his tyrannical leadership, quickly drained his democracy and cooperation rhetoric. Meanwhile, publication scrutiny escalated. Strict censorship laws were heavily imposed, and many publications were forced to shut down (P.-k. Yu 1975, 30). As scrutiny and censorship became intensified, the growing appeal for press freedom and resentment against high-pressure control fermented into increasing protests and movements.

One of the best remembered media activist movements during this postwar period was *Jujian Yundong* launched in the GMD-occupied territory in August 1945. Newspapers, journals and commercial publishing houses in major cities openly refused to abide by any form of censorship rules and orders. Not only did they reject censorship orders, but also stopped sending print copies to government scrutiny agencies. Statements and editorials were issued to denounce the GMD censorship regime. *Jujian Yundong* became a milestone of media activism by openly rubbishing the censorship rules, orders, and apparatus. Moreover, apart from staging strongly worded criticisms, *Jujian Yundong* featured ideological consensus, political engagement, and broad participation by democratic intellectuals, political groups, and news outlets. It completely rebuked the government censorship apparatus and demanded incorporation in the constitution of the rights to freedom of speech.

The *Jujian Yundong* started with Huang Yanpei's open refusal to hand in for scrutiny his book, *Return from Yan'an*, before its publication on August 7, 1945. This book recorded favorably the democracy and freedom Huang had witnessed and experienced during his visit to Yan'an in July 1945 (E. S. K. Fung 2000, 257). Following Huang's non-compliance, a statement was jointly drafted by Zhang Zhirang, Yang Weigong, and Fu Binran on behalf of and endorsed by sixteen political journals in Chongqing, then provisional capital city of the nationalist GMD government, and was published on August 17.[5] The statement declared that these journals would stop sending in print copies for scrutiny from September 1 (F. Yao 1990, 422). Ten journals in Chongqing jointly issued an additional edition on September 15, reiterating that they would stop applying to the government authority for registration of newly established newsprints and sending in any script for scrutiny.[6] Among the fewer than forty journals in Chongqing, thirty-three had joined the *Jujian Yundong* by August 27 (Fu 2006, 77). Furthermore, the movement in Chongqing was quickly and strongly echoed by twenty-seven newspapers and journals in Chengdu, eleven in Kunming, and many others in Guilin, Xi'an, Peking, and Shanghai. An overwhelming wave of protest and defiance nationwide was rising against the GMD's control.

Ten political journals and magazines including *Xianzheng* and *Guoxun* jointly published on September 15 a four-page *United Supplementary Edition*. Huang Yanpei, chief editor of *Guoxun*, declared at the editorial meeting on August 27 that his Guoxun bookstore would publish the special edition without applying to the GMD propaganda authority for registration or sending in editions for scrutiny (Shang 1990, 115). Ye Shengtao, chief editor of *Zhongxuesheng*, drafted *An Open Letter from Seventeen Cultural Organizations to the Journals in Chongqing* to support the *Jujian Yundong* there. On September 9, Ye published, in the second issue of the *United Supplementary Edition,* one of his most quoted articles, titled "We Never Want Censorship of Publication and Journalism." In the article, Ye stated that:

> We don't need such a system. It is not because my thought and speech was banned or deleted, or your thought and speech was banned or deleted, or someone else's thought or speech was banned or deleted. Even if my thought and speech or yours as well as that of anyone else was not banned or deleted, or our speech is not to be banned or deleted in the future, we still don't need such a system. As long as such a system exists, there will always be someone suffering from spiritual persecution. We and those people are spiritually connected, and their persecution is our suffering too. (Fu 2007, 189)[7]

To manifest his hatred towards any restraint on free publication, Ye Shengtao condemned censorship and stated that:

> Censorship is a manufactured criteria and yardstick to which thoughts and speeches have to conform before getting published. This means some thoughts and speeches cannot be published and people cannot express themselves freely. Think about it. How unreasonable is that? (Pang 2001, 192)

Ye's distaste of censorship was also echoed in the open letter jointly issued by sixteen newspapers, journals, and news agencies in Chengdu in support of the Chongqing initiative. The letter targeted "all rules and systems that may limit the freedom of speech of the people" and demonstrated the determination of the news industry to "eliminate for good the censorship system and prevent it from reviving in any form in any part of the Chinese territory" (Xihua Zhao and Ding 1992, 100).

## Broad Participation, Ideological Consensus, and Political Engagement

Ostensibly, *Jujian Yundong* was the result of the widely spread social disillusionment and deteriorating national economy and living conditions. Fundamentally, it stemmed from the ideological and political dispute between the GMD one-party dictatorship and the popular pursuit of freedom and democracy. Following the end of the Anti-Japanese War in 1945, the GMD decided to reconstitute administration alone, as reaching consensus on a coalition government grew dimmer (Dillon 2009, 250). The dictatorship, iron-fist rule, and corruption of Jiang's regime as well as his indifference to the widespread disease and starvation of the Chinese people bothered both the domestic public and the United States, the latter being the major source of financial and military aid for the GMD (Donovan 2007, 10).

This dispute eventually alienated the non-GMD political groups and the intelligentsia (Groot 2004, 27). Their broad engagement in *Jujian Yundong* was attributed, at least in part, to the pervasive disillusion among democratic political personages, groups, and the media. Huang Yanpei, the leading figure, was one of the "disillusioned" democratic academics (E. S. K. Fung 2010 136). He was a prominent democrat [*minzhu renshi*], chairman of the Democratic National Construction Association in 1945, activist of the Democratic Salvation Movement, and a founding member of the China Democratic League. Huang's disillusion was broadly echoed within the news and publication industry when the public voice was stifled by the GMD. The intellectuals and middle class were deeply frustrated not only because their livelihood was worsened beyond despair but also because their political engagement was denied. As Lawrence Kaelter Rosinger (1945, 65) has observed, pandemic inflation imposed a deadly effect on their livelihood while democracy and freedom had never been operative at any time. "Incompetent and corrupt" was the common phrase increasingly heard from journalists in describing the GMD regime that had to resort heavily to the wartime censorship system in its attempt to silence critical voices (Pepper 1991, 306).

Among the first sixteen journals that endorsed the statement of rejecting scrutiny came from various backgrounds that shared Huang's position, *Minzhu Shijie* was associated with leftist GMD background, and *Xiandai Funu* and *Zhongsu Wenhua* related to the CCP. The rest of the fourteen journals were sponsored either by a minor party group (MPG), intellectual associations, or commercial publication businesses.[8] The CCP official mouthpiece, *Qunzhong* [*The Mass*] made its first official declaration on September 18 to stop abiding by the censorship rules. As a result, the vast ideological consensus on democracy and freedom among the CCP, MPGs and the non-GMD media constituted a strong opposition to the GMD dictatorship and its censorship apparatus.[9]

In contrast with their growing anti-GMD sentiment, the democratic political groups, intelligentsia and leftist GMD media were increasingly attracted to the freedom and democracy that the CCP promised and exhibited in its Yan'an governance. Ideologically at least, the Yan'an model offered an alternative model for the liberal intelligentsia to pursue their political ideals. Strategically, *Jujian Yundong* aimed at a policy outcome to substantiate this ideal of rights to freedom of speech.

Yan'an was the place of birth and practice for Mao's "New Democracy," which provided an effective platform for the CCP United Front Work (Chai 1970, 232). After the Anti-Japanese War, the new democratic united front aimed to unite as many social political forces as possible including, at times, the national bourgeoisie and big landlords, against the imperialist and feudal forces (Groot 2004, 25). The democratic intelligentsia were increasingly attracted by Yan'an democracy and Mao's comprehensive proposal of coalition government as they were disillusioned by deteriorating living conditions and the GMD's dictatorship (Groot 2004, 26). Many of them either left their metropolitan life behind to pursue their future in Yan'an or paid exploring visits to seek answers there.

During his visit to Yan'an, Huang Yanpei had a conversation with Mao Zedong. Huang raised a question of the cycle of life and death in politics. He argued that history was made up of cycles of success and failure, and no one was able to escape that cycle (Ding 1994, 27). Mao answered that:

> We have found the new path. We can jump out of such a cycle. The new path is democracy. The government dare not slacken off provided that it is subject to the people's supervision. The political system will not perish after the death of the leaders provided that everybody takes responsibility.[10]

Agreeing with Mao, Huang took the Yan'an model of democracy as a valid alternative to the GMD's dictatorship. He commented in his 1945 book *Return from Yan'an* that:

> Mao Zedong is right. The cult of personality will not happen so long as major policies are decided by the public. Only when everything is disclosed to the people, can this place flourish with the people and the people can engage themselves in the cause. I am convinced that the cycle of success and failure can be effectively broken by such democracy. (Ding 1994, 27)

Encouraged by what he had witnessed in Yan'an and his refreshed political faith in democracy promised by the CCP, Huang Yanpei stood up first to reject the GMD censorship apparatus and initiated the *Jujian Yundong*. To Huang and many others, freedom and democracy were not just an empty promise or abstract concept but ideas that could be substantiated and put into practice. Such consensus took shape among democratic political groups and the intelligentsia and subsequently fermented into collective actions against censorship and dictatorship.

Strategically, the participants of *Jujian Yundong* demanded policy outcomes. The target of *Jujian Yundong* was specifically the GMD wartime censorship system. Unlike the skylights which were relatively passive and reserved protests, open rejection of the censorship system was by no means a mild and individual appeal aiming at incremental progress of press freedom, but rather an outburst of systematic attacks nationwide against government control. Furthermore, not only did *Jujian Yundong* demand abolition of the wartime censorship system but it also called for prevention of any legislation that might lead to enforcement of censorship in the future.

The protests forced the government into a situation where it had to make a choice between enforcing fiercer clampdowns and abolition of the censorship system. The *Jujian Yundong* succeeded, at least temporarily, in realizing its two policy goals, namely abolition of the wartime censorship system and reinforcement in the constitution of rights to freedom of speech. As a direct policy outcome, a resolution was passed at the Tenth Standing Committee of the GMD Central Committee on September 22 that the wartime censorship system was to be repealed on October 1, 1945 in the territory ruled by the GMD.[11] Section Four of the *October Tenth Agreement* between the CCP and the GMD stated that:

> As to the freedom of the people, it is unanimously agreed that the government should safeguard the freedom of personal liberty, religion, speech, publication, assembly and association that the people in a democracy can enjoy on daily basis. The present laws and orders (against this principle) should be abolished or modified according to this principle. (Youyu Zhang 1986, 220)[12]

The abolition of wartime censorship and modification of publication laws was reaffirmed in chapter 2 and the annex of the *Heping Jianguo Gangling Cao'an* proposed by the CCP and the Democratic League, passed on January 24, 1946 at the Political and Consultative Conference, and finally legislated in the *Constitution of the Republic of China* at the National Constitutional Assembly on December 25, 1946.[13] The biggest difference between the constitutional rights to freedom of speech stipulated in the May 5, 1936 version and the 1946 version lies in the conditional limits to the rights. The 1936 version stated that "Every citizen shall have freedom of speech, writing and publication. Such freedom shall not be restricted except *in accordance with law*" (Shih and Chang 1936, 285).[14] The legalistic condition made it possible for the government to make laws and orders at its discretion against the freedoms and rights. The 1946 version, however, stated that the freedoms and rights enumerated in the preceding articles shall not be restricted by law, except in case where a restriction is necessary . . . for . . . promoting the public interest" (Kirby 2004, 116). The latter version, largely based on the draft proposed by the CCP and the Democratic League despite some "unilateral KMT revisions," made it possible to minimize the legitimacy of state interference against such freedoms and rights (Pepper 1999, 138).

The activism and dynamic journalism following the end of the Anti-Japanese War was fundamentally a result of broad political engagement empowered by the ideological consensus among the CCP, democratic political groups, intelligentsia, and the press. It was more a political movement aiming for policy outcome than a spontaneous response to restriction of individual rights. China was at a time when the nation had to make a choice of where to go next. By the end of Anti-Japanese War, the CCP had grown into a powerful force and controlled many areas of China and therefore exerted considerable influence on the liberal intelligentsia, the public and the media. The GMD government was not able to establish effective control of the whole country, let alone the disputed ideological superstructure.

The practice of democracy and freedom in Yan'an offered a laudable alternative to the GMD's censorship and dictatorship realities. While the democratic political groups, intelligentsia, and the general public had been increasingly disillusioned by the GMD dictatorship and worsening living conditions, they had fostered genuine sympathy for and agreement with the CCP, and shift their political engagement and prospects to the latter's political agenda. This sympathy and agreement was rooted in the common pursuit of freedom and democracy, and consequently constituted and consolidated a broadly participated socio-political base for the pre-1949 media activism exerting effective impact on the GMD censorship apparatus and regime legitimacy.

## SKYLIGHTS IN THE REFORM ERA

Skylights did not re-emerge until the 1980s when ideological consensus on the nature of socialism started to break up and the economy started to diverge from the Maoist socialist path. The Party-state's priority was that the CCP must restructure its ideological system and re-establish its control over the media system (Brady 2008, 44) to keep public opinions in line. This ideological change gave rise to the problem of censorship. After a short period of press freedom reaching its peak and end on the eve of the 1989 Tiananmen clampdown, dissident voices were suppressed. Unlike those before 1949, a typical skylight in the early years of the reform era was not one opened in newspapers but a blank space left in a journal or a book. This was because, at least in part, documentary literature was the most active public domain in the 1980s. Moreover, as the media found its prosperity in the transformed mass media such as commercialized newspapers, broadcasting services, and digital networks, the twenty-first century has seen a steady rise of blank spaces both in commercial publications and sometimes even official mouthpieces.[15]

However, the so-called skylights in the reform era could hardly parallel those before 1949 in terms of political participation and ideological consensus. Unlike the democratic and left-wing press that dared to articulate clearly their political conviction before 1949, the media in the reform era are much more cautious, carefully avoiding direct and open confrontation with the authorities, even when a skylight is allegedly opened. Three prominent examples of skylights will be examined to show how media activism in the reform era is different from that in the pre-1949 years.

The first skylight in the reform era was no more than an *operational negligence*. The Chinese central government staged on the Anti-Bourgeois Liberalism Campaign after its clampdown on the pro-democracy student movement in late 1986 (Y.-l. Yu 1991, 71). A number of dissident liberals, including the journalist Liu Binyan, the astrophysicist Fang Lizhi, and the writer Wang Ruowang, were deprived of Party membership, and their publications banned (Sleeboom-Faulkner 2007, 88). The January 1987 issue of the *Literary Review* [*Wenxue Pinglun*] carried in its content list the title of an article by Liu Binyan, even though the article had been removed according to censorship orders from the central propaganda authority. Given the liberal stand of Liu Zaifu, then chief editor, retaining the title in the content list has been interpreted as a sign of liberal media protesting against the Party censorship regime (H. Y. He 2001, 221).

However, this well-celebrated incident turned out to be no more than an accident. Liu Zaifu acknowledged that he had duly followed the ban and ordered that the article be removed (Z. Liu 2010). Hu Sheng, the head of the China Academy of Social Sciences (CASS), was furious though. At a CASS internal meeting, Hu accused the journal of "using skylights against the Party." Liu, however, defended himself by insisting that it was a sheer operational negligence by the printing house staff who had forgotten to remove the title from the index. In an interview with *Jingji Guancha Bao* [*The Economic Observer Newspaper*] on August 21, 2009, Liu Zaifu reiterated that the whole skylight saga was "absolutely an operational negligence" (Y. He 1992, 435; Z. Liu 2009).

Although he has been sympathetic toward Liu Binyan to the extent that his journal did not publish any article critical of the dissident liberal during the 1987 anti-liberalism campaign (H. Y. He 2001, 221), Liu Zaifu has never set himself against the party-state or openly questioned the legitimacy of its censorship apparatus. As described by his daughter Liu Jianmei, Liu has always been a mild reformist who would resort to amelioration, compromise, and dialogue rather than confrontation (Jianmei Liu 2008). It is obvious that some are willing to celebrate with a sense of pride such negligence as an intentional skylight (B. Liu 1990, 380). The irony is that neither the chief editor nor the journal was dissident or keen to use any skylight to overtly challenge the Party on purpose. It was neither an editorial decision nor intentional and open protest against the censorship or the Party-state. It does not conform to either aspect of Henry Yuhuai He's definition of the pre-1949 skylights. There has been no evidence that Liu Zaifu or his journal has had any political agenda different from that of the Party-state. The asserted grievance against the banning orders, if any at all, was reserved, unuttered, and largely imaginary.

Another well-known skylight is seen in Ba Jin's *A Book Telling the Truth* published by Sichuan Wenyi Chubanshe [Sichuan Art and Literature Publishing House] in 1990. The book collected articles that the author had written between 1977 and 1990. Ba Jin, a writer profusely honoured by the Party, wrote an essay titled "Cultural Revolution Museum" in 1986. The article proposed the establishment of a museum as a historical reminder to prevent tragedies that many had experienced in the political movement from happening again. The content was far from divergent from the official holocaust [*haojie*] discourse when addressing the Cultural Revolution. However, Ba Jin connected the ongoing *Qingwu Yundong* [Eliminating Spiritual Pollution Campaign], an ideological campaign against liberalism in the mid-1980s, with his memory of the Cultural Revolution. He warned of a possible repetition of the purge he had experienced. The article implied objection to the massive clampdown by violence and ideological controls, which the Party-state happened to be using against the rising debate over China's ideological divergence, lest it went out of control. Ba Jin's alert became something the media administrative authority found sensitive and inappropriate in such a circumstance. As a result, the article was taken out of the 1990 version and the 1991 reprint of the book. But the title was deliberately retained in the content list and the corresponding page left blank, physically qualified a skylight.

However, neither the publishing house nor Ba Jin was dissident. The so-called skylight was the result of a well-informed compromise agreement between the provincial media administrative authority, the author, and the publisher, with a full knowledge and understanding of the matter by all rather than an outburst of protest or agony. Li Zhi, deputy director of the Propaganda Department of CCP Sichuan Provincial Committee in charge of journalism and publication work, is Ba Jin's nephew. He urged the publishing house and Ba Jin to withdraw the article many times and sought opinions from higher administrative hierarchy by reporting the case to He Jingzhi, then Deputy Minister of Culture. He Jingzhi responded with a vague remark, stating that he trusted that this matter could be appropriately handled (Gong 2007). The publishing house then contacted Ba Jin and suggested removal of the article and retention of the title in the content list (J. Tang and Zhang 2004, 557). Ba Jin completely understood the situation and agreed, because he "would not like to have the rest of the book kept out of the reach of the readers because of two or three articles" (Z. Li 2005, 225), for which he felt sorry (Y. Fan 2005). Besides, Ba Jin insisted that "it is not my intention to open a skylight" (J. Tang and Zhang 2004, 557).

Although Ba Jin had personally suffered from violence and persecution during the Cultural Revolution, he had never attributed his suffering to the Party. Also, there is no evidence that the publishing house was trying to use a skylight for any protest purpose. According to Ba Jin, the publisher was worried that the publication of his article might lead to some undesirable consequences (Gong 2007). By suggesting removal of the article and retaining the title in the content list, the publisher was trying to find a balance between avoiding possible political risks and respecting the prestigious author. The media administrative authority, given Li Zhi's kinship with Ba Jin, gave tacit consent to the compromise. Such compromise was acceptable to the cultural administration in Beijing, which rather took an ambiguous non-interventionist attitude. In such a situation, removal of the article and retention of its title in the content list might became a relatively easy choice for the publisher, the author, and the administrative authority as no one was getting hurt. Mutual understanding between the three parties was indispensible in making peace out of such a compromise. Therefore, little can be drawn out of the so-called skylight to support any allegation of protest or demonstration of political dissidence against the Party or its publicity apparatus. Nor does it bear any pre-1949 ideological pursuit of freedom and democracy or mean to lead to a nationwide media activism and shake the censorship apparatus.

The third case appeared on *Huashang Bao* [Chinese Business View] in 2011. The CBV is a commercialized, state-owned metropolitan newspaper based in Xi'an. David Bandurski (2011a) salutes the CBV with his hat off for its bold editorial style exhibited in reporting the Wen-Yong high speed train collision on July 23, 2011, which claimed forty lives. From the day of the accident, the paper had joined a one-week nationwide media quest for open investigations. This quest culminated on July 29 with "the new high point of degree of variety and professionalism" (Bandurski 2011a). It was alleged that the CBV had prepared to publish three pages of editorials in its July 30 edition, but these pages were withdrawn due to the censorship orders from the Party's publicity authority. As a result, the commentaries on page B3, which were supposed to call for independent investigation and a constitutional path to the truth, were replaced by irrelevant articles while parts of pages B2 and B4 were left blank. Page B2 carried a square blank with the title

"When you lie, your nose grows," alluding that the officials from the Ministry of Railway were trying to lie to the public (Bandurski 2011a). The page B2, particularly, is widely quoted as a newly opened skylight against the censorship apparatus.

However, the pages, which were alleged to plan to carry bold content, were never included in the publicly released newsprints. Only draft copies were posted on the Internet without the possibility of verifying their authenticity. The CBV reportage over the previous week was just as feverish as many other media. Its silence after July 30 was also no different from anyone else. The media being muzzled, if so, is as tragic an outcome as the collision accident itself. This might be the reason that many commentators admire the courage and boldness of the outlets, even if their efforts were short-lived and case-specific. But, the reality is that the CBV and other outlets followed censorship orders and withdrew their follow-up reports, if any. Although CBV appeared to be keen to produce editorials and commentaries as timely as its competitors, it chose to refrain from going any further when censorship orders arrived. To such an extent, whether the outlet deserves a "hat-off" salutation remains an arguable myth.

Not only were the allegedly censored pages replaced, but the newspaper also stopped following up its investigations and making further commentaries. According to Henry Yuhuai He's definition, a skylight should be an editorial decision that uses blank space as an openly uttered protest. It is noted that the blank spaces on the withdrawn CBV pages were not explicitly skylights. As Bandurski (2011a) recognizes, "the spaces were waiting for other content, in one case a cartoon, before they had to be pulled altogether." There has been no evidence that the CBV has made any editorial decision that openly goes against the censorship regime.

Moreover, the CBV, like many other commercialized outlets, is by no means free from the influence of local politics. In contrast with its aggressive involvement in the one-week extensive report of the train collision, its editorial strategy has been much cautious in reporting issues concerning local politics. Although the paper bitterly condemned the Ministry of Railways for its high-speed train fervor and lack of transparency, it has taken an ambiguous editorial attitude when dealing with the problematic construction of local transport infrastructure. Despite its inferred grievance against the censorship orders regarding the Wen-Yong collision case,[16] it exhibited much enthusiasm in positive promotion in favor of the local Xi'an government.

The CBV spared no efforts in hailing the new subway in Xi'an, which was officially opened on September 16, on its front pages on September 5, 8, 9, 16, and 17, 2011, respectively. Contrary to the celebration on the CBV headlines, however, the subway has been haunted by various construction quality problems since its start of operation, such as failed cabin doors, cracks, and water leakage at platforms. These problems, while having been extensively covered by the media outside Xi'an, were largely ignored by the CBV and other local media. The paper kept silent until for unknown reasons the glass door on the platform at the Zhouloutai Stop cracked on September 27, 2011, resulting in considerable public concern about structural safety of the facilities. CBV reported on its website that only minor problems had occurred when a driver failed to stop a train with its doors accurately docking against the glass doors on the platform (K. Ren 2011). Other local media also made similar reports (T. Wang 2011). These reports were far from investigative but redirected the public concern about possible construction quality issue to the discussion of similar problems with the subway in Shanghai. The report finishes with reassurance of the quality of glasses chosen for the Xi'an subway, without showing any intention of further and deeper investigation.

As many outlets pose to ignore some Party's guidelines such as the CPD and SAFRT's prohibition from practicing media supervision outside their home jurisdiction (Liebman 2011, 165), most media outlets usually choose to stay on the safe side by keeping editorial content within the tolerance of local officialdom. Expressions of resentment against inhibited editorial suppression, if any, are case-specific, temporary, and fragmentary, and soon swamped by positive publicity and pervasive submission.

The CBV case shows that, rather than engaging the public sphere as a public information resource with public conviction and representation commitment, the commercialized media tend to commoditize everything that can be commoditized for profit or public relations purposes while "playing a safe game" is essential. In contrast with the ambiguity with which the media play for attracting public speculation around skylights, market rating has always played a clear role in promoting "bold" journalism. Yuezhi Zhao (2004b, 57) maintains, "Social problems, if articulated within the confines of Party-sanctioned investigative reporting, seem to be profitable both for the media and for the management of social tensions." In an age when readers have access to unprecedented number of sources and amount of information, no commercialized outlets can afford to neglect newsworthy opportunities generated by such events as the Wen-Yong train collision. Being unable to attract the readers' attention and meet their expectation of timely reportage means losing subscriptions and the market. As most of the urban newsprints were distributed at prices lower than cost or even free, the marginal profit generated by selling more copies is no longer the point of marketing strategies. Instead, as advertising has become the major source of profits, it becomes crucial for the media to appeal to the niche market where craving for sensation and satisfaction with curiosity becomes the focus of content production. It will not be such a difficult editorial decision to publish eyebrow-raising or so called reader-oriented content when there is a market share to win and the political alarm is relatively remote. The heated-up media discussion around the Wen-Yong accident before the arrival of censorship orders was, at least in part, motivated by market performance, or as discussed in chapter 3, positive self-presentation. Relatively, however, it is a much harder decision for senior management to make to take a rebellious stand when censorship orders arrive and political risk becomes high. Note that what is to be published is always an editorial decision made by the senior management, who are not necessarily public intellectuals but Party bureaucrats. Few of these officials would care about journalistic commitments to the public interest, but their own existing interests sanctioned by the party-state (Y. Zhao 2008a, 106).

The three skylight stories, like many other similar ones such as the 2009 *Southern Weekend* skylight saga, appeared in the form of blank spaces without carrying any ostensible statement related to censorship. None of them has articulated any political agenda different from that of the Party-state and corporate interest. The content is either de-politicized or commoditized version of the stories that follow the niche market demand. When censorship orders arrived, utter obedience can also be consumerized by keeping curious silence and self-discipline, profiting on public sympathy and speculation alluded to the pre-1949 media activism. Nevertheless, these blank pages are easily interpreted to be hinting at a protest. It might be true that these outlets would not object to the idea of having some degree of editorial autonomy, particularly when they have "found lucrative news material by joyfully sniping at the travails of other areas" (Esarey 2007, 8), but to say that they are willing to repudiate the party-state media administrative system and thereby embark on a new stage of activism is, based on current evidence, unwarranted.

## MEDIA ACTIVISM, WHOSE ACTIVISM?

As demonstrated above, there has been no real skylight activism in the post-Mao period as there was in the GMD period. Media activism before 1949 was driven by political convictions and based upon broad participation by democratic groups, the press, and intelligentsia and vast consensus on democracy and freedom, and encouraged by Mao's communist practice in Yan'an. This consensus was not only reached when living conditions, as described by Joseph K. S. Yick (1995, 106), kept deteriorating under the GMD dictatorship and bureaucratic capitalism, but more significantly empowered by a common political cause toward freedom and democracy. This broad participation and political consensus had led to the collective anti-censorship campaign of the *Jujian Yundong*.

However, rooted in de-politicized professionalism rather than political conviction, the skylights in the post-Mao era are no more than physical resemblance of the pre-1949 ones. Neither do the commercialized media carry any ostensible explication of the existence of censorship, nor do they openly declare any protest or disobedience against the censorship apparatus. At best, these blank spaces trigger the pre-1949 memories and borrow the latter's revolutionary legacy to allude to the existence of censorship and create room for public sympathy and speculation in their favor. More pragmatically, these blank spaces can be used by the profit-driven and de-politicized media for building brand and securing market share. While the profit-seeking outlets' implied disobedience is ambiguous and largely unuttered, obedience is pervasive and obvious, particularly when the media managers have developed a vested interest in sustaining the current political economic order by following the party line while pursuing financial gains (Y. Zhao 2008a, 82).

The pre-1949 broad participation and political consensus are tellingly absent in the post-Mao era, and the absence reflects the major weakness of media activism today. Activism, if any, exists only among the few journalists and editors who dare to cross the line while they barely have any political or organizational support. They are considered activists because they try to practice journalism despite that this practice constitutes civil disobedience and defies the Party-state-media consensus. However, individual efforts are far from effective in changing the censorship reality as their de-politicized professionalism, when isolated from political purpose or significance in the interest of the public, is unable to find its pivot and social base in the vast majority of the grassroots population. As a middle-class slogan, professionalism thrives in catering for the niche market in producing sensation related to various kinds of urban stories of pleasure and sorrow, excitement and melancholy, success and individualistic struggle. Such de-politicized professionalism is only part of the new urbanism confined to the straightjacket of political and market control.

On the other hand, a new consensus on political control and pursuit of profit has been established between the Party-state and the media. It is demonstrated by how these activist professionals are treated as disposable labor and how the media is in line with the Party-state. One has to place the individual effort of professionalism within the restructured labor relationship in order to understand its frustration. The Nanfang Daily Press Group and its subsidiary outlets are known in the West as being rebellious and combative.[17] *Nanfang Dushi Bao* [*Southern Metropolis Daily*], one of its subsidiaries for example, is considered "gutsy" and noted for its "trenchant and critical approach" (Dillon 2009, 98; P. P. Pan 2009, 235). The SMD owes its reputation, at least in part, to the 2003 in-depth reporting of "the case of Sun Zhigang" that resulted in the abolition of the *Chengshi Liulang Qitao Renyuan Shourong Qiansong Banfa* [*Custody and Repatriation Procedures*].[18] This policy outcome is celebrated as a textbook example of media activism against corruption, enhancing governance capability and winning support from the people (P. P. Pan 2009, 255).

However, just because the SMD has become a celebrated outlet does not mean that the activist professionals who have helped the SMD and the conglomerate build up their brand are also able to share this success. On the contrary, many of them have ended up being suspended, fired, or even persecuted. Below are some examples:

- Deputy Chief Editor Xia Yitao was removed from his position on December 27, 2005 for a front-page report of the deputy governor of Guangdong Province being punished for a mining accident (J. Tong 2011, 112).
- General Manager Yu Huafeng and editor Li Minying were fired, arrested, and accused of corruption in January 2004. Both of them had been actively engaged in reporting the case of Sun Zhigang and SARS in 2003, which annoyed the provincial leadership (P. P. Pan 2009, 263).
- Cheng Yizhong is known as a hardcore activist heavily engaged in reporting the case of Sun Zhigang and SARS in 2003. He was removed from his positions as chief editor of *Xin Jing Bao* in March 2004 and chief editor of the SMD in October 2004. He was then transferred to another department that was not related to journalism. Later, Cheng Yizhong and his fellow management team members, Yu Haifeng and Lin Minying, were arrested for alleged "corruption and embezzling public funds" (Beach 2005).
- Jiang Yiping, deputy chief editor of the press group in charge of the SMD, was demoted from her position in December 2008. Jiang is known for her objective editorial style, both as a writer and editor (J. Tong 2011, 58).
- Zhu Di, editor of a historical column, was suspended in April 2010 for the publication of an article by Hong Zhenkuai titled "Patriotism Does Not Mean Love for the Royal Court."[19]

The list goes on. These are the professionals who have been the contributory factor for the aggressive journalism that has accredited the SMD as an outspoken outlet. However, the fact that these people have been purged demonstrates that one can hardly expect a commercialized, market-oriented, and so-called rebellious outlet to protect its professionals who go against the new consensus. As discussed previously in chapter 5, although some of the activists hold higher editorial positions, their careers are still in the hands of the Party-state's media administrative authority and subject to the powerful *Sheweihui* governance. Their elite urban professionalism without public political conviction withers like a flower shallowly planted in barren soil.

As far as the new consensus goes, the SMD's success lies in its common stance shared with the Party-state in terms of political and market control. The primary goal of the SMD is making profits and playing a politically safe game. Chief Editor Zhuang Shenzhi (2003) claimed that the paper has been "making the best newspapers across the country." The SMD (2011) boasts the seventh-largest paper in China with a circulation volume of 1.85 million copies per issue and an annual advertising turnover for 2.8 billion yuan in 2010.[20]

As for the secret to such success, Zhuang (2003) reiterates that the SMD has stayed strictly in line with the Party's guidelines. He acknowledges that it was true that the SMD was a bit bold in its early stage, but its recent success should be attributed to its wisdom in handling the boundaries. Such wisdom, according to Zhuang, comes out of its commitment to the official discourse of "pushing the social progress in a steady and harmonious way," or in other words, maintaining the social order and political stability. Its corporate structure has consolidated this commitment and consequently the political control and ensures the consensus on the leadership of Party logic and promotion of market logic at the same time. According to Zhuang, the corporate structure of the SMD since 2003 features three parallel operational boards under the supreme leadership of *Sheweihui*. The three boards are editorial board [*bianweihui*], management board [*jingweihui*], and administrative board [*xingzheng weiyuanhui*]. As a subsidiary of the Nanfang Daily Press Group, the SMD is ultimately subject to the leadership of the conglomerate's *Sheweihui* and Party committee.

The new consensus on political and market control between the Party-state and the media has been reached in the context of capitalism, marketization, and commercialism. Activism, if any, has been doomed by its conflict with this consensus. The profit-seeking outlets and their senior management have unswervingly stayed in line with censorship orders and political commitment and are unlikely and unwilling to risk their positions and prosperity for their fellow professionals, particularly when political risk becomes patent. To these senior management officials, there is no such thing as journalism on behalf of the public free of political control and market influence. Consequently, implications of the new consensus are threefold.

Firstly, this Party-state-media consensus diminishes the potential predicted by Qian Gang and David Bandurski (2011) that "commercialization, emerging professionalism and technological advance are shifting the press agenda-setting power from the Party-state to the media." In fact, the consensus has actually rendered such shift of power, if any, meaningless because the assumption of such a shift is made upon binary and dualistic consideration of the state and media to be two natural opposites against each other. Such consideration is something that Yuezhi Zhao warned of in 1998 in addressing the limitations of a heavily commercialized media system. She argues that the risks of such binary considerations lie in:

> . . . the reduction of freedom of the press to either unaccountable Party or corporate control of the media, the conflation of democracy of either the rule

of a vanguard Party or the market, and the conceptualization of the media as either an instrument of the Party propaganda or as generating an objective value-free reflection of reality and public opinion. (Y. Zhao 1998, 9)

The celebrated shift of agenda-setting power to the marketized media according to Western liberal model has failed to result in any viable activism. Zhao (2008b, 11) also rightfully points out that the liberal journalistic values and their application are more often than not defined and determined by the social political forces that possess the greatest political and economic power and discourse hegemony that define social political realities. Such interlocking of political and corporate control of the media is just as true in the capitalized authoritarian China as in liberal democracies like the United States.

Secondly, the new consensus results from and, in turn, reinforces the Party-state's adaptive management of the incompatibility of communist ideology with a new capitalist economic base, as well as the conflict between the public sphere and the influence of politics and profit incentives. This incompatibility and conflict have given rise to justification problems of information control because it is largely the voices of the weak and poor that have been stifled (G. Chen and Wu 2006, 94). As the justification problem escalates, adaptation is made to steer the media from public watchdogs to profit generators under the Party-state's political sanction and capitalist market agenda. As Christopher A. McNally (2008a, 132) has observed, a number of adjustments have been made accordingly: some topics once considered taboo became tolerated; new administrative structures have been adopted to oversee a much bigger expanse of the media industry; the Chinese populace have access to choices of media outlets and media content unprecedented in the PRC history; the media flourishes both in number and revenue; and yet, the media system overall remains in a period of significant contraction.

In turn, this adaptation has consolidated the new consensus, which is very similar to the way in which a consensus has been reached in the North America. On the one hand, the U.S. media is plagued by what Hackett and Zhao (1998, 165) have identified to be the long-standing tension and logical contradiction between free market capitalism and democracy. On the other, these contradictions are mediated in the consensus established upon political and financial interests between the government, corporations, and the media system (Goodman and Goodman 2003, 2006). As a result, the political and market status quo is kept under control in a dynamic way. Sharing the same insight, Noam Chomsky has argued that the economy and the social and political life are dominated by domestic elements that are sensitive to the needs of corporations and the government (Chomsky 1989, 108). What Chomsky reveals in the United States is happening in China in a similar manner. The Chinese media is politically steered and profit-driven as much as its American counterparts. Given the effective control by politics and market forces, there are no contradictions in the liberal capitalist democracies like United States (Chomsky 1989, 108). Similarly, there are no contradictions in the capitalist market-liberal agenda prescribed by the Chinese authoritarian Party-state if the media activism in the post-Mao era should be interpreted from Chomsky's perspective. The liberal prediction of press freedom based on a free market misses what the Party-state-media consensus is trying to mitigate: the logical contradictions between communist ideology and capitalist economic base as well as between free market capitalism and democracy, a problem embedded both in Western liberal democracies and capitalized authoritarian China. Hence, how can media activism thrive without contrarieties?

Thirdly, this new consensus reflects and aggravates the political disjuncture of representation of the Party-state and the media. Political control is intensified to maintain the media as part of the Party-state's mechanism of power. Market control is encouraged by profit incentives. Such control has denied the media's functionality as a public sphere, which, as Wang Hui (2006, 235) argues, is closely related to the basic way in which the public's rights to know and social communication are realized and politics is operated. The denial of the media's public nature is manifested as the irrelevance of media boom to the expansion of public sphere (H. Wang 2011b, 68) and the absence of subjectivity of the workers and peasantry in the media content production (Eyferth 2006, 14).

Such denial is embedded in the broader picture of the socioeconomic marginalization of the workers and peasantry in the reform era, in which, as Wanning Sun (2009) has exemplified, the discourse and imaging shaping in media content is well beyond the reach of those from the lower strata of the society. Besides, the public nature of the media becomes suspicious because, as Wang Hui (2006, 237) maintains, the representation proclaimed by the Party-state is increasingly blurred and unwarranted. Wang Hui (2009, 6; 2011a, 83) also argues that disjuncture of representation in journalism manifests the fact that workers and peasants do not have any agent of their own on the political arena; instead, the state has transformed itself into the agent of global capital and a mere mechanism of power, and the relationship between the workers and the state has changed from a representation one into a conflicting one. The officially promoted and even forced privatization of the national and collective economy have exerted profound impact on or to some extent destroyed the lifestyle and culture of the people from bottom strata of the society including ethnic groups in remote areas (H. Wang and Xu 2006, 243). This conflicting nature of the relationship between the Party-state and the workers and peasantry has determined the disjuncture of the former's political representation and given rise to the need to increase political control.

Furthermore, the irrelevance of media prosperity to the workers and peasantry, absence of their subjectivity, and their conflicting relationship with the state have not only resulted from the media's disjuncture of their public nature and political representation but have also resulted in the media's pervasive reluctance to confront the Party-state. For example, the rural population, where social tension and massive incidents have become alarming, has little representation in the media although satellite and digital networks have covered most of the regional communities. They now have unprecedented access to television broadcasting since the initiation of the *Cuncuntong* [village to village connection] rural direct broadcast satellite [DBS] project in 1998 (Kumar 2010, 503). By the end of 2004, television broadcasting service has covered 94.3 percent of the rural area, and people in these areas spend 166 minutes in average per day before the screen, forty-six minutes more than urbanites, according to a CCTV investigation (Ying Li and Tuo 2007a, 17). However, this access is irrelevant to the rural concerns. Only 1 percent of the programs are associated with rural issues such as villages, peasants, agriculture, and migrant workers from rural areas (Ying Li and Tuo 2007b, 37). Similar irrelevance is seen in newsprints and online portals. Among more than 9,000 journals and magazines, only 187 are related to the rural community; among the approximately 2,000 newspapers, only a handful are targeted at farmer readers (Ying Li and Tuo 2007b, 37). Market-oriented newspapers, as Yanhong Li (2008, 58) has expounded, target readers with the spending power that advertising clients value and cannot champion the interests of the marginalized groups at the expense of their main market.

In contrast to the media's indifference to the absence or loss of subjectivity of the workers and peasantry is the embracement of globalization and manufacture of transnational imagination (W. Sun 2002), middle-class and elite-oriented programs (Y. Zhao 2004b, 53), and proliferation of non-political content that basically ignore the needs, concerns, and petitions of the workers and the peasantry. The chance for the latter two to have their voices heard *through* the media is diminished. The media's political submission, sensitive obedience so as to avoid confrontation, and profit-driven commercialism have paved the way for political and market control. Lu and Zhao (2010, 16) have argued that as the Party's representation becomes ambiguous, the problems of the mass media epitomize the crisis of contemporary social democracy; and no public interests are possible in the public sphere when the participation and competition in this domain is based upon anything but equality and freedom. The dominance by the powerful has resulted in the collapse of the public sphere and hollowed out the latter's public nature (Lu and Zhao 2010, 16). Since the de-politicized and niche-market-oriented media and their professionalism do not represent the vast majority, or the weak, poor, victimized, and disenfranchised groups at the bottom of the social strata, whose interests have been victimized by the elite politics and capitalized market, how can anyone expect the commercialized outlets to initiate activism in the way that the pre-1949 media had been politically engaged?

## CONCLUSION

Comparing the media activism before 1949 and in the reform era, this chapter maintains that current media activism, skylights, for example, is drastically different from that before 1949, in terms of purpose, process, and practice. *Jujian Yundong* staged a protest against censorship and dictatorship and made an outspoken quest for its political mission. The movement was participated in by a broad range of democratic political groups, intelligentsia, and the media, and based upon their consensus on freedom and democracy, which had laid down the foundation for *Jujian Yundong*'s policy outcomes.

In contrast, such a consensus and political commitment is tellingly absent in the reform era. Instead, the Party-state and the media have reached a new consensus on political control and pursuit of profit. The three skylight examples have demonstrated and helped explain the media's reluctance to confront the Party-state. News outlets in post-Mao China are restructured to suit unrestrained commercialization and political control, intertwined with the fusion of Party logic and market logic (Y. Zhao 1998, 2). The consensus between the Party-state and the media is rooted in such a fusion and constitutes a coercive pressure on the vast majority of professionals, particularly when some disobedient individuals have been severely punished (Y. Zhao 1998, 160). Such a consensus is responsible for the absence of political representation of the workers and the peasantry in journalism and demonstrates the disjuncture of the media from its public nature.

As a result, the officially promoted concept of transparency and supervision by public opinion has been hollowed out by this confusion of Party logic and market logic. State power and the reformed media are not necessarily in diametrical opposition to each other. Even in a most outspoken outlet, the editorial board is but part of the political and market control agenda. Besides, most news outlets, following or driven by the tide of commercialization and busy with making profits, do not seem to have any activist blueprint beyond the Party line. The media, in general, do not have a clear, consistent and persistent pursuit for policy outcome that aims for journalism free from political and market control and in the interest of the disenfranchised groups. Media activism, therefore, withers under such control (Latham 2007, 37), and the contemporary transparency and supervision by public opinion rhetoric is no more than empty and de-politicized concepts catering for elite politics and market forces.

The skylights in the post-Mao era have demonstrated how the de-politicized and niche-market-oriented media have been profiting on the sympathy and speculation drawn from the revolutionary legacy of the pre-1949 media activism. In reality, while the Party-state and the media have been colluding on their new consensus, such consensus has been well concealed and packaged in a state-versus-media dichotomy so that sympathy and speculation can be fostered in a political and media culture that features lack of transparency. That said, the post-Mao media activism rooted in de-politicized professionalism does not have the empowerment or social base to rock the new ties between the Party-state and the media, both are disjunct from their nominal political representation of the public. Reciprocally, as Wang Hui implied, the hollowed-out ideological and political values are compensated with reinforced power structure and mechanism (H. Wang 2009), which in turn diminishes the likelihood of revival of the pre-1949 media activism in a capitalist authoritarian context.

## NOTES

1. Translation by author.
2. Yuan Shikai (1859–1916) was former president of the Republic of China from 1912 to 1915. He restored Monarchism on January 1, 1916 and declared himself Emperor Hong Xian. His imperial reign lasted only eighty-three days in the midst of uprising nationwide against the restoration before he died of uremia. See (J. Z. Gao 2009, 135).
3. Jiang Jieshi is also known as Chiang Kai-shek (1887–1975), former president of the nationalist GMD regime. See Groot 2004, 16.
4. Translation by author.
5. Chongqing was the capital city of the nationalist GMD government from November 20, 1937 to May 4, 1946.
6. The ten journals were *Xianzheng, Guoxun, ZhonghuaLuntan, MinzhuShijie, Minxian, Zaisheng, DongfangZazhi, XinZhonghua, Zhongxuesheng,* and *WenhuiZhoubao*. Notably, the communist *ZhongsuWenhua* and *XiandaiFunv* did not partake in the jointly issued additional edition, showing that the CCP did not want to impress the GMD government with any leading role in the *Jujian Yundong*.
7. Translation by author.
8. The MPG refers to the democratic parties [*minzhudangpai*]. See Gerry Groot, *Managing Transitions: The Chinese Communist Part, United Front Work, Corporatism, and Hegemony* (London: Routledge, 2004). Please refer to appendix 7 for a detailed list of the sixteen outlets.
9. The CCP, having to have its newspapers and publications constantly censored, had kept calling for major modification to the censorship system. In a statement drafted by Guo Moruo on February 22, 1945, the CCP appealed that "Censorship system, except for that concerning military secret, should not exist any longer. All laws and orders that impose limit on the people should be abolished so that the people can have the freedom of assembly, association, speech and publication." See Shaoci Zhang, Tian, and Chen 1995, 496.
10. Translation by author.
11. However, the wartime censorship system still applied in the territory recovered from the Japanese occupation, which is also known as *shoufuqu*.
12. Translation by author.
13. The *Heping Jianguo Gangling Cao'an* [*Draft Programme for Peacefully Building the Country*] is also known as *Administration Programme of the Political and Consultative Conference* [*zhengxieshizheng gangling*].

14. Italics mine.

15. For example, the official *Dalian Daily* opened a skylight on the front page of its electronic version of its August 15, 2011 edition. The blank space was originally carrying an official decision made by CCP Dalian Committee and Dalian government to remove the Fujia Chemical Plant from suburban residential area. The decision was made in response to a massive demonstration on August 14 by the Dalian residents requesting the removal of the Plant that produces paraxylene. It is reported that the chemical plant restored production in late September, and that the promise to remove the chemical plant was repealed in December. See (Bandurski 2011b) and (VOA 2011). The *Dalian Daily* skylight is not discussed in this chapter as it involves more faction fight within the Party-state than relationships within the public sphere.

16. See Yitian Liu 2011.

17. *Nanfang Daily* is the official media of the CCP Guangdong Provincial Committee and the Guangdong Provincial Government.

18. *Chengshi Liulang Qitao Renyuan Shourong Qiansong Banfa* [Custody and Repatriation Procedure for Vagrants and Beggars in Urban Areas], or briefly as the Custody and Repatriation Procedure, was established on May 12, 1982 by the State Council and abolished in 2003. It was an administrative procedure that gave the urban police the discretionary power to detain and repatriate migrants from rural areas if they failed to produce on demand hukou [household registration] information, temporary living permits or identity cards. See Beach 2005; S. Hu 2011; Jakes 2003.

19. The article was published on the April 11, 2011 edition of the SMD. But the online version of the article has been removed from the official website of the newspaper. It is reposted to various social media platform and is available from blog.caijing.com.cn/expert_article-151289-4873.shtml. See Borders 2010.

20. However, the SMD figure of distribution and advertising turnover is different from that from non-SMD resources. According to Lin Yao's investigation, the SMD distribution statistics is 1.4 million copies per issue and advertising sales turnover is two billion yuan in 2010. See L. Yao 2011.

*Chapter Seven*

# Transparency Illusion and Disjuncture of Representation

This book argues that the transparency illusion, the gulf between the official transparency rhetorics and the information control reality should not be simply understood as being a conflict between state power and the media, or merely as a matter of censorship. This illusion stems from the hope that political control would ensure social stability and the market-oriented capitalist economic development would eventually enable solutions to all societal problems, and that once the problems are solved there would be no need for censorship or any other form of information control. The government seems to have no hesitation in promoting transparency in its official discourse as being part of its efforts to shift to "scientific development" and build up a "harmonious society" and "Chinese dreams," giving hope that someday in the future there will be transparency and freedom of information along the current track. Such a hope, however, rests on the intrinsic incompatibility of communist ideology with the Party-state's elite politics and capitalist economic base, characterized by heavy exploitation of the fundamental interests of the populace, particularly that of the disenfranchised and dispossessed groups who are supposedly the Party-state's source of legitimacy and social base.

This incompatibility makes it increasingly difficult for the post-Mao Party-state to substantiate the concept of transparency and its promised supervision by public opinion, inevitably leaving the concept and promise hollowed and emptied out. Some may prefer the Western term of "transparency" for its more modern connotation to the long existing traditional metaphoric concept of "*mingjing gaoxuan*" ("clear mirror hung aloft," meaning honesty and justice). Or "transparency" can at least be used to gloss over the capitalized and marketized public sphere, where the labor relationships within the media system have been fundamentally restructured in both state-owned and private sectors in favor of the Party-state's political and market control agenda. The control agenda aims to maintain the institutional status quo, from which powerful political and capital elites have been drawing power and profits. Such an agenda has managed to maintain strategic balance between the Party-state and the media within a win-win framework while the truth of the collusion between the elite politics and capital has been made ambiguous by public attention being steered to the state-versus-media dichotomy, and the media is able to further make profits by playing martyr of press freedom on the one hand and thriving on the capitalist niche market on the other. Thus, it is from a transparency perspective that this book unfolds its main argument from chapters 2 to 6, each of which discusses one sub-argument related to various factors that have impact on the openness, credibility, accountability, and relevance of China's reformed journalism.

Chapter 2 conceptualizes media transparency as a multi-faceted concept. The chapter refuses to downsize the problem of the Chinese media system to be a mere matter of censorship within the dichotomous state-media framework. The profit-seeking media, including those most financially successful and editorially influential ones, are not necessarily victimized and martyred propaganda puppets to the opposite of state power. On the contrary, the Party-state and the profit-seeking media have reached a win-win consensus on political and market control and hence loathe substantiating the concepts of transparency and supervision by the media. The chapter explains what media transparency is and what the major constraints on media transparency are. It also specifies media transparency on the basis of the fundamental principles of transparency, namely openness, accountability, credibility and relevance.

Chapter 3 examines the meta-censorship rationale, or censorship of censorship itself, in the censorship and self-censorship practice. Censorship is applied by both the Party-state apparatus and the media outlets, yet by all means denied due to its intrinsic justification problem. Various strategies, including positive self-presentation, defensive attack against accusation, mitigation, moral blackmail, and denial of relevant legal construction, are adopted in an attempt to bypass the justification difficulty. In particular, such rationale is well used by the market-oriented news outlets that rigorously apply self-censorship and yet pose to be victims of the censorship regime. However, none of the strategies has been able to gloss over the fact that the meta-censorship rationale is rooted in the interest of the powerful and rich and thrives on the culture of secrecy. Such a culture of secrecy may foster various kinds of elite conceptual framework from Party-state legalism to no-holds-barred developmentalism but will always hate and hinder transparency.

Chapter 4 identifies the causes of the pandemic media malpractice to be a dilemmatic situation resulting from political and market control rather than the state ownership. The chapter argues that it is the Party-state-controlled and profit-seeking media system that should be responsible because this system fosters exploitative management and loss of journalist subjectivity. This chapter rejects the principal-agent analogy which leads to privatization and niche market domination of the media. The problem does not lie in state-ownership per se but in the suppression imposed by political and market control on the public representation which is supposedly paired with state-ownership. What have been shaping the media industry to what it is today is "the powerful market imperative that has already been set in motion by the Party-state itself and the domestic and transnational capitalist class interests" (Y. Zhao 2008a, 347). The collusion between the Party-state and the market imperative has formed mutually accommodating and beneficial relationships that have realigned the Party-state and capitalist interests in win-win prosperity.

To facilitate this prosperity, the labor relationships within the media system have been fundamentally restructured and reduced to a sheer capital-labor model. While the journalist professionals are mere wage earners, both their personal subjectivity and public representation have been suppressed, distorted, and alienated from official ideologies and professional ethical standards. As the ethical dome collapses and professionalism thrives on selective and relative journalism, a strange middle-class sense of pride flourishes among the urban journalist practitioners. Journalism becomes either a means for quick money by practicing various malpractices or a premise for fame and personal gains. For example, Zhao Pu, who has been an ace CCTV anchor-man for years yet still employed as an informal laborer whose salary is barely enough for making his ends meet (B. Xie and Gao 2013), has managed to make a fortune by selling his calligraphies and paintings. One of his calligraphy works was sold at a charity auction for 400,000 yuan (Qiu 2013). Such celebrity effect is not uncommon in commercial auctions for well-known media personages such as Dong Hao, Ni Ping, Zhu Jun, Zhao Zhongxiang and Bi Fujian, to mention just a few. Others, such as Chai Jing, rank themselves among bestseller authors in the book market. However, few grassroots journalists have the luxury to make a fortune by selling art pieces or books. More have resorted to "gray income" from receiving "red pack [*hongbao*]" (Stockmann 2013, 80) to extortion and blackmailing (Y. Zhao 1998, 91). Rather than a problem due to lack of ideological or ethical awareness at individual level from official or professionalism perspectives, corruption and malpractices are rooted in the system which has been dominated by Party-state-media collusion which aims at power and profits but remain antithetical to the "development of the culture of the working people" (Y. Zhao 2008a, 347).

Chapter 5 discusses how marketization and the new corporate governance adopted in media conglomerates have considerably consolidated the political and market control by restructuring organizational infrastructure and labor relationship. Contrary to the illusion that press freedom can be predicated on market imperatives, this new governance has reinforced the Party-state's grip over the newsrooms. This new consensus has diminished the space for public participation and denied the subjectivity of the workers and the peasantry in the public domain, and hence considerably squeezed the social base of the public sphere. This is a process of what Habermas has called refeudalization (Habermas 1991, 231; Holub 1991, 4), or in some scholars' eyes, double-feudalization (Zhan 2005, 9). The consolidation of the new consensus has demonstrated the Party-state's and the media's further disjuncture from their political representation.

Chapter 6 examines the "skylights" phenomena in the reform era to demythologize the activism illusion borne on an expectation on market imperative and professionalism. The illusion tries to draw from the revolutionary legacy in the past to interpret and speculate on the present while ignoring the fact that the combative and laudable past was built on clearly articulated political convictions, broad public participation, and ideological consensus on freedom and democracy against dictatorship and censorship. These critical elements, however, are curiously absent in the so-called skylights on the depoliticized and niche-market-oriented media as well as among the professionals who tend to uphold professionalism that considers political representation a source of bias. The absence of public subjectivity and political commitment has determined the major weakness of the media activism today and its doomed impotence in front of the formidable Party-state and market control.

Most marketized outlets play a critical role in selling official rhetoric, making media products and behavior look like a response to market demand rather than ideological indoctrination. Although many of them are no longer branded as official mouthpieces, they are in effect loyal messengers of the elite discourse posing as non-official media or market-oriented outlets (Y. Zhao 1998, 158). The outlets and their senior management are the major beneficiaries of commercialization and conglomeration and, therefore, loathe confronting the Party-state. Although sometimes they may pose to explore the boundaries, they seldom mean to cross the line. This has engendered, at least in part, the irony that "media challenge to state control can boost the ability of the state to manipulate public opinion" (Stockmann 2011, 182).

As summarized above, this book has provided answers to the questions raised in the opening chapter:

- Media transparency is defined as a multifaceted concept that includes openness, accountability, credibility, and relevance in administration,

management, and operation. The concept of transparency does not bear any substance unless it is rooted in the purpose to expand the public sphere in the interests of the underrepresented and disenfranchised groups and hold both politics and the media system accountable.
- The meta-censorship rationale, or censorship being censored, stems from the difficulties in justifying the censorship and self-censorship apparatus. These difficulties are due to the fact that the Party-state and the media have reached consensus on political control and ceased to represent the workers and peasantry. This consensus has demonstrated that the Party has metamorphosed into a mere mechanism of power and agent of capitalism, which in turn determines Party-state's and the media's disjuncture from their public representation and political commitment.
- Pandemic media malpractice results from the market imperatives set in motion by the Party-state, which have fundamentally altered the labor relationships, distorted the journalist subjectivity, and inevitably caused ethical confusion. The collapse of official ethical standards and the weakness of professionalism have further demonstrated the disillusionment as the grassroots professionals are increasingly alienated from the Party-state transparency rhetoric and market discourses.
- Adopting full-fledged niche-market imperatives and a profit-driven management through restructured corporate governance and conglomeration, the CCP has actually strengthened its control over journalism. Contrary to the illusion that press freedom is predicated on market forces and financial autonomy, the Party-state and the media have reached consensus on political control and pursuit of profit on the bandwagon of commercialization and conglomeration. Such a consensus is antithetical to journalism for the populace, particularly those who are weak and poor and, therefore, hates and hinders transparency.
- The "skylights" in the reform era are by no means signalling activism parallel with pre-1949 scale and significance. The major weakness of the former lies in its lack of political conviction, broad participation, and vast ideological consensus on democracy and freedom that were distinctive in the latter. Misinterpretation of the media activism today is rooted in the illusion that market forces and depoliticized professionalism will be able to lead to massive rebellion against state power. The weakness, on the other hand, shows that the media is disjunct from its public nature and political representation.

The discussion of the transparency illusion, therefore, has generated a picture of transparency disillusion. However, this book does not focus on the disillusion per se but considers the causes of the illusion and disillusion to be the discrepancy between the Party-state's capitalist nature and communist representation on which it posits its legitimacy. Given this discrepancy and disjuncture, the Party-state and the media loathe substantiating the rhetoric of transparency.

The government transparency rhetoric is so promoted and widespread that it has been not only integrated into the mainstream elite ideal and public discourse but also has an overwhelmingly stifling effect that hampers questioning of the rationale of the rhetoric. Such rhetoric is part of the Party-state politics and the market discourses because it is an autocratic, exclusive, compulsory, and brain-washing parlance, sweetened with modern linguistic pragmatism, and manufactured and manipulated by the very small number of elites in power. Such rhetoric and discourses built upon the consensus on political and market control suppress any discussion that aims for expansion of the public sphere and prevents the delivery of the voices of the underrepresented and disenfranchised groups.

## DISJUNCTION OF POLITICAL REPRESENTATION

The transformation from "the People's Dictatorship" in Mao's era to the current consensus on political and market control should not be conveniently seen as "a result of negotiation" (Ho 2008, 37) between the Party-state and market forces, because negotiation implies conflict of interests and contrarieties. However, given the consensus, there is no such thing as fundamental contrarieties between the Party-state, the market, and the profit-driven media. Rather, the transformation has been a process of the power and profit mechanism departing from its supposed representation, resulting from a trend of de-politicization within which both China and the West are deeply involved (H. Wang 2009, 6). Wang Hui (2009, 7) maintains that "China's de-politicization process has had two key characteristics: firstly, the 'de-theorization' of the ideological sphere; secondly, making economic reform the sole focus of party work." Unlike the depoliticized democracy in the West, which features "weakened party systems" and "the decline in the parliamentary-democratic systems" (H. Wang 2009, 6), de-politicization in China has seen the Party-state and the media gain power and increasingly disjunct from the public nature of their representation, particularly of those victimized and disenfranchised groups. This disjuncture of representation is manifested in how the CCP has transformed into an agent of capitalism, the consequent loss of substance in its ideological system, and its impact on the media's political representation.

Firstly, that China remains a one-party rule state does not necessarily mean the ruling party remains unchanged. On the contrary, the intensified political control is attributed to the changing of the Party into a power mechanism representing bureaucratic and capitalist interests. China today is considered to be a capitalist country in terms of the structure of its national economy regardless of its alleged socialist ideology (M. Gao 2008, 185). Some observers, such as Elisabeth Alles (2012, 3) drawing on Marx's description of the nineteenth-century England, and Laurence Coates ( 2000 ) mapping the dominant social grouping, have identified China's economy as "wild capitalism."

According to Christopher A. McNally (2008b), capitalism entails three elements including a distinctive drive to extract and accumulate capital, the structuring role of the market, and, more importantly, emergence of a capital-oriented class. These three elements have unmistakeably dominated the economic and political reality of China today. One cannot attribute China's problems to socialism when the capitalist market has been playing a dominant role in allocating resources and the public sector keeps decreasing and is responsible for less than 30 percent of the national economy (H. Wang 1998, 9), not to mention that the majority of the critical state-owned industries have fallen to the hands of a few "red families" (Walter and Howie 2012; Weil 1996). Not only have the political and capital elites established a tight alliance to solidify their status but such alliance has also provided space for their mutual accommodation.

Moreover, capital has been politically recognized (McNally 2008b, 21), while its exploitative nature has been depoliticized and glossed over by the media as if capitalism is the only game in town (Sun 2008, 31). The political recognition of capital has been escalated to the extent that capitalist entrepreneurs are recruited to the Party membership since the reign of Jiang Zemin. Liang Wengen, CEO of private-owned SANYI Corp and one of the wealthiest capitalist entrepreneurs in China, gained his Party membership in 2004 although his initiative to join the Party was to "multiply his chances to attract girls in the countryside" upon his first submission of application eighteen years before (Z. Zhu 2011 ).[1] In September 2011, Liang was nominated for a candidate of alternate member of the Party's Central Committee (Rein 2012, 15). Although Liang's 2011 attempt was eventually frustrated by scandals and faction fights in industrial competition and conspiracies involving the Party princelings located in the same city, Liang remains one of the most favorable capitalists in Xi Jinping's administration. His political ambition and foreseeable opportunities mark the start of sharing, if not taking over yet, the central state power with the capital elites and capitalism. Besides, the political elites have made considerable fortunes either for themselves, or more commonly and pragmatically, for their family members (M. Gao 2012, 176). Their way of devouring the social fortune has given birth to crony capitalism (McNally 2007, 199), and network capitalism (McNally 2008b, 106 12), which is responsible for increasing social inequality, polarization, and disturbance.

As a result, the Party has been disconnected from its communist values and representation and metamorphosed into a mere mechanism of power.

Wang and Chen (2005, 132) argue, citing Habermas (1991, 231), that "with the linking of public and private realms, not only certain functions of the sphere of commerce and social labor are taken over by political authorities, but conversely political spheres are taken over by the societal powers," which will lead to "refeudalization" of the public sphere and politics. This refeudalization diminishes the possibility for the workers and peasantry to engage the public sphere and have their voice heard because the base and space for these underrepresented and marginalized groups have largely collapsed (Lu and Zhao 2010, 10). The public sphere has turned into an amphitheatre where the state, market forces, and interest groups compete for power (Lu and Zhao 2010, 6). As Wang Hui (2009, 6) maintains,

> The party is no longer an organization with specific political values, but a mechanism of power. Even within the party it is not easy to carry on real debate; divisions are cast as technical differences on the path to modernization, so they can only be resolved within the power structures.

The change of social production methods and the nature of the Party, therefore, have engendered the disjuncture of representation of the Party-state and the state-owned media, and such disjuncture is pervasive in the public domain. As Wang Hui (2011b, 69) maintains,

> The social base of the disjuncture of the representative politics lies in the reality that the political, economic and cultural elites and their interests are disconnected with the social mass. Such disjuncture is directly manifested when the political party, media and legal system fail to represent relevant social interests and public opinions. It is a multifaceted crisis of the party politics, public sphere and legal system.[2]

Disequilibrium has been widened between rural and urban areas, coastal and inland regions, the rich and the poor, the powerful and the weak (Shirk 2007, 30). The failure of socialism and democracy and the crisis of the party legitimacy are revealed in not only the unequal distribution of social fortune and polarization but also the sinking status of labor in the process of production and the social stratification (H. Wang 2011b, 78), which has also been discussed in chapter 4 and 5.

Secondly, loss of substance has characterized official rhetoric because there is no room for conciliation between communist ideology and exploitative capitalism. As a result, the Party-state has to coin ambiguous conceptual terminologies such as "touching the stones while crossing the river," "Three Represents" and "Scientific Development" to blur the fronts of the conflicting values and interests within China's contradictory modernity, trying to create an overlapping or at its best a consensus zone. Hence is the creation of "socialism with Chinese characteristics" in the reality of capitalism with

Chinese characteristics (M. Gao 2008, 185). When one leadership and its concept fails to provide solutions to social political problems, successive leaderships will have to coin one concept after another to further blur the ideological perceptibility and carry on the current modernization fervor. The Party has to constantly make adjustment to its official ideology to the extent that it ends up opposing or debasing its very original political ideals.

Following the seizure of state power in 1949, the CCP has increasingly changed into a bureaucratic machine that no longer possesses its own distinctive evaluative standpoint or social goals, and its relationship with the state has become a structural-functionalist one (H. Wang 2009, 9). This is a process of statification of the party, or changing the Party from an organization of particular political values into a machinery of state power. This process has ultimately excluded the workers and peasantry from leadership positions in the party, the government, and largely the People's Congress today (H. Wang 2009, 10). The short-lived communist practice in the mid-1960s, including "efforts at social remobilization and stimulation of political life outside the Party-state context," re-organization of factories to bring about workers' management, and various social experiments, have been totally abandoned (H. Wang 2009, 9). Instead, politics in the reform era has been dominated by political and capital elites who represent powerful interest groups. These elite interest groups are able to facilitate private capture of the state properties in a relatively strong state because the Party has managed to maintain the continuity of its power structures by altering its official ideologies (Y. Sun 2004, 8).

Before 1949, the political ideal of the CCP was to establish a "new democracy" distinct from the Guomingdang's "fake democracy" and dictatorship (Gilley 2004, 17). It promised democracy and freedom, which were political ideals shared and echoed by the minor party groups (Groot 2004), intelligentsia, and the populace. The legitimacy of the Party-state was based on increased representation of workers and peasantry and its alliance with the minor party groups through the United Front Work. However, the statification of the party, a process that Wang Hui defines as "from Party-state to state-party" (H. Wang 2009, 8), started soon after the CCP came to power. The early stage of the Cultural Revolution, which called for re-examination of the party's political values, re-organization of factories for "democratic management," and social experiments in various schools and work units, was "possibly the last" attempt to change the course of the statification, which failed because it conflicted with the fundamental interests of the ruling elites and therefore fell to a renewed enforcement of the Party-state system (H. Wang 2009, 9).

Statification of the Party and weakening its official ideology were fast-tracked since Deng Xiaoping decided to shelve the "capitalism or socialism" debate over the nature and direction of the reform (H. Y. He 2001, 24).

Socialism with Chinese Characteristics turns out to be no more than Capitalism with Chinese Characteristics (M. Gao 2008, 185), or "the use of socialism to build capitalism" (Weil 1996). The seizure of state property and various forms of corruption by the political elites and their family members, which had triggered the student movements in the 1980s, has developed into a rampant social phenomenon. No new political countermeasures or initiatives were institutionalized against corruption during the successor Jiang Zemin's term of office, although anti-corruption was included in the official discourse (Dittmer 2000, 45). It was also during Jiang Zemin's reign that the Party membership was opened to private entrepreneurs, justifying the political alliance between the political and capital elites within the state-party framework. The road map for the reform was so ambiguous that the communist party ideology was gradually hollowed out. Developmentalism and market economy, therefore, became the only answer.

Consequently, open discussion, not to mention critical journalism, was stifled. Meanwhile, Deng Xiaoping Theory, including his "no debate resolution," was written into the constitution and became the leading ideology after de-legitimization of Marx-Leninism and Mao Zedong Thoughts (Dittmer 2000, 45). This is not only a deliberate blurring of ideological concepts but also, more significantly, contempt for public discussion on the part of the Party-state. The disruption of public debate over the direction of the reform led to policies of suppression which have practically destroyed the media's public representation and political commitment.

To gloss over the ideological confusion and the social reality plagued by increasing problems of inequality, polarization, corruption, and emerging disjuncture of the Party-state's representation, a new vocabulary of party terminology "Three Represents" was coined by Jiang Zemin as his brand of leadership and updated leading ideology. However, not only was the "Three Represents" self-contradictory and therefore unable to draw a clear picture of the Party, but it also further hollowed out the Party's political values. It almost goes without saying that "the most advanced productive forces" suggest non-state capital and capitalism, and that "the most advanced culture" is the discourse hegemony manipulated at the discretion of the political, capital and intellectual elites who have benefited the most from the status quo of the social political order (Sorman 2010, 186).

Before the "Three Represents," the Party had, at least theoretically, positioned itself as the avant-garde of the workers, peasants, and soldiers. Afterward, however, it proclaimed representation of the fundamental interests of "the largest number of Chinese People." The debased representation has practically included capitalist productive forces and method and officially recognized their vanguard status. The attempt to represent everyone aims to conceal the fact that the representative nature of the Party has drastically changed. Hence the previous representation of workers, peasants, and soldiers is quietly replaced and practically denied. The self-contradictory simultaneous representation of the exploiters and the exploited has rendered the communist political values of the Party null and void and yet failed to give the new ideology any substantial political meaning. This hollow proclamation of representation has not only in effect denied the existence of increasing social stratification and polarization but also exhibited the Party elites' indifference to the suffering of the victimized and disenfranchised groups.

The Hu Jintao–Wen Jiabao administration exhibited a certain degree of concern about the suffering workers and peasantry at the early stage of their office. They apparently realized the consequences of the overexploitation of the labor and the environment. They appeared to have recognized the needs of the people from lowest strata of the society and increasing social grievance. The abolition of agricultural taxes in 2006 was a milestone of their new governance. However, this progress was soon offset by re-emerging "random charges" heavily laden on the farmers by local officials and kept outside the government's bookkeeping (Dillon 2009, 36), not to mention the massive land deprivation and forced dislocation at saddening cost of lives and livelihood, which have caused numerous massive incidents in rural China. While the locomotive of the capitalist economy keeps powering on, the social problems which were unsolved and expanding during the Jiang–Zhu administration remained so and even deteriorated under the Hu-Wen leadership.

It is within such a context that the transparency rhetoric, promise of supervision by public opinion, and pledge to reform the political system are unprecedentedly disseminated via the media and official discourse. Efforts were made to put forth a new set of political terminologies to try to distinguish the Hu-Wen administration's political vision from that of the Jiang–Zhu leadership. Following the short-lived slogan of "Eight honors and eight shames," the abstract concepts of "scientific development perspective" and "harmonious society" were launched in 2003. These concepts can even hardly be called "ideology" because they do not convey any ideological ideals or political values. At best, they can be regarded as the Hu-Wen administration's conscious theoretical adjustment to the single-minded developmentalism during the Jiang-Zhu administration. At worst, they are as empty and hollow as the echo one can hear from a wishing well. As Mobo Gao (2012, 185) puts it so well:

> But there is no such thing as "scientific development." You can have balanced or unbalanced development, depending on what you mean. You can have development that favours the rich and the powerful only or development that brings along the poor and the advantaged. You can have development that harms the environment and exhausts the resources or you can have sustainable development that protects the environment and leave resources for future generations. But neither of these is either "scientific" or "non-scientific." Science

may aim to pursue the truth; but what is perceived or agreed to be "scientific" does not mean it is good for human society. Furthermore, there is no such thing as the holy grail of the "scientific."

Nor is there such a thing as "harmonious society." People can be taught to behave toward each other civilly and politely; but there are always tensions and conflicts among different sectors and different strata of any society. A successful leadership is one that has the power and the imagination to allocate resources in such a way that innovation and creativity is encouraged and at the same time even the most disadvantaged feel that there is something worth living for, or at least feel that they are cared for.

The political slogans, emerging in an endless stream and posing as pragmatic party ideologies or values, are so abstract and hollow that people have no idea what they are all about and simply don't pay attention (Hewitt 2008, 416). The hollowed and/or blurred political ideals have epitomized what Max Weber defined as a "crisis of rationality" in that the structure of cognition, instrumentality, and morality is manipulated by elite politics and literati (H. Wang 1997, 5), which reflects the gap between the populace and the cultural experts whose manufactured culture does not have practical meaning in everyday life.

Thirdly and consequently, the disjuncture of political representation of the Party-state and its embracement of capitalism has exerted considerable impact on the media. Contrary to common intuitive, the commercialized news media, reaping financial success yet posing as victims of information control, has been steadily transformed from public utility into a profit-making mechanism. This mechanism sees the media heavily invest in the middle-class niche market and lose interest in facilitating the voices of those from the lowest strata of the society who are the real victims of the intensified political control and market filtering of information. The irrelevance of growth of the media market to expansion of the public sphere has exemplifies the "depoliticized politics" in the media when the outlets are allowed and encouraged to adopt business management, marketize its profit-seeking divisions and maximize their profits (H. Wang 2009), as long as they stay between "the Party line and bottom line, between commercial success and political correctness" (Y. Zhao 1998, 144).

It is a process of modernization or, more pragmatically interpreted, adaptation to market logic sanctioned by Party-state politics. From Max Weber's "the disenchantment of the world" perspective (Wulf 2003, 26), the irrelevance of growth of the media to the expansion of public sphere is the result of the development at the expense of the ideological substance. Loss of ideological substance leads to loss of ideological consensus and suppression of rising disputes. The loss of ideological consensus thereby must be compensated by certain changes in order to maintain order and control. Therefore, a new set of market discourse has been established to promote capitalist marketization and new ideological terminology "in its most potent expressions in the worship of reason; in its faith in economic development, the market system and the legal-political system" (H. Wang 2009, 75).

The media's disjuncture of representation of the public is, therefore, manifested in the former's role as a Party-state's messenger in the marketplace. While the editorial rigidity of official outlets, a self-evident cause of loss of readership and audience, remains largely unchanged, the commercialized media have taken over the committed role posing as client-oriented commercial outlets (Y. Zhao 1998, 158). Official messages are mingled with reportage that pertains to entertainment, sports, finance, and other middle-class-oriented content with easy and relaxed editorial style, or in a depoliticized manner (Lee 2003, 8). This is so because the semi-official media is perceived, from a niche market point of view, to be more credible than the official ones, as the result of the former's dissociation from the government, and the Party publicity authorities are fully aware of this reality (Stockmann 2011, 181).

The disjuncture of political representation shows that the Party-state and the media keep moving on into their future in a way that Habermas (1990, 72) would call a "future without relationship to their origins." This process of diremption has not only rendered official rhetoric and market discourses increasingly irrelevant to the social realities but has also disconnected the media from its public nature and representation of those who desperately need to have their voices heard. The media reform, therefore, has functioned as a systematic arrangement to shift the role of shaping public opinion from official mouthpieces to commercialized outlets. Meanwhile, the financial benefits are so enormous that both the media and their senior management have developed considerable vested interests in the current system (Y. Zhao 2008a, 82). These interests, in turn, have constituted obstacles to progress of substantive media transparency.

## IMPACT OF MEDIA TRANSPARENCY ON THE PUBLIC SPHERE TODAY

Given the consensus between the Party-state and the media and their re-aligned relationship, transparency becomes more important than mere press freedom. Mere freedom does not reduce the media's desire for profit and, as also discussed in chapter 1, is not adequate enough to hold politics and the market accountable, either in a liberal democracy or capitalized autocracy. In contrast, transparency does not predicate on market imperatives but aims to expose all factors that may hinder the freedom of information and to hold the politics, the media, and the market answerable to those who have no power and money to do so.

Media transparency calls for legislations, rather than legalism, that substantiate the concept of transparency regarding media policies, rules, and practice. Its primary goal is to clarify the public nature of the media as an indispensable part of the public sphere without being undermined by any political and market control. While "the rule of law" has become a legal maxim almost as popular as the transparency rhetoric, it cannot be immediately embraced as a progress of modernization in contrast to the "rule of man" before it clarifies in what interest the rule is built upon. The codification of rules and construction of legal institution are more often than not driven by the CCP's pursuit of more power over its citizens (Clarke 1985), and the policy innovation is heavily involved with conflict and preservation of the power shared by various interest groups (Shirk 1993, 88). The procedures of proposing, drafting, revision, finalizing, and passing of rules and law related to journalism should be transparent and relevant to the public interest. Any progress of rule of law in ideal or rule by law in reality will be meaningless if it does not substantiate openness, credibility, accountability, and relevance.

One case in point is the legislation of the Law of Response to Emergencies (draft). The draft was proposed to the National People's Congress Standing Committee in June 2006. Its article 57 forbade the news media from publishing news concerning industrial accidents, natural disasters, and public health and security crises without prior authorization of the government (L. Yang 2006). The first hearing of the draft in June 2006 incurred a huge wave of criticism both at home and abroad. The enormous scale of objections was such that the draft had to be revised. Under the pressure of the public opinion, the article 57 was deleted in the revised final draft which was passed in 2007. The deletion was hailed as a victory of the media power (Zhan 2007, 36).

This particular case shows that there is no such thing as benevolence under political control. This is so because of disjuncture of the Party-state political representation from the public interest. The consensus between the Party-state and the media on political control and pursuit of profits is in essence against the spirit of transparency and democracy. Therefore, the state power and censorship apparatus are constantly alert and nervous to the extent that they will keep producing legislation processes that legalize government actions against the expansion of public sphere in the name of keeping social stability or even promoting transparency. Hence, it is important that the intention of policies and their making process must be made transparent to the public before these policies may claim to improve the media environment.

Another aspect of media transparency lies in the performance of the media in terms of its own transparency. Although news outlets tend to prefer editorial autonomy, this autonomy does not necessarily lead to media transparency. It is about whom and what the media represent. Freedom without transparency can contribute to what Noam Chomsky is critical of "media control" and "manufactured consent" (Chomsky 2002), whether in a liberal democratic country like the United States or an authoritarian country like China. Without adequate media transparency that aims to substantiate the public nature of the media, the concept of public sphere remains what Vincent Mosco (1996, 152) calls an "idealism of the phantasm and the false materialism of the public sphere as a space to be defended by defining the public as a set of social processes that carry out democracy, namely advancing equality and the fullest possible participation in the complete range of economic, political, social, and cultural decision-making..."

For this reason, the journey toward media transparency can be seen as a constant struggle against political and market control. The *Jujian Yundong* in 1945 has established a role model for the news outlets, professional practitioners, and the intelligentsia. Following the combative role models, increasing numbers of activist journalists, editors, academics, and their supporters today have paid and are paying the price for advocating serious journalism and professional ethics. Also, there has been considerable and increasingly dynamic online participation by the very ordinary people via various e-media from semi-official to underground platforms, which "has significant democratization effects" (M. Gao 2011, 151). Nevertheless, we have to understand that media activism celebrated by commercialized media does not necessarily aim at transparency, and a market-oriented free media can always commoditize almost every aspect of the socio-political life, even their own hypocritical victim status in a state-media confrontation cliché. Therefore, it comes as no surprise that activism without transparency is compromised in a media ecosystem dominated by political control and niche market discourses.

Constant struggle for media transparency calls for bottom-up efforts, challenging the authority of the elite politics and the authoritarian political culture. Closest to this rationale in China's history of modernity is the "mass line" democracy in Mao's era that features mobilizing the power of the mass to attain collective goals (Tse and Lee 2003, 112). Such mass line, however, failed in the post-Mao power struggle and has been degraded and substituted in the reform era with modernization discourse and elite ideals promoted in the name of good of individuals. Yet, challenging the political and market control is not something that can be accomplished without broad participation and ideological consensus on the public nature of the public sphere in the ultimate interest of the public, which were the major ingredients for the success of the 1945 *Jujian Yundong*.

Given the constraints on media transparency, this book presents the concept of media transparency and aims to identify the undermining problems. Media transparency is difficult yet promising because it is rooted in the popular social base of the interests of those who have no power or money, and the underrepresented and disenfranchised groups whose voices could not be heard otherwise. Media transparency is relevant because it aims to hold both politics and the media accountable. It is vibrant because its power lies in the substance rather than positive connotations implied yet suppressed by the official rhetoric and market discourses. The substantiated idea of transparency will become more and more powerful because it not only facilitates freedom of the press but also further holds this freedom public and transparent.

## NOTES

1. Translation by author.
2. Translation by author.

# Afterword

This book has examined issues surrounding the question of media transparency and considered it to be a central topic regarding press freedom in a capitalist authoritarian context intertwined with transparency rhetoric and stifled public sphere reality. The discussion has mainly focused on traditional media, particularly on newspapers and passing by radio and television broadcast. Other forms of new media based on digital and web 2.0 technologies, microblog and social networks, for example, and their impact on media transparency and democratization are less explored. This "oversight" might lend credence to criticism from various perspectives such as technological determinism or even its opposite—social construction of technology (technological constructivism). The former believes that digital revolution is able to knock down the wall of information control (M. Y. Zhang and Stening 2010, 57). The latter believes that human action, such as quest for press freedom, shapes technology. For example, former U.S. Vice President Al Gore (1995) proclaimed that the historical genesis of information technology is "inseparable from our (the Americans') quest for freedom—from the printing press that Thomas Paine used to print 'Common Sense' to the explosion of talk radio and the growth of the Internet."[1]

The author is aware that public participation with the help of the Internet and wireless accessibility is a dynamic and indispensible part of the media environment and public sphere as a whole. Its democratizing effect should by no means be made light of. However, discussion of the impact of the new media and technological advance cannot be valid until it is placed in a certain social political framework, which is the political and market control that has been discussed herein. In this regard, two explanations might be made in response to possible criticism of my inadequate discussion of new media and online technology: 1) the Party-state does not pay any less attention to the growth of traditional media than to that of the new media. Both traditional and new media are governed in the same social political environment and subject to political and market control in similar way. Research in the traditional media remains highly relevant and referential to the discussion of the new media. 2) Online technology can be used by anyone who has access to it, be it the strong or the weak, the informed or ill-informed, the elite and the disenfranchised. However, the bigger the gap between the strong and the weak, the more likely the media is controlled by powerful elite political and market forces. With the growth of online public participation comes increasingly sophisticated censorship and self-censorship mechanisms. Talks on technology and new media cannot make any fundamental difference without addressing the cause and impact of such control, which is discussed in this book as a problem of media transparency undermined by the disjuncture of political representation of the Party-state and the media. Nevertheless, the author does not intend to make any light of the new media and its impact on press freedom or democratization. The debate over the "online revolution" and its implications for media transparency is so important yet complex that I would prefer developing further arguments in this respect in another project to devoting to just one chapter or fragmental texts.

Most of the pages of this book have been spent on discussion of media transparency as a multifaceted concept. The discussion aims to lead to consideration of the Party-state and the media's disjuncture of political representation that is causal to the problems. However, due to the limit of length, this book has been far from adequate in unfolding the solution part, which is significant and worth further research with much deliberation. Future research is intended to concentrate on how media transparency is to be institutionalized in the interest of the public and particularly of the weak and poor in the given social political context. Inevitably, the role of the mass media as the media of the mass in democratization of China through transparency will not be bypassed. More attention is to be paid to the differences between nominalism and essentialism and their implications for the Party-state politics and the mass media. These questions will form an interesting ground for further exploring the nature, essence, and ultimate goal of media transparency and its connection with democratization in contemporary China's social political context.

## NOTE

1. (the Americans') is added by author.

# Bibliography

Abouharb, M. R., and Cingranelli, D. L. (2007). *Human Rights And Structural Adjustment*. New York: Cambridge University Press.
Alles, E. (2012). Class Struggles in China Today: Towards a Third Chinese Revolution? *China Perspectives*(1), 3–4.
An, G. (1982). *Xinwen Lunji [Essays on Journalism]*. Tianjin: The Tianjin People's Press.
An, L. (2010). Mama Pingshentuan Zhaomu Chengyuan, Zhuanmen Jiankong Wangluo Buliang Xinxi [Recruiting the Mothers Reviewers Group, Specifically Targeting Unhealthy Online Information] Retrieved February 14, 2011, from report.qianlong.com/33378/2009/12/26/118@5388518.htm
Andrew, D. P. S., Pederson, P. M., and McEvoy, C. D. (2011). *Research Methods and Design in Sport Management*. Champaign: Human Kinetics.
Ang, P. H., and Wang, G. (2010). The Principal-Agent Problem in Chinese State-owned Media. *China Media Research, 6*(1), 108–17.
Bagdikian, B. H. (1997). *The Media Monopoly*. Boston: Beacon Press.
Bai, R. (1998). *Zhongguo Xinwen Tongshi Gangyao [General History of Journalism in China]*. Beijing: Xinhua Press.
Baker, H. K., and Powell, G. E. (2009). Management Views on Corporate Governance and Firm Performance. In M. Hirschey, K. John and A. K. Makhija (Eds.), *Corporate Governance and Firm Performance*. Bingley: Emerald Group Publishing Limited.
Balkin, J. M. (1999). How Mass Media Simulate Political Transparency. *Cultural Values*, 3(4), 1–19.
Ball, C. (2009). What Is Transparency? *Public Integrity, 11*(4), 293–307.
Bandurski, D. (2010). Are Chinese Media a Public Nuissance? Retrieved January 1, 2012, from cmp.hku.hk/2010/12/06/8762/
Bandurski, D. (2011a). Chinese Media Muzzled after Day of Glory. Retrieved October 11, 2011, from cmp.hku.hk/2011/07/31/14332/
Bandurski, D. (2011b). Dalian Protests Erased from Social Media. Retrieved October 12, 2011, from cmp.hku.hk/2011/08/14/14785/
Bandurski, D., and Hala, M. (Eds.). (2010). *Investigative Journalism in China: Eight Cases in Chinese Watchdog Journalism*. Hong Kong: Hong Kong University Press.
Bao, Y. (2009, 10th June). Xin Diannao Bixu Zhuang Shangwang Guolv Ruanjian [News Computers Must be Installed with Online Information Filtering Software], *Xin Jin Bao*, p. A06.
Barlow, A. (2010). The Citizen Journalist as a Gatekeeper: A Critical Evolution. In J. Rosenberry and B. S. John (Eds.), *Public Journalism 2.0: the Promise and Reality of a Citizen-engaged Press*. New York: Routledge.

Baum, R. (2008). Political Implications of China Information Revolution: The Media, the Minders and Their Message. In C. Li (Ed.), *China's Changing Political Landscape: Prospects for Democracy.* Washington D.C.: Brookings Institution Press.

Baynes, K. (2004). The Transcendental Turn: Habermas's "Kantian Pragmatism." In F. L. Rush (Ed.), *The Cambridge Companion to Critical Theory* (pp. 194–218). Cambridge: Cambridge University Press.

BBC. (2012). Phone-Hacking Scandal: Timeline. Retrieved November 4, 2013, from www.bbc.co.uk/news/uk-14124020.

BBC. (2013). Q&A: UK filters on Legal Pornography. Retrieved September 8, 2013, from www.bbc.co.uk/news/technology-23403068.

Beach, S. (2005). Rise of Rights? Retrieved October 11, 2011, from chinadigitaltimes.net/2005/05/rise-of-rights/

Béja, J.-P. (2007). The Chinese Communist Party in Reform. *The China journal (Canberra, A.C.T.)*(58), 209–11.

Bennett, W. L. (1990). Toward a Theory of Press-State Relations in the United States. *Journal of Communication*, 40(2), 103–27.

Bentham, J. ([1790s] 2001). In M. Quinn (Ed.), *Writings on the Poor Laws* (Vol. 1). Oxford: Clarendon Press.

Belsey, A. (1998). Journalism and Ethics: Can They Co-exist? In M. Kieran (Ed.), *Media Ethics* (pp. 1–14). New York: Routledge.

Blasi, V. (1996). Milton's Areopagitica and the Modern First Amendment. *Ideas*, 4(2).

Borders, R. W. (2010). Propaganda Department Sets Rule for Covering Shanghai Expo and Qinghai Earthquake. Retrieved April 28, 2011, from en.rsf.org/china-shanghai-expo-earthquake-qinghai-censorship-29-04-2010,37231.html.

Bovard, J. (2000). *Lost Rights: The Destruction of American Liberty.* New York: Palgrave.

Brady, A.-M. (2008). *Marketing Dictatorship: Propaganda and Thought Work in Contemporary China.* Lanham: Rowman and Littlefield Publishers Inc.

Bristow, M. (2009). China Defends Screening Software. Retrieved May 8, 2011, from news.bbc.co.uk/2/hi/asia-pacific/8091044.stm.

Brodsgaard, K. E. (2006). Bianzhi and Cadre Management in China: the Case of Yangpu. In K. E. Brodsgaard and Y. Zheng (Eds.), *The Chinese Communist Party in Reform* (pp. 103–21). Abingdon: Routledge.

Brown, H. I. (2007). *Conceptual Systems.* Abingdon: Routledge.

Buckley, C. (2009). China Demotes Editor after Obama Interview: Sources. Retrieved October 11, 2011, from www.reuters.com/article/2009/12/13/us-obama-china-censorship-idUSTRE5BC0BM20091213.

Bunkenborg, M. (2012). Organizing Rural Health Care. In A. Bislev and S. Thogerson (Eds.), *Organizing Rural China, Rural China Organizing.* Lanham: Lexington Books.

Burd, G. (1978). Newspapers as Civic Participants and Observers: Dilemmas in Journalistic Objectivity/ Subjectivity. Paper presented at the the Annual Meeting of the Association for Education in Journalism, Washington, D.C.

Burgess, R. (2012). Google Transparency Report Reveals Global Political Censorship Trend. Retrieved June 20, 2012, from www.techspot.com/news/49029-google-transparency-report-reveals-global-political-censorship-trend.html.

Burns, J. P. (1989). *The Chinese Communist Party's Nomenklatura System.* Armonk: M.E. Sharpe, Inc.

Cai, C. (2008). *Women's Participation as Leaders in the Transformation of the Chinese Media: A Case Study of Guangzhou City.* Ann Arbor: ProQuest LLC.

Cai, Y. (2008). Disruptive Collective Movements in China. In K. J. O'Brien (Ed.), *Popular Protest in China* (pp. 163–78). Cambridge: Harvard University Press.

Cai, Y. (2010). *Collective Resistance in China: Why Popular Protests Succeed or Fail.* Stanford: Stanford University Press.

Cao, C. (2010a). Yong Geming Jieshu Zhonggong Baozheng [To Terminate Chinese Dictatorial Regime by Revolution]. Retrieved May 10, 2010, from www.observechina.net/info/artshow.asp?ID=66795.

Cao, C. (2010b). Dangjin Zhongguo You "Baoli Geming" ma? [Is There Violent Revolution in China Today?]. Retrieved May 10, 2010, from caochangqing.com/big5/newsdisp.php?News_ID=2120.
Cao, C., and Seymour, J. D. (Eds.). (1998). *Tibet through Dissident Chinese Eyes: Essays on Self-Determination*. Armonk: M.E. Sharpe Inc.
Cao, P. (1999). *Zhongguo Baoye Jituan Fazhan Yanjiu [Study on the Development of China's Press Groups]*. Beijing: Xinhua Press.
Carlson, B. (2013). Average Chinese are Awash in Consumer Bliss. Retrieved October 20, 2013, from www.globalpost.com/dispatch/news/regions/asia-pacific/china/130703/awash-consumer-bliss.
Castells, M. (2009). *Communication Power*. Oxford: Oxford University Press.
Caton, H. (1973). *The Origin of Subjectivity: An Essay on Descartes*. New Haven: Yale University Press.
Center for Public Integrity, Global Integrity, and Public Radio International. (2012). State Integrity Investigation. Washington, DC: Center for Public Integrity.
Chai, W. (1970). *Essential Works of Chinese Communism*. Santa Barbara: Pica Press.
Chan, K.-B., Ku, A. S., and Chu, Y.-W. (2009). *Social Stratification in Chinese Societies*. Leiden: Koninklijke Brill NV.
Chao, L. (2009). China Squeezes PC Makers. Retrieved May 8, 2011, from online.wsj.com/article/SB124440211524192081.html.
Cheek, T. (1997). *Propaganda and Culture in Mao's China: Deng Tuo and the Intelligentsia*. Oxford: Oxford University Press.
Chen, B., and Jia, Y. (2005). 2004 Nian Shida Jiaxinwen [Top Ten Fake News in 2004]. *Journalism Review*(1), 33–8.
Chen, F. (2009a). Liushi Nian Shehui Zhuyi Fazhi Jianshe Chengjiu Xianzhu [Legal Construction Has Made Prominent Achievements Over 60 Years]. Retrieved August 5, 2010, from theory.people.com.cn/GB/10136002.html.
Chen, F. (2009b). Xin Zhongguo Liushi Nian Shehui Zhuyi Fazhi Jianshe Budan Jiaqiang Chengjiu Xianzhu [Prominent Achievements Have Been Made in the Construction of Law Over the Sixty Years of New China]. Retrieved August 5, 2010, from www.gov.cn/jrzg/2009-09/28/content_1428931.htm.
Chen, G., and Chun, T. (2004). *Zhongguo Nongmin Diaocha [An Investigative Report on the Chinese Peasantry]*. Beijing: Renmin Wenxue Chubanshe.
Chen, G., and Wu, C. (2006). *Will the Boat Sink the Water?: The Life of Chinese Peasants* (H. Zhu, Trans.). New York: Public Affairs.
Chen, L. (2008). *Zhongguo Gongchandang Lingdao Tizhi de Kaocha:1921–2006 [Observation on the Leadership System of the CCP: 1921–2006]*. Shanghai: Shanghai People's Press.
Chen, Y., Jiang, P., and Wang, Y. (2003). *Lao Xinwen: 1912–1920 [Old News: 1912–1920]*. Tianjin: Tianjin People's Press.
Chen, Z. (2010). 2010 Nian Shijie Ribao Faxingliang Qian 100 Ming Paihangbang [Top 100 Best Selling Dailies Worldwide in 2010]. *Xinwen Jizhe*(9), 13.
Cheng, J. Y. S. (1998). Introduction. In J. Y. S. Cheng (Ed.), *China in the Post-Deng Era* (pp. 1–20).
China Radio and TV Year Book Compiling Committee. (2002). *China Radio and TV Year Book*. Beijing: Zhongguo Guangbo Dianshi Chubanshe.
Cho, L.-F. (2006). News Crusaders: Constructing Journalistic Professionalism within the Confines of State Control and Commercial Pressure. *Media Asia, 33*(3–4), 130–41.
Chomsky, N. (1989). *Necessary Illusions: Thought Control in Democratic Societies*. Cambridge: South End Press.
Chomsky, N. (2002). *Media Control: The Spectacular Achievements of Propaganda* (2 ed.). New York: Seven Stories Press.
Cimino, A. (2012). Die Performative Grundbestimmung der Menschlichen Subjektivitat. In v. d. Heiden Gert-Jan, Novotny Karel, and L. Tengelyi (Eds.), *Investigating Subjectivity: Classical and New Perspectives* (pp. 165–80). Leiden: Koninklijke Brill NV.
Clarke, D. C. (1985). Political Power and Authority in Recent Chinese Literature. *The China Quarterly, 102*(June), 234–52

CNNIC. (2013). Di 32 Ci Zhongguo Hulian Wangluo Fazhan Tongji Baogao [The 32nd Statistical Report on the Development of China's Internet]. Beijing: China Internet Network Information Centre.
Coates, L. (2000). *Is China Capitalist?* Umeå: Förlaget Rättviseböcker.
Compiling Committee of the *Annals of Guangzhou*. (1999). *Guangzhou Shizhi [Annals of Guangzhou]* (Vol. 16). Guangzhou: Guangzhou Publishing House.
Compiling Committee of the *Annals of Harbin*. (1994). *Annals of Harbin: Newspapers, Radio and Television*. Harbin: Heilongjiang People's Press.
Cotterrell, R. (1999). Transparency, Mass Media, Ideology and Community. *Cultural Values, 3*(4), 414–26.
Couldry, N., and Curran, J. (2003). The Paradox of Media Power. In N. Couldry and J. Curran (Eds.), *Contesting Media Power: Alternative Media in a Networked World* (pp. 3–16). Lanham: Rowman and Littlefield Publishers Inc.
Critchley, S. (1999). *Ethics, Politics, Subjectivity: Essays on Derrida, Levinas and Contemporary*. London: Verso.
Crossick, S. (2010). Corruption Threatens Chinese Communist Party Rule. Retrieved October 11, 2010, from crossick.blogactiv.eu/2010/03/12/corruption-threatens-chinese-communist-party-rule/.
Croteau, D., and Hoynes, W. (2006). *The Business of Media: Corporate Media and the Public Interest*. Thousand Oaks: Pine Forge Press.
Cui, B. (2005). *2004–2005 Nian: Zhongguo Chuanmei Chanye Fazhan Baogao [2004–2005: Report on Development of China's Media Industry]*. Beijing: Social Sciences Academic Press (China).
Cui, B. (Ed.). (2009). *2009: Report on the Development of China's Media Industry*. Beijing: Social Sciences Academic Press (China).
Cui, B., and Zhang, X. (2010). *Zhongguo baozhi chanye fazhan gaikuang [Outline of the Development of China's Newspapers]*. Beijing: Social Sciences Academic Press (China).
Cui, B. (2013). *Report on the Development of China's Media Industry*. Beijing: Social Sciences Academic Press (China).
Curran, J. (2012). *Media and Power*. London: Routledge.
Curran, J., and Seaton, J. (2010). *Power without Responsibility: The Press, Broadcasting and the Internet in Britain* (7 ed.). Abingdon: Routledge.
Curry, J. L. (2005). Eastern Europe's Postcommunist Media. In R. A. May and A. K. Milton (Eds.), *Uncivil Societies: Human Rights and Democratic Transitions in Eastern Europe and Latin America* (pp. 139–62). Lanham: Lexington Books.
Curtis, M. (1997). *Marxism: The Inner Dialogues* (2 ed.). New Brunswick: Transaction Publishers.
Davidson, D. (2005). *Meaning, Truth, Language and Reality*. Oxford: Oxford University Press.
Davis, E. L. (Ed.). (2005). *Encyclopedia of Contemporary Chinese Culture*. Abingdon: Routledge.
Davis, S. L., Weisgal, H. G., and Neggers, W. (2001). Trial Techniques. In P. W. Iyer (Ed.), *Nursing Malpractice* (pp. 773–806). Tucson: Lawyers and Judges Publishing Company.
Dayangwang. (2010). Wangyi Youdao Zhuwei 2010 Guangzhou Yayunhui [2010 Guangzhou Asian Games Assisted by Netease.com's Search Engine Youdao]. Retrieved May 30, 2012, from news.dayoo.com/sports/201008/25/54235_13694697.htm.
de Burgh, H. (2003a). *The Chinese Journalist: Mediating Information in the World's Most Populous Country*. London: RoutledgeCurzon.
de Burgh, H. (2003b). Kings without Crowns? The Re-emergence of Investigative Journalism in China. *Media, Culture and Society, 25*(6), 801–20.
de Burgh, H. (2005). Introduction: Journalism and the New Cultural Paradigm. In H. De Burgh (Ed.), *Making Journalists: Diverse Models, Global Issues* (pp. 1–22). Abingdon: Routledge.
Dean, J. (2009). Obama's China Interview Mystery. Retrieved October 11, 2010, from blogs.wsj.com/chinarealtime/2009/11/19/obama%E2%80%99s-china-interview-mystery/.
Deibert, R., Palfrey, J., Rohozinski, R., and Zittrain, J. (Eds.). (2011). *Access Contested: Security, Identity, and Resistance in Asian Cyberspace*. Cambridge: The MIT Press.

# Bibliography

Deng, X. (1983). Muqian de Xingshi he Renwu [The Present Situation and Tasks]. In X. Deng (Ed.), *Selected Works of Deng Xiaoping*. Beijing: The People's Press.

Di, M. (2011). Between Propaganda and Commercials: Chinese Television Today. In S. L. Shirk (Ed.), *Changing Media, Changing China* (pp. 91–114). Oxford: Oxford University Press.

Dickson, B. J. (2003). *Red Capitalists in China: The Party, Private Entrepreneurs, and Prospects for Political Change*. Cambridge: Cambridge University Press.

Dillon, M. (2009). *Contemporary China: An Introduction*. Abingdon: Routledge.

Ding, S. (1994). *Zhongguo Lidai Zouyi Dadian [Dictionary of Chinese Political History]*. Harbin: Harbin Press.

Dittmer, L. (2000). Sizing up China's New Leadership: Division over Labour, Political Background and Policy Orientation. In H.-m. Tien and Y. Zhu (Eds.), *China under Jiang Zemin* (pp. 33–54). Boulder: Lynne Reinner Publishers Inc.

Donald, S. H., and Keane, M. (2002). Media in China: New Convergences, New Approaches. In S. H. Donald, M. Keane and Y. Hong (Eds.), *Media in China: Consumption, Content and Crisis*. London: RoutlegeCurzon.

Dong, T., and Feng, F. (2004). Xinwen Sheying Bixu Jianchi Zhenshixing Yuanze—"Hesai Huojiang Zuopin Zaojia Shijian" Toushi [The Principle of Truth Must be Adhered to in Journalist Photography: Looking through the "Fake WPP Award Winning Photo" Event]. *Journalism Review*(7), 35–7.

Donovan, S. (2007). *Madame Chiang Kai-Shek: Face of Modern China*. Mankato: Compass Point Books.

Douglas A., V. B. (2000). *Press Freedom and Global Politics*. Westport: Praeger Publishers.

Dubben, N., and Williams, B. (2009). *Partnerships in Urban Property Development*. West Sussex: John Wiley and Sons Ltd.

Dykstra, C. A. (1939). The Quest for Responsibility. *American Political Science Review, 33*(1), 1–25.

Edelmann, N., Hochtl, J., and Sachs, M. (2012). Collaboration for Open Innovation Processes in Public Administrations. In Y. Charalabidis and S. Koussouris (Eds.), *Empowering Open and Collaborative Governance: Technologies and Methods for Online Citizen Engagement in Public Policy Making*. Heidelburg Springer.

Eigen, P. (2002). Measuring and Combating Corruption. *Journal of Policy Reform*, 5(4), 187–201.

Elliott, A. (2004). *Social Theory Since Freud: Traversing Social Imaginaries*. Abingdon: Routledge.

Esarey, A. (2007). Cornering the Market: State Strategies for Controlling China's Commercial Media. In D. L. Yang (Ed.), *Discontented Miracle: Growth, Conflict, and Institutional Adaptations in China* (pp. 1–48). Singapore: World Scientific Publishing Co. Pte. Ltd.

Ewing, K. (2011). Murdoch's Misery, China's Delight. Retrieved November 15, 2011, from www.atimes.com/atimes/China/MG26Ad01.html.

Eyferth, J. J. K. (2006). Introduction. In J. J. K. Eyferth (Ed.), *How China Works: Perspectives on the Twentieth-Century Industrial Workplace* (pp. 1–24). Abingdon: Routledge.

Fake News Research Project Team. (2012). 2012 Nian Xujia Xinwen Yanjiu Baogao [Research Report on the Fake News in 2012]. *Journalism Review* (1), 44–52.

Fan, H. (2006, November 7). Zhongguo Dui Hulianwang Guanli Yongde shi Guoji Tongxing Zuofa [China Regulates the Internet According to International Practice], *Beijing Youth Daily*, p. A3. Retrieved from bjyouth.ynet.com/3.1/0611/07/1958002.html.

Fan, S., Kanbur, R., and Zhang, X. (Eds.). (2009). *Regional Inequality in China: Trends, Explanations and Policy Responses*. Abingdon: Routledge.

Fan, Y. (2005). *Nitu Jiaoyin Xubian [Footprint on Earth (Continued Edition)]*. Beijing: Sanlian Shudian.

Fang, H. (2000). Zhongguo Xinwen Shiye Bainian [One Hundred Years of Chinese Journalism]. *Xinwen Sanwei*(12), 44–6.

Fang, H., and Chen, C. (Eds.). (2002). *Zhengzai Fasheng de Lishi: Zhongguo Dangdai Xinwen Shiye [History That Is Happening: Chinese Contemporary Journalism]* (Vol. 2). Fuzhou: Fujian People's Press.

Facsar, F. (2010). China's Censorship Could Lead to a Brain Drain. Retrieved June 23, 2010, from edition.cnn.com/2010/TECH/web/06/03/hong.kong.students.google/index.html.

Farganis, J. (2000). *Readings in Social Theory: The Classic Tradition to Post-Modernism*. New York: McGraw Hill.

Feldman, S. M. (2008). *Free Expression and Democracy in America: A History*. Chicago: University of Chicago Press.

Feng, C., and Dong, J. (2008). Xuexi Hu Jintao Zongshuji Zai Renmin Ribaoshe Kaocha Gongzuo shi de Jianghua [Learning the Speech by Secretary General Hu Jintao on his Visit to People's Daily Press]. Retrieved January 4, 2011, from media.people.com.cn/GB/40628/7563891.html.

Feng, R. (2009). "Nanfang Zhoumo" Fouren Xiangxi Diaozhi yu Chuli Aobama Zhuanfang Youguan [The *Southern Weekend* Denied Connection between Xiangxi's Demotion with the Treatment of the Interview with Obama]. Retrieved November 13, 2010, from www.rfa.org/cantonese/news/china_media_obama-12092009122326.html/story_main?encoding=traditional.

Fewsmith, J. (2001). *Elite Politics in Contemporary China*. Armonk: M.E. Sharpe Inc.

Finel, B. I., and Lord, K. M. (2002). *Power and Conflict in the Age of Transparency*. New York: Palgrave MacMillan.

Fischer, D. (2009). Censorship and Marketization: Institutional Change within China's Media. In T. Heberer and G. Schubert (Eds.), *Regime Legitimacy in Contemporary China* (pp. 175–96). Abingdon: Routledge.

Fitton, L., Gruen, M., and Poston, L. (2010). *Twitter for Dummies*. Hoboken: John Wiley and Sons.

Foucault, M. (2000). *Ethics: Subjectivity and Truth* (R. Hurley, Trans. Vol. 1). London: Penguin.

Freund, J. C. (1992). *Smart Negotiating: How to Make Good Deals in the Real World*. Cammeray: Simon and Schuster.

Friedman, M. (2002). *Capitalism and Freedom: Fortieth Anniversary Edition* Chicago: University of Chicago Press.

Friend, C., and Singer, J. B. (2007). *Online Journalism Ethics: Traditions and Transitions*. New York: M.E. Sharpe.

Fu, G. (2006). *Bidi Bolan: Bainian Zhongguo Yanlunshi de Yizhong Dufa [Waves Under the Pen: Reading the Centennial History of Freedom of Speech in China]*. Nanning: Guangxi Normal University Press.

Fu, G. (2007). *Wenren de Diqi: Bainian Zhongguo Yanlunshi Jianying [Backbone of Intellectuals: A Centennial Silhouette of the History of Freedom of Speech in China]*. Kunming: Yunnan People's Press.

Fulga, G. (2005). *Social Change and Political Culture*. Liege: Les Editions de l'Universite de Liege.

Fung, A. (2003). Marketing Popular Culture in China: Andy Lau as a Pan-Chinese Icon. In C.-C. Lee (Ed.), *Chinese Media, Global Context* (pp. 252–64). London: RoutledgeCurzon.

Fung, E. S. K. (2000). *In Search of Chinese Democracy: Civil Opposition in Nationalist China, 1929–1949*. Cambridge: Cambridge University Press.

Fung, E. S. K. (2010). *The Intellectual Foundations of Chinese Modernity: Cultural and Political Thought in the Republican Era*. Cambridge: Cambridge University Press.

Gao, J. Z. (2009). *Historical Dictionary of Modern China (1800–1949)*. Plymouth: Scarecrow Press, Inc.

Gao, M. (2003). Book Review. *Australian Journal of International Affairs, 57*(2), 390–1.

Gao, M. (2004a). Media Ownership: One Case Studies and Two Perspectives. *The International Journal of Humanities, 2*(3), 2103–12.

Gao, M. (2004b). Reviews. *The China Journal*(52), 113–6.

Gao, M. (2005). A Boom Financed by Taxes on the Poor. *New Statesman*(1), 19–20.

Gao, M. (2008). *The Battle for China's Past: Mao and the Cultural Revolution*. London: Pluto Press.

Gao, M. (2011). Netizenship and Its Implication on Democratization in China. In J. Y. S. Cheng (Ed.), *Whither China's Democracy? Democratization in China since the Tiananmen Incident* (pp. 151–76). Hong Kong: City University of Hong Kong Press.

Gao, M. (2012). The Transitional Role of the Hu-Wen Leadership in China: A Case Study of Liu Xiaobo. In J. Cheng (Ed.), *A New Stage of Development for an Emerging Superpower* (pp. 175–92). Hong Kong: City University of Hong Kong Press.

GAPP. (2009). *Jizhe Zheng Guanli Banfa* [Measures for the Administration of the Press Cards]. Retrieved September 24, 2010, from www.gapp.gov.cn/cms/html/21/397/200908/465942.html.

GAPP. (2013). 2012 Nian Xinwen Chuban Chanye Fenxi Baogao [2012 Analytical Report on the Journalism and Publication Industry]. Beijing: General Administration of Press and Publication.

GAPPRFT. (2013a). *Zhongguo Guangbo Dianying Dianshi Fazhan Baogao* (2013) [Annual Report on Development of China's Radio, Film and Television (2013)]. Beijing: General Administration of Press, Publication, Radio, Film, and Television.

GAPPRFT. (2013b). *Zhongguo Shiting Xinmeiti Fazhan Baogao 2013* [Annual Report on the Development of China's Audio-visual New Media 2013]. Beijing: General Administration of Press, Publication, Radio, Film and Television.

George, C. (Ed.). (2008). *Free Markets Free Media?: Reflections on the Political Economy of the Press*. Singapore: AMIC.

Gilley, B. (2004). *China's Democratic Future: How It Will Happen and Where It Will Lead*. New York: Columbia University Press.

Goldman, A. J., and Sigismond, W. D. (2010). *Business Law: Principles and Practices*. Mason: Cengage Learning Inc.

Goldstein, R. J. (1989). *Censorship of Political Caricature in Nineteenth-Century France*. Kent: Kent State University Press.

Goldstein, T. (2007). *Journalism and Truth: Strange Bedfellows* Evanston: Northwestern University Press.

Goldstone, R. L., Feng, Y., and Rogosky, B. J. (2005). Connecting Concepts to Each Other and the World. In D. Pecher and R. A. Zwaan (Eds.), *Grounding Cognition: The Role Of Perception And Action In Memory, Language and Thinking* (pp. 282–314). Cambridge: Cambridge University Press.

Gong, M. (2007). Sanjian Ba Jin [Three Visits to Ba Jin]. Retrieved October 12, 2011, from blog.tianya.cn/blogger/post_read.asp?BlogID=206048&PostID=8453909.

Goodman, A., and Goodman, D. (2003). *The Exception to the Rulers: Exposing America's War Profiteers, the Media That Love Them and the Crackdown on Our Rights*. Crows Nest: Allen and Unwin.

Goodman, A., and Goodman, D. (2006). *Static: Government Liars, Media Cheerleaders, and the People Who Fight Back*. New York: Hyperion.

Google. (2012). Transparency Report. Retrieved June 20, 2012, from www.google.com/transparencyreport/removals/government/.

Google. (2014). Google's Mission is to Organize the World's Information and Make it Universally Accessible and Useful. Retrieved July 14, 2014, from www.google.com.au/about/company/.

Gordon, N. S. (2008). *Media and the Politics of Culture: The Case of Television Privatization and Media Globalization in Jamaica (1990–2007)*. Boca Raton: Universal Publishers.

Gore, A. (1995). *Remarks of Vice President Al Gore as Delivered to the Federal-State-Local Telecomm Summit*. Paper presented at the The Federal-State-Local Telecomm Summit, Washington D.C.

Graen, G. B., and Graen, J. A. (1992). *Predator's Game-Changing Designs: Research-Based Tools*. Charlotte: JHU Press.

Graham, J. R., and Tesh, L. (2009). *Free, Sovereign, and Independent States: The Intended Meaning of the American Constitution*. Gretna: Pelican Publishing Company, Inc.

Gray, J. (1996). *Enlightenment's Wake: Politics and Culture at the Close of the Modern Age*. London Routledge.

Green, J., and Karolides, N. J. (2005). *Encyclopedia of Censorship*. New York: Facts on File, Inc. (Reprinted from: 1990).
Groot, G. (2004). *Managing Transitions: The Chinese Communist Part, United Front Work, Corporatism, and Hegemony*. London: Routledge.
Gu, E. X. (2004). Social Capital and Institutional Change. In E. X. Gu and M. Goldman (Eds.), *Chinese Intellectuals between State and Market* (pp. 1–42). New York: RoutledgeCurzon.
Guerrero, M. A. (2009). *Empowering Citizenship through Journalism, Information, and Entertainment in Iberoamerica*. Mexico City: Universidad Iberoamericana.
Guo, C. (1997). *Houshe Lun [On Tongue and Throat Argument]*. Beijing: Xinhua Press.
Habermas, J. (1974). The Public Sphere: An Encyclopedia Article (1964). *New German Critique*(3), 49–55.
Habermas, J. (1990). *The Philosophical Discourse of Modernity: Twelve Lectures* (F. G. Lawrence, Trans.). Cambridge: First MIT Press.
Habermas, J. (1991). *The Structural Transformation of the Public Sphere: An Inquiry into a Category of Bourgois Society*. Cambridge: MIT Press.
Habermas, J. (2005). *Truth and Justification* (B. Fultner, Trans.). Cambridge: The MIT Press.
Hackett, R., and Zhao, Y. (1998). *Sustaining Democracy?: Journalism and the Politics of Objectivity*. Toronto: Garamond Press.
Hallahan, K. (1996). Product Publicity: An Orphan of Marketing Research. In E. Thorson and J. Moore (Eds.), *Integrated Communication: Synergy of Persuasive Voices* (pp. 305–30). Mahwah: Lawrence Erlbaum Associates, Inc.
Hardt, H. (2000). Karl Marx on Press Freedom and Censorship. *The Public*, 7(4), 85–100.
Hazell, R. (1998). Balancing Privacy and Freedom of Information: Policy Options in the United Kingdom. In A. McDonald and G. Terrill (Eds.), *Open Government, Freedom of Information and Privacy* (pp. 67–85). Basingstoke: Macmillan.
He, D., Zhang, S., and Wang, W. (2012). *2011 Nian Zhongguo Chuanmei Hangye Fazhan Gaikuang* [Outline of the Development of China's Media Industry in 2011]. In B. Cui (Ed.), *2011 Nian: Zhongguo Chuanmei Chanye Fazhan Baogo* [2011: Report on the Development of China's Media Industry] (pp. 22–29). Beijing: Social Sciences Academic Press (China).
He, H. Y. (2001). *Dictionary of the Political Thought of the People's Republic of China*. Armonk: M.E.Sharpe Inc.
He, Y. (1992). *Cycles of Repression and Relaxation: Politco-Literary Events in China, 1976–1989*. Bochum: N. Brockmeyer.
He, Z. (2000). Chinese Communist Party Press in a Tug-of-War: A Political-Economy Analysis of the Shenzhen Special Zone Daily. In C.-C. Lee (Ed.), *Power, Money, and Media: Communication Patterns and Bureaucratic Control in Cultural China* (pp. 112–51). Evanston: Northwestern University Press.
Heald, D. (2006a). Varieties of Transparency. In C. Hood and D. Heald (Eds.), *Transparency: The Key to Better Governance?* (pp. 25–46). Oxford: Oxford University Press.
Heald, D. (2006b). Transparency as an Instrumental Value. In C. Hood and D. Heald (Eds.), *Transparency: The Key to Better Governance?* (pp. 59–74). Oxford: Oxford University Press.
Herman, E. S., and Chomsky, N. (1994). *Manufacturing Consent: The Political Economy of the Mass Media*. London: Vintage Books.
Hewitt, D. (2008). *Getting Rich First: Life in a Changing China*. London: Vintage.
Hicks, A., and Goo, S. H. (2008). *Cases and Materials on Company Law* (6 ed.). Oxford: Oxford University Press.
Ho, P. (2008). Self-imposed Censorship and De-politicized Politics in China. In P. Ho and R. L. Edmonds (Eds.), *China's Embedded Activism: Opportunities and Constraints of a Social Movement* (pp. 20–43). Abingdon: Routledge.
Holden, T. J. M., and Scrase, T. J. (2006). *Medi@sia: Global Media/tion in and out of Context*. Abingdon: Routledge.
Holtz, S., Havens, J. C., and Johnson, L. D. (2009). *Tactical Transparency: How Leaders can Leverage Social Media to Maximize Value and Build their Brand* (2 ed.). Hoboken: John Wiley and Sons.
Holub, R. C. (1991). *Jürgen Habermas: Critic in the Public Sphere*. London: Routledge.

Hood, C. (2006). Transaprency in Historical Perspective. In C. Hood and D. Heald (Eds.), *Transparency: The Key to Better Governance?* Oxford: Oxford University Press Inc.

Howarth, D. R., and Stavrakakis, Y. (2000). Discourse Theory and Political Analysis: Identities, Hegemonies and Social In D. R. Howarth, A. J. Norval and Y. Stavrakakis (Eds.), (pp. 1–23). Manchester: Manchester University Press.

Howarth, V. (1991). Social Work and the Media: Pitfalls and Possibilities. In B. Franklin and N. Parton (Eds.), *Social Work, the Media and Public Relations* (pp. 116–28). London: Routledge.

Hsing, Y.-t., and Lee, C. K. (2010). *Reclaiming Chinese Society: the New Social Activism*. Abingdon: Routledge.

Hu, H., and Chen, X. (2009). *Zhongguo Wenhua Chanye Pinglun [Review of China's Cultural Industry]* (Vol. 9). Shanghai: Shanghai People's Press.

Hu, S. (2011). The Rise of the Business Media in China. In S. L. Shirk (Ed.), *Changing Media, Changing China* (pp. 77–90). New York: Oxford University Press.

Huang, F. (2008). Zhongguo Yahu Xiangyou Aoyun Caifangzheng, Fabu 2008 Aoyun Zhanlue [Yahoo China Enjoys Journalist Permits for the Olympic Games, Releasing 2008 Olympic Strategies]. Retrieved October 10, 2011, from news.sohu.com/20080318/n255771508.shtml.

Huang, S., and Zhou, Y. (Eds.). (2003). *Zhongguo chuanmei shichang da bianju*. Beijing Citic Publishing House.

Hübner, Z., and Kosicka, J. (1988). *Theater and Politics*. Evanston: Northwestern University Press.

Hujiang English. (2009). Beijing Shifan Daxue 2009 Nian Boshisheng Zhaosheng Jianzhang [2009 Doctoral Students Recruitment Adverstisement of Beijing Normal University]. Retrieved June 14, 2012, from www.hjenglish.com/kaobo/p343000/.

Hunansheng Difangzhi Bianzuan Weiyuanhui. (1993). *Hunan Shengzhi Baoye [Annals of Hunan Province, Newspapers]*. Changsha: Hunan Chubanshe.

Institution of Journalism of China Academy of Social Sciences. (1989). *Zhongguo Xinwen Nianjian*. Beijing: Chinese Academy of Social Sciences Press.

Institution of Journalism of China Academy of Social Sciences. (1999). *Zhongguo Xinwen Nianjian [Almanac of China's Journalism]*. Beijing: China Social Sciences Press.

Institution of Journalism of Chinese Academy of Social Sciences. (1994). *Zhongguo Xinwen Nianjian*. Beijing: Chinese Academy of Social Sciences Press.

Ip, H.-y. (2005). *Intellectuals in Revolutionary China, 1921–1949: Leaders, Heroes and Sophisticates*. Abingdon: RoutledgeCurzon.

Ishihara, N., and Tarone, E. (2009). Subjectivity and Pragmatic Choice in L2 Japanese: Emulating and Resisting Pragmatic Norms. In N. Taguchi (Ed.), *Pragmatic Competence* (pp. 101–28). Berlin: Mouton de Gruyter.

Jakes, S. (2003). Hostages of the State. Retrieved October 11, 2011, from www.time.com/time/magazine/article/0,9171,458835,00.html#ixzz1aj6DjY7i.

Jakubowicz, K. (2011). *Media Revolution in Europe: Ahead of the Curve*. Paris: Council of Europe.

Jamieson, K. H., and Campbell, K. K. (2000). *The Interplay of Influence: News, Advertising, Politics, and the Mass Media* (V ed.). Belmont: Wadsworth Publishing Company.

Jansen, S. C. (1988). *Censorship: The Knot That Binds Power and Knowledge*. Oxford: Oxford University Press.

Jia, Y. (2000). "Wumian Zhiwang" Anran Wuyang Hu? Shanghaishi Xinwen Congye Renyuan Jiankang Zhuangkuang Chouyang Diaocha Baogao ["Uncrowned Kings," Are You Alright?—A Sampling Report on the Health Status of Journalist Practitioners in Shanghai]. *Journalism Review*(6), 6–9.

Jiang, S. (2013). Bo Xilai Found Guilty on All Charges, Sentenced to Life in Prison. Retrieved September 22, 2013, from edition.cnn.com/2013/09/21/world/asia/china-bo-xilai-verdict/?hpt=hp_t2.

Jiang, Z. (1999). *Jiang Zemin Lun Shehui Zhuyi Jingshen Wenming Jianshe [Jiang Zemin's Talks on Construction of Socialist Spiritual Civilization]*. Beijing: Zhongyang Wenxian Chubanshe.

Jiang, Z. (2001). *Lun "Sange Daibiao"* [On the "Three Represents"]. Beijing: Zhongyang Wenxian Chubanshe.
Jing, Y. (2012, 18th November). Xiang "Baipai" Zhilei de Xingshi Zhuyi Shuo "Bu" [Say "No" to All Formalism including Photo Orchestration], *Xinjing Bao [the Beijing News]*.
Jordan, T. (2002). *Activism!: Direct Action, Hacktivism and the Future of Society*. London: Reaktion Books Ltd.
Kaarbo, J., and Beasley, R. K. (1999). A Practical Guide to the Comparative Case Study Method in Political Psychology. *Political Psychology*, 20(2), 369–91.
Kamenka, E. (1962). *The Ethical Foundations of Marxism*. London: Routledge and Kegan Paul Ltd.
Kang, J. (2004, 18th July). Mohu de Heli Huaiyiquan Yibei Guanyuan Zuankongzi [Officials May Find Loopholes in the Ambiguious Stipulation of the Rights to Reasonable No-Fault Suspicion], *Yanzhao Dushibao*. Retrieved from news.xinhuanet.com/comments/2004-07/18/content_1610880.htm.
Kant, I. (2006). *Fundamental Principles of the Metaphysic of Morals*. Teddington: The Echo Library.
Keane, M. A. (2001). Broadcasting Policy, Creative Compliance and the Myth of Civil Society in China. *Media Culture and Society, 23*, 783–98.
Kesselman, M., Joseph, W. A., and Krieger, J. (2009). *Introduction to Politics of the Developing World*. Boston: Cengage Learning.
Kirby, W. C. (2004). The Chinese Party-State under Dictatorship and Democracy on the Mainland and on Taiwan. In W. C. Kirby (Ed.), *Realms of Freedom in Modern China* (pp. 113–38). Standford: Standford University Press.
Klyueva, A., and Yang, A. (2009). *Media Transparency in Action: A Case Study of Media Coverage of a Controversy between ENGOs and a Paper Company in China*. Paper presented at the the Annual Meeting of the International Communication Association, Chicago.
Kolstø, P. (2009). *Media Discourse and the Yugoslav Conflicts: Representations of Self and Other*. Surrey: Ashgate Publising Limited.
Kondo, S. (2002). Fostering Dialogue to Strengthen Good Governance *Public Sector Transparency and Accountability: Make It Happen* (pp. 7–12). Paris: OECD.
Korsgaard, M. C. (1996). *Creating the Kingdom of Ends*. Cambridge: Cambridge University Press.
Kovach, B., and Rosenstiel, T. (2001). *The Elements of Journalism: What Newspeople Should Know and the Public Should Expect*. New York: Three Rivers Press.
Kretchmar, J. (2009). Conflict Theory. Retrieved March 10, 2010, from EBSCO Publishing Inc vidaka.home.mruni.eu/wp-content/uploads/2009/09/gendsoci.pdf.
Kumar, A. (2010). *Implementing Mobile TV: ATSC Mobile DTV, Mediaflo, Dvb-H/Sh, Dmb, Wimax, 3g Systems and Rich Media Applications*. Burlington: Elsevier Inc.
LaFraniere, S., and Ansfield, J. (2009, 19th November). In Obama Interview, Signs of China's Heavy Hand. *New York Times*.
Lagerkvist, J. (2008). China's Online News Industry: Control Giving Way to Confucian Virtue. In E. Thomson and J. Sigurdson (Eds.), *China's Science and Technology Sector and the Forces of Globalisation* (pp. 191–206). Singapore: World Scientific Publishing Co. Pte. Ltd.
Lai, X. (2005). *Meiti Fazhan yu Guojia Zhengce: Cong Yanlun Ziyou yu Xinwen Ziyou Sikao Chuanbo Chanyi Quanli*. Taipei: Wu-nan Tushu Chuban Gufen Youxian Gongsi.
Lamble, S. (2002). Freedom of Information, a Finnish Clergyman's Gift to Democracy. *Freedom of Information Review*, 97, 2–8.
Lan, H. (1995). *Mianxiang xinwenjie*. Beijing: Jingguan Jiaoyu chubanshe.
Lang, J. (2003). *Zhongguo xinwen zhengce tixi yanjiu*. Beijing: Xinhua Publishing House.
Latham, K. (2007). *Pop Culture China!: Media, Arts, and Lifestyle*. Santa Barbara: ABC CLIO, Inc.
Lee, C.-C. (1994). Ambiguities and Contradictions: Issues in China's Changing Political Communication. In C.-C. Lee (Ed.), *China's media, media's China* (pp. 3–22). Boulder: Westview Press.
Lee, C.-C. (2000). China's Journalism: The Emancipatory Potential of Social Theory. *Journalism Studies, 1*(4), 559–75.

Lee, C.-C. (2000). Chinese Communication: Prisms, Trajectories, and Modes of Understanding. In C.-C. Lee (Ed.), *Power, Money, and Media: Communication Patterns and Bureaucratic Control in Cultural China* (pp. 3–44). Evanston: Northwestern University Press.

Lee, C.-C. (2001). Servants of the Party or of the Market: Journalists and Media in China. In In J. Tunstall (Ed.), *Media Occupations and Professions* (pp. 240–52). Oxford: Oxford University Press.

Lee, C.-C. (2003). The Global and the National of the Chinese Media: Discourse, Market, Technology and Ideology. In C.-C. Lee (Ed.), *Chinese Media, Global Contexts* (pp. 1–31). London: RoutledgeCurzon.

Lee, C.-C. (2004). The Conception of Chinese Journalists: Ideological Convergence and Contestation. *Perspectives: Working Papers in English and Communication, 16* (1).

Lee, C.-C. (2005). The Conception of Chinese Journalists: Ideological Convergence and Contestation. In H. De Burgh (Ed.), *Making Journalists: Diverse Models, Global Issues* (pp. 107–26). Abingdon: Routledge.

Lee, C.-C., He, Z., and Huang, Y. (2008). "Chinese Party Publicity Inc." Conglomerated: The Case of the Shenzhen Press Group. In K. Sen and T. Lee (Eds.), *Political Regimes and the Media in Asia* (pp. 11–30). Abingdon: Routledge.

Lenin, V. I. (2005). *Lenin's Fight against Economism* (Vol. I). Chippendale: Resistance Books.

Li, B., and Niu, Y. (2010, July 13). Lvba Ruanjian Xiangmuzu Quefa Jingfei Zao Qiansan [The Green Dam Project Dismissed Due to Shortage of Fund], *Jinghua Shibao*, p. B46. Retrieved from epaper.jinghua.cn/html/2010-07/13/content_567823.htm.

Li, C. (2000). Promises and Pitfalls of Reform: New Thinking in Post-Deng China. In T. White (Ed.), *China Briefing 2000: The Continuing Transformation* (pp. 123–58). Armonk: M E Sharpe Inc.

Li, G. (2005). "Shenzhen Yufan Zhiwu Fanzui Tiaoli" Qicaoren Jieshi Weihe Shanqu "Zhiqingquan he Heli Huaiyi Quan" [Draftsman Explained Why the "Rights to Know and Rights to Reaonsable Suspicion" Were Deleted]. Retrieved September 24, 2011, from zqb.cyol.com/content/2005-04/25/content_1074368.htm.

Li, H., and Shen, R. (2010). Cong shuju kan gaige kaifang sanshi nian zhongguo de dianshiye. In B. Cui (Ed.), *Report on Development of China's Media Industry (2009)*. Beijing: Social Sciences Academic Press (China).

Li, L. (1994). The Historical Fate of "Objective Reporting" in China. In C.-C. Lee (Ed.), *China's Media, Media's China* (pp. 225–38). Boulder: Westview Press.

Li, L. (2009). Woguo Jiang Jianli Zhengfu Lifa Tingzheng Zhidu, Baozheng Tingqu Minyi Changtaihua [Our Country is to Establish Hearing System for Government Legislation to Ensure Adoption of Public Opinions]. Retrieved May 1, 2012, from politics.people.com.cn/GB/1026/10502318.html.

Li, M., and Bray, M. (2007). Cross-border Flows of Students for Higher Education: Push-pull Factors and Motivations of Mainland Chinese Students in Hong Kong and Macau. *Higher Education*, 53, 791–818.

Li, Y. (2008). Representing the Underpriviledged? Reporting on the Rights of the "Peasant Labourers" under Market Forces. In C. George (Ed.), *Free Markets Free Media?: Reflections on the Political Economy of the Press in Asia* (pp. 48–58). Singapore: Asian Media Information and Communication Centre.

Li, Y., and Song, Y. (2010). Anhui Yanyi Jituan, Anhui Guangdian Chuanmei Chanye Jituan Jinri Chengli [Anhui Performance Art Group and Anhui Radio and Television Media Group are Established Today]. Retrieved June 27, 2012, from ah.anhuinews.com/system/2010/02/22/002665673.shtml.

Li, Y., and Tuo, J. (2007a). Nongmin Pingdeng Huayuquan de Shixian Tujing [Ways to Realize the Peasants' Equal Rights to Speech]. *Dangdai Chuanbo*(3), 16–18.

Li, Y., and Tuo, J. (2007b). Ruhe wei Cunmin Fafang "Kuoyinqi": Luelun Nongming Pingdeng Huayuquan de Shixian Tujing [How to Distribute "Speakers" to the Peasants: Brief Discussion on Ways to Realize the Peasants' Equal Rights to Speech]. *Xinwen Jizhe*(1), 36–8.

Li, Z. (2005). Cong "Cunmu" Tanqi [A Talk Started with "Title Retained"]. In S. Chen and C. Li (Eds.), *Shengming de Kaihua: Ba Jin Yanjiu Jikan Juanyi [Blossom of Life: Collective Research on Ba Jin Volume I]*. Shanghai: Wenhui Publishing House.

Li, Z. (2008). *The Past Revisited: Popular Memory of the Cultural Revolution in Contemporary China*. (PhD.), Northwestern University, Evanston.
Liang, J. (1984). *Zhongguo Xinwen Ye Shi: Gudai Zhi 1949 Nian [History of Chinese Journalism: From Ancient Times to 1949]*. Nanning: Guangxi People's Press.
Liebman, B. L. (2011). Changing Media, Changing Courts. In S. L. Shirk (Ed.), *Changing Media, Changing China*. Oxford: Oxford University Press.
Lin, F. (2008). *Turning Gray: Transition of Political Communication in China, 1978–2008*. (PhD), The University of Chicago, Ann Arbour.
Lin, H. (2004). *Wei Wancheng de Lishi: Zhongguo Xinwen Gaige Qianyan [Unfinished History: Front of the Journalism Reform in China]*. Shanghai: Fudan University Press.
Liu, B. (1990). *Liu Binyan Zizhuan [Autobiography of Liu Binyan]*. Taipei: China Times Publishing Company.
Liu, J. (1998). *Gonghe Minzhu Xianzheng: Ziyou Zhuyi Sixiang Yanjiu [Republic, Democracy, Constitutional Rule: Study on Liberal Thoughts]*. Shanghai: Sanlian.
Liu, J. (2005). *Zhongguo Xinwen Tongshi [History of Chinese Journalism]* (2 ed.). Wuhan: Wuhan University Press.
Liu, J. (2008). Bo Yu Jie: Shenchu Nide Shetai Kongkong Dangdang [Refuting Yu Jie: Show Your Coated Tongue, Empty]. Retrieved February 16, 2012, from www.ftchinese.com/story/001022870.
Liu, S., and Li, B. (2009, June 10). Diaocha Cheng Bacheng Wangyou Renwei Diannao Zhuang Guolv Ruanjian Qinfan Yinsi [Eighty Percents Netizens Believe Installation of Filtering Software Violate Their Privacy], p. A42. Retrieved from epaper.jinghua.cn/html/2009-06/10/node_43.htm.
Liu, W. (2003). Dushilei Baozhi Zhuxuanlv Baodao de Chuangxin [Innovation of Mainstream Reportage]. *China Journalists*(10), 27–9.
Liu, W. (2006). Zuo Jianshexing de Jiandu Yunlun—Huaxi Dushibao Yulun Jiandu de Shijian yu Duice [Be Constructive in Media Surveillance: Huaxi City Newspaper's Strategies and Practice in Media Surveillance]. Retrieved October 11, 2011, from www.360doc.com/content/09/0511/15/111008_3458108.shtml.
Liu, W. (2007). Transparency Key to Public Faith. Retrieved November 15, 2010, from www.chinadaily.com.cn/china/2007-07/16/content_5435353.htm.
Liu, Y. (2011, August 17). Wangyangbulao Qianchezhijian, Zhongguo Gaotie Quanmian Jiangsu [China High-speed Trains Slow Down for Previous Accidents]. *Huashang Bao*, p. B2.
Liu, Y., and Cai, Q. (2010). 2008 nian guangbo guanggao jingying gaikuang. In B. Cui (Ed.), *Report on Development of China's Media Industry (2009)*. Beijing: Social Sciences Academic Press (China).
Liu, Z. (2009). Nashi Fuyou Huoli de Niandai [That Was a Dynamic Age], *Jingji Guancha Bao [The Economic Oberser Newspaper]*. Retrieved from book.ifeng.com/special/dushuwujinqu/200908/0821_7799_1314005_4.shtml.
Liu, Z. (2010). Aiyuan Jiaozhi de Wangshi: Hu Sheng Jishi [Past Interwined with Love and Hate: Hu Sheng in Memory]. *Du Shu*(12), 96–105.
Lo, V. I., and Tian, X. (2009). *Law for Foreign Business and Investment in China*. Abingdon: Routledge.
Louden, R. B. (2011). *Kant's Human Being:Essays on His Theory of Human Nature*. Oxford: Oxford University Press.
Louw, E. (2010). *The Media and Political Process* (2 ed.). London: SAGE Publication Ltd.
Lu, X. Ritual, Television, and State Ideology: Rereading CCTV's 2006 Spring Festival Gala. In Y. Zhu and C. Berry (Eds.), *TV China* (pp. 111–28). Bloomington: Indiana University Press.
Lu, X., and Zhao, Y. (2010). Zhongguo de Xiandaixing, Dazhong Chuanmei yu Gonggongxing de Chonggou [Reconstruction of China's Modernity, Public Media and Their Public Nature]. *Chuanbo Yu Shehui Xuekan*(12), 1–24.
Lubman, S. B. (1999). *Bird in a Cage: Legal Reform in China After Mao*. Stanford: Stanford University Press.
Luo, Y., Zhang, J., and Shan, B. (2005). *Zhongguo Meiti Fazhan Yanjiu Baogao [Report on the Development of China's Media]*. Wuhan: Wuhan University Press.

Luo, Z. (2010). Zhongfang Duncu Meifang Zhengque Kandai Zhongguo Xinwen Ziyou Zhuangkuang [China Urges the United States to Hold Correct View on China's Press Freedom Status]. Retrieved May 20, 2011, from news.xinhuanet.com/world/2010-05/07/c_1279935. htm.
Mansfield, N. (2000). *Subjectivity: Theories of the Self from Freud to Haraway* New York: New York University Press.
Marshall Cavendish Corporation. (2010). *Sex and Society* (Vol. 1). Kuala Lumpur: Marshall Cavendish Reference.
Marx, K. (1967). *Writings Of The Young Marx On Philosophy And Society* (L. D. Easton and K. H. Guddat, Trans. 1997 ed.). Indianapolis: Hackett Publishing Company, Inc.
Maslen, G. (2007). Chinese Students to Dominate World Market. Retrieved June 23, 2010, from www.universityworldnews.com/article.php?story=20071101150549773.
Maurer, H., Balke, T., Kappe, F., Kulathuramaiyer, N., Weber, S., and Zaka, B. (2007). Report on Dangers and Opportunities Posed by Large Search Engines, Particularly Google. Graz: Graz University of Technology.
McConnell, T. C. (1981). Moral Blackmail. *Ethics, 91*(July), 544–67.
McDonald, A. (2006). What Hope for Freedom of Information in the UK? In C. Hood and D. Heald (Eds.), *Transparency: The Key to Better Governance?* (pp. 127–44). Oxford: Oxford University Press.
McLaren, M. A. (2013). Feminism, Foucault, and Globalized Subjectivity. In R. W. Tafarodi (Ed.), *Subjectivity in the Twenty-First Century: Psychological, Sociological, and Political Perspectives* (pp. 210–44): Cambridge University Press.
McNally, C. A. (2007). China's Capitalist Transition: the Making of a New Variety of Capitalism. In L. Mjoset and T. H. Claus (Eds.), *Capitalisms Compared* (Vol. 24, pp. 177–204). Oxford: Elsevier Ltd.
McNally, C. A. (2008a). *China's Emergent Political Economy: Capitalism in the Dragon's Lair*. Abingdon: Routledge.
McNally, C. A. (2008b). Reflections on Capitalism and China's Emergent Political Economy. In C. A. McNally (Ed.), *China's Emergent Political Economy: Capitalism in the Dragon's Lair*. Abingdon: Routledge.
Melton, O., and Pillsbury, A. (2005). Get a (Non-teaching) Job: Workin' for the Man. In A. Pillsbury (Ed.), *The Insider's Guide to Beijing 2005–2006* (Second ed., pp. 585–7). Beijing: True Run Media, Inc.
Mendonça, M., and Kanungo, R. N. (2007). *Ethical Leadership*. Berkshire: Open University Press.
Mente, B. D. (2012). *China Understanding and Dealing with the Chinese Way of Doing Business!*. Essex: Phoenix Books and Publishers.
Merrill, J. C., Gade, P. J., and Blevens, F. R. (2008). *Twilight of Press Freedom: The Rise of People's Journalism*. Mahwah: Lawrence Erlbaum Associates, Inc.
Metzinger, T. (2004). *Being No One: The Self-model Theory of Subjectivity*. Cambridge: The MIT Press.
Miaozi. (2009). Zhongguo Guanyuan Fouren Cunzai Xinwen Shencha Zhidu [Chinese Officials Denied Existence of Censorship System]. Retrieved August 5, 2010, from www.dw-world.de/dw/article/0,,4801458,00.html.
Milligan-Whyte, J., and Min, D. (2010). Consensus Building in China and America Retrieved 8th May, 2011, from english.people.com.cn/90001/90780/91342/6917450.html.
Mills, C. W. (2000). *The Power Elite* (Second ed.). Oxford: Oxford University Press.
Moeller, S. D., Melki, J., Lorente, R., Bond, M., and Cutler, J. (2006). *Openness and Accountability: A Study of Transparency in Global Media Outlets*. College Park: International Centre for Media and Public Agenda.
Mommsen, W. J., and Steinberg, M. (1984). *Max Weber and German Politics, 1890–1920*. Chicago: The University of Chicago Press.
Montague, R. (2010). *Live for Today! Plan for Tomorrow*. Victoria: Trafford Publishing.
Mosco, V. (1996). *The Political Economy of Communication* (2009 ed.). London: SAGE Publications Ltd.

Mueller, M., and Tan, Z. (1997). *China in the Information Age: Telecommunications and the Dilemmas of Reform*. Westport: Praeger Publishers.
Mulgan, R. (2000). "Accountability": An Ever-Expanding Concept? *Public Administration 78*(3), 555–73.
Muncaster, P. (2012). Chinese Social Network to Recruit In-House Censor: Job Ad for "Monitoring Editor" Points to Web Crackdown. Retrieved June 25, 2012, from theregister.co.uk/2012/05/22/sina_censor_job_ad/.
Neuhouser, F. (1990). *Fichte's Theory of Subjectivity*. New York: Cambridge University Press.
Ngo, T.-W. (2009). *Rent Seeking in China*. New York: Routledge.
NG'Weno, H. (1978). All Freedom is at Stake. In P. C. Horton (Ed.), *The Third World and Press Freedom* (pp. 127–34). New York: Praeger Publishers.
Nikoltchev, S. (2004). *Political Debate and the Role of the Media: the Fragility of Free Speech*. Strasburg: European Audiovisual Observatory.
Nordenstreng, K. (2011). Free Flow Doctrine in Golobal Media Policy. In R. Mansell and M. Raboy (Eds.), *The Handbook of Global Media and Communication Policy* (pp. 79–94). West Sussex: Blackwell Publishing Ltd.
Norris, P. (Ed.). (2010). *Public Sentinel: News Media and Governance Reform*. Washington D.C.: World Bank.
NSB. (1980). Public Report on the Implementation of the 1979 Plan of National Economy. Beijing: National Statitics Bureau.
Oakes, T. Building a Southern Dynamo: Guizhou and State Power. In D. S. G. Goodman (Ed.), *China's Campaign to "Open Up the West": National, Provincial, and Local Perspectives* (pp. 153–73). Cambridge: Cambridge University Press.
OECD. (1999). *Environment in the Transition to a Market Economy: Progress in Central and Eastern Europe and the New Independent States*. Paris: OECD Publishing.
Olesen, T. (2011). *Power and Transnational Activism*. Abingdon: Routledge.
Oliver, R. W. (2004). *What Is Transparency?* Columbus: The McGraw-Hill Companies, Inc.
O'Neill, O. (2006). Transparency and the Ethics of Communication. In C. Hood and D. Heald (Eds.), *Transparency: The Key to Better Governance?* New York: Oxford University Press.
Onyegam, S. A. (2006). *Historical Comparative Case Study of Emerging Hegemonic Behavior: Perspectives on the People's Republic of China*. Little Rock: University of Arkansas Press.
Palermo, P. F. (1978). *Lincoln Steffens*. New York: Twayne Publishers.
Palmer, J. (2000). *Spinning into Control: News Values and Source Strategies* London: Leicester University Press.
Pan, P. P. (2009). *Out of Mao's Shadow: The Struggle for the Soul of a New China* (II ed.). New York: Simon and Schuster Paperbacks.
Pan, Z. (2005). Media Change through Bounded Innovations: Journalism in China's Media Reforms. In A. Romano and M. Bromley (Eds.), *Journalism and Democracy in Asia* (pp. 96–107). London: Routledge.
Pan, Z., and Chan, J. M. (2003). Shifting Journalistic Paradigms: How China's Journalists Assess "Media Exemplars." *Communication Research, 30*(6), 649–82.
Pang, Y. (2001). *Ye Shengtao he Tade Jiaren [Ye Shengtao and His Family]*. Shenyang: Chunfeng Wenyi Chubanshe.
Park, M.-J., and Curran, J. (2000). *De-Westernizing Media Studies*. London: Routledge.
Pearson, M., and Polden, M. (2011). *The Journalist's Guide to Media Law*. Crows Nest: Allen and Unwin.
Peerenboom, R. P. (2002). *China's Long March toward Rule of Law*. Cambridge: Cambridge University Press.
Pei, M. (1998). *From Reform to Revolution: The Demise of Communism in China and the Soviet Union*. Cambridge: Harvard University Press.
Pepper, S. (1991). The KMT-CCP Conflict, 1945–1949. In L. E. Eastman, J. Ch'en, S. Pepper and L. P. V. Slyke (Eds.), *The Nationalist Era in China, 1927–1949* (pp. 291–356). Cambridge: Cambridge University Press.
Pepper, S. (1999). *Civil War in China: The Political Struggle, 1945–1949*. Oxford: Rowman and Littlefield Publishers, Inc.

Petersen, K. (1999). Censorship! Or Is It? In A. C. Hutchinson and K. Petersen (Eds.), *Interpreting Censorship in Canada* (pp. 3–18). Toronto: University of Toronto Press Inc.

Philo, G., and Miller, D. (Eds.). (2001). *Market Killing: What the Free Market Does and What Social Scientists Can Do About It*. Harlow: Longman.

Picard, R. G. (2007). A Media Management Framework for China. In M. Kops and S. Ollig (Eds.), *Internationalization of the Chinese TV Sector* (pp. 109–22). Berlin: LIT Verlag Münster.

Power, M. (1997). *The Audit Society: Rituals of Verification*. Oxford: Oxford University Press.

Qian, G., and Bandurski, D. (2011). China's Emerging Public Sphere: The Impact of Media Commercialization, Professionalism and the Internet in an Era of Transition. In S. L. Shirk (Ed.), *Changing Media, Changing China* (pp. 38–76). Oxford: Oxford University Press.

Qiu, J. (2013, October 15). Zhaopu Shufa Zuopin Paichu 40 Wanyuan, Zicheng Lianshufa Yi 30 Nian [Zhaopu's Calligraphy Sold for 400,000 Yuan at Auction, He Claims 30 Years of Experience in Calligraphy]. *Chengdu Shangbao [Chengdu Business News]*.

Qu, J. (2011). Xinwen Chuban Zongshu: Jiaqiang Xinwen Caibian Guifan, Yanfang Xujia Shishi Baodao [GAPP: Strengthen Standards of News Collection and Editing, Prevent Fake and False News]. Retrieved June 11, 2012, from news.xinhuanet.com/legal/2011-11/10/c_111158795.htm.

Quick, M. C. (2003). *World Press Encyclopedia: A*. Florence: Gale.

Quinn, E. (2006). *A Dictionary of Literary and Thematic Terms*. New York: Infobase Publishing.

Ragin, C. C. (1987). *The Comparative Method: Moving beyond Qualitative and Quantitative Strategies*. Berkeley: University of California Press.

Randall, D. (2000). *Universal Journalist* (2nd ed.). Kenwyn: The University of Cape Town Press Ltd.

Rein, S. (2012). *The End of Cheap China: Economic and Cultural Trends That Will Disrupt the World*. Hoboken: John Wiley and Sons.

Ren, J., and Liang, L. (1999). *Gongheguo Jigou Gaige yu Bianqian [The Institutional Reform and Changes of the People's Republic]*. Beijing: Sino-Culture Press.

Ren, K. (2011). Xi'an Ditie Zhantai Yi Pingbimen Boli Turan Baolie, Yuanyin Buming [A Glass Safety Door at the Platform of the Subway in Xi'an Cracked. Cause Remains Unknown]. Retrieved December 15, 2011, from news.hsw.cn/system/2011/09/27/051114552.shtml.

Ren, W. (2010, October 25). Woguo Gongmin Xiangyou Yanlun Chuban Ziyou Shi Buzheng de Shishi [It Is an Undisputable Fact That Our Citizens Enjoy Rights to Free Speech and Publication], *People's Daily*, p. 11. Retrieved from politics.people.com.cn/GB/30178/13051097.html.

Reporters Without Borders. (2009). Sixty Years of News Media and Censorship. Retrieved May 30, 2010, from en.rsf.org/spip.php?page=article&id_article=34630.

Ritzer, G. (2008). *Sociological Theory*. New York: McGraw Hill.

Robison, R., and Goodman, D. S. (1996). The New Rich in Asia: Economic Development, Social Status and Political Consciousness. In D. S. Goodman and R. Robison (Eds.), *The New Rich in Asia: Mobile Phones, McDonald's and Middle Class Revolution* (pp. 1–18). Abingdon: Routledge.

Rodan, G. (2004). *Transparency and Authoritorian Rule in Southeast Asia*. London: Routledge Curzon.

Rollins, P. C. (2003). *The Columbia Companion to American History on Film: How the Movies Have Portrayed the American Past*. New York: Columbia University Press.

Rose, M. A. (1978). *Reading the Young Marx and Engels: Poetry, Parody, and the Censor*. Totowa: Rowman and Littlefield.

Rosinger, L. K. (1945). *China's Crisis*. New York: Alfred A. Knopf.

Russell, N. (2006). *Morals and the Media: Ethics in Canadian Journalism*. Vancouver: University of British Columbia Press.

Saich, T. (2006). China in 2005: Hu's in Charge. *Asian Survey*, 46(1), 37–48.

Schiller, H. (2013). *Information Inequality: The Deepening Social Crisis in America*. Abingdon: Routledge.

Schilpp, P. A. (Ed.). (1968). *The Philosophy of C. I. Lewis*. Chicago: Open Court.
Schneider, B. R., and Maxfield, S. (1997). Business, the State and Economic Performance in Developing Countries. In S. Maxfield and B. R. Schneider (Eds.), *Business and the State in Developing Countries* (pp. 3–35). Ithaca: Cornell University Press.
Scotton, J. F. (2010). Xinhua: The Voice of the Party. In J. F. Scotton and W. A. Hachten (Eds.), *New Media for a New China* (pp. 115–27). Chichester: John Wiley and Sons Ltd.
Shang, D. (1990). *Huang Yanpei* (2 ed.). Beijing: The People's Press.
Shanghai Culture Yearbook Compiling Committee. (2007). *Shanghai Culture Yearbook*. Beijing: Encyclopedia of China Publishing House.
Shao, W. (1994). *Henan Shengzhi: Wujia Zhi*. Zhengzhou: Henan People's Press.
Shaw, Y.-m. (1988). *Changes and Continuities in Chinese Communism: The economy, society, and technology*. Boulder: Westview Press.
Shibowang. (2010). Tengxun Shibo Zhanluo Jiexiao, Jiang Dazao Quanqiu Zuida Shibo Wangluo Shequ [Tencent-Expo Strategic Ties will Create the Biggest Online Expo Community in the World]. Retrieved May 30, 2012, from www.expo2010.cn/a/20091030/000035.htm.
Shih, C.-y., and Chang, C.-h. (1936). *The Chinese Year Book, Part II*. Shanghai: The Commercial Press, Limited.
Shirk, S. L. (1993). *The Political Logic of Economic Reform in China*. Berkeley: University of California Press.
Shirk, S. L. (2007). *China: Fragile Superpower*. Oxford: Oxford University Press.
Shirk, S. L. (2011). Changing Media, Changing China. In S. L. Shirk (Ed.), *Changing Media, Changing China* (pp. 1–37). Oxford: Oxford University Press.
Shrader-Frechette, K. (1991). *Risk and Rationality: Philosophical Foundations for Populist Reforms*. Berkeley: University of California Press.
Silverman, C., and Jarvis, J. (2009). *Regret the Error: How Media Mistakes Pollute the Press and Imperil Free Speech*. New York: Sterling Publishing Co., Inc.
Sleeboom-Faulkner, M. (2007). *The Chinese Academy of Social Sciences (CASS): Shaping the Reforms, Academia and China*. Leiden: Koniklijke Brill NV.
SMD. (2011). Nangfang Dushibao Jianjie [Brief Introduction to the SMD]. Retrieved February 20, 2012, from g2.oeeee.com/index.php?m=Esindex&a=intro&.
Smith, A. E. (1901). *New Outlook* (Vol. 68). New York: Outlook Publishing Company
Soley, L., and Feldner, S. B. (2006). Transparency in Communication An Examination of Communication Journals' Conflicts-of-Interest Policies. *Journal of Communication Inquiry*, 30(3), 209–28.
Song, C., and Zhu, J. (1988). *Zhongguo Gongchandang Cidian [Dictionary of the Chinese Communist Party]*. Changchun: Jilin Wenshi Chubanshe.
Song, R. (2006). *Christianity and Liberal Society*. Oxford: Oxford University Press.
Sorman, G. (2010). *Empire of Lies: The Truth about China in the Twenty-First Century*. New York: Encounter Books.
Sparks, C., and Reading, A. (1998). *Communism, Capitalism, and the Mass Media*. London: SAGE Publications Ltd.
Stasavage, D. (2006). Does Transparency Make a Difference? The Example of the European Council of Ministers. In C. Hood and D. Heald (Eds.), *Transparency: The Key to Better Governance?* (pp. 165–82). Oxford: Oxford University Press.
Steele, P. (1999). *Censorship*. London: Evans Brothers Limited.
Sterling, C. H. (2009). *Encyclopedia of Journalism* (Vol. 1). Thousand Oaks: SAGE Publications, Inc.
Stockmann, D. (2011). What Kind of Information Does the Public Demand? Getting the News during the 2005 Anti-Japanese Protests. In S. L. Shirk (Ed.), *Changing Media, Changing China* (pp. 175–201). New York: Oxford University Press.
Stockmann, D. (2013). *Media Commercialization and Authoritarian Rule in China*. Cambridge: Cambridge University Press.
Su, N. (2012). Jinri Zaobao Touban Kandeng Nubing Xuexi Shibada Jingshen Baipaizhao. Retrieved October 11, 2013, from media.people.com.cn/n/2012/1118/c40606-19613436.html.

Sun, P. (2004). *Dangdai Zhongguo Xinwen Gaige [Reform of Journalism in Contemporary China]*. Beijing: The People's Press.
Sun, W. (2002). *Leaving China: Media, Migration, and Transnational Imagination*. Lanham: Rowman and Littlefield Publishers, Inc.
Sun, W. (2008a). The Curse of the Everyday: Politics of Representation and New Social Semiotics in Post-Socialist China. In K. Sen and T. Lee (Eds.), *Political Regimes and the Media in Asia* (pp. 31–48).
Sun, W. (2008b). Sexuality, Domesticity, and Citizenship in the Chinese Media: Man's Needs, Maid's Rights. *Information*, 22(2), 221–44.
Sun, W. (2009a). Suzhi on the Move: Body, Place and Power. *Positions*, 17(3), 617–42.
Sun, W. (2009b). *Maid in China: Media, Morality, and the Culture Politics of Boundaries*. Abingdon: Routledge.
Sun, W. (2012). Localizing Chinese Media: A Geographic Turn in Media and Communication Research. In W. Sun and J. Chio (Eds.), *Mapping Media in China: Region, Province, Locality* (pp. 13–28). Abingdon: Routledge.
Sun, W. (2013). Inequality and Culture: A New Pathway to Understanding Social Inequality. In W. Sun and Y. Guo (Eds.), *Unequal China: The Political Economy and Cultural Politics of Inequality* (pp. 27–42). Abingdon: Rougtledge.
Sun, X., and Michel, E. C. (2001). *An Orchestra of Voices: Making the Argument for Greater Speech and Press*. West Port: Praeger Publishers.
Sun, Y. (2002). *Baoye Zhongguo [Journalism in China]*. Beijing: Sanxia Publishing House.
Sun, Y. (2004). *Corruption and Market in Contemporary China*. Ithaca: Cornell University Press.
Sylvie, G., Hollifield, C. A., and Sohn, A. B. (2009). *Media Management: A Casebook Approach*. New York: Taylor and Francis Group, LLC.
Tamanaha, B. Z. (2004). *On the Rule of Law: History, Politics, Theory*. Cambridge: Cambridge University Press.
Tang, J., and Zhang, X. (2004). *Ba Jin de Yige Shiji [Ba Jin's Century]*. Chengdu: Sichuan Wenyi Chubanshe.
Tang, W. (2005). *Public Opinion and Political Change in China*. Stanford: Stanford University Press.
Tang, X., and Zhuo, Y. (2009). 2008 Nian Baoye Guanjianci [Key Words for the Press in 2008]. In B. Cui (Ed.), *Report on the Development of China's Media Industry (2009)* (pp. 62–71). Beijing: Social Sciences Academic Press (China).
Tapscott, D., and Williams, A. D. (2010). *MacroWikinomics*. London: Atlantic Books.
Telegraph, T. (2008). China Fakes Reports from Space. Retrieved May 30, 2012, from www.telegraph.co.uk/news/worldnews/asia/china/3082804/China-fakes-reports-from-space.html.
Tilt, B., and Xiao, Q. (2010). Media Coverage of Environmental Pollution in the People's Republic of China: Responsibility, Cover-up and State Control. *Media, Culture and Society*, 32(2), 225–45.
Tomkins, A. (2002). In Defense of the Constitution. *Oxford Journal of Legal Studies*, 22(1), 157–75.
Tong, B., and Lin, H. (2001). *Ershi shiji zhongguo xinwenxue yu chuanboxue: lilun xinwenxue juan [Chinese Journalism and Communication: Theoretical Journalism]*. Shanghai: Fudan University Press.
Tong, J. (2011). *Investigative Journalism in China*. London: The Continuum International Publishing Group.
Tse, T. K.-C., and Lee, J. C.-K. (2003). China: Defending Socialism with Chinese Characteristics. In M. Williams and G. Humphrys (Eds.), *Citizenship Education and Lifelong Learning: Power and Place* (pp. 103–18). Hauppauge: Nova Science Publishers, Inc.
Tsetsura, K. (2009). The Development of Public Relations in Russia: A Geopolitical Approach. In K. Sriramesh and D. Vercic (Eds.), *The Global Public Relations Handbook: Theory, Research and Practice* (Revised Edition) (pp. 655–76). New York: Routledge.
Tsou, T. (1986). *The Cultural Revolution and Post-Mao Reforms: A Historical Perspective*. Chicago: The University of Chicago Press.
Tubilewicz, C. (2006). *Critical Issues in Contemporary China*. Abingdon: Routledge.

UNESCO Institute for Statistics. (2006). *Global Education Digest 2006: Comparing Education Statistics Across the World*. Montreal: UNESCO.
Unger, J. (1991). Whither China? Yang Xiguang, Red Capitalists, and the Social Turmoil of the Cultural Revolution. *Modern China, 17*(1).
Van Dijk, T. A. (1992). Discourse and the Denial of Racism. *Discourse and Society, 3*(1), 87–118.
Varghese, N. V. (2008). *Globalization of Higher Education and Cross-border Student Mobility*. Paris: International Institute for Educational Planning.
Verbik, L., and Lasanowski, V. (2007). *International Student Mobility: Patterns and Trends*. London: The Observatory on Borderless Higher Education.
Vernon, R. (1998). Beyond the Harm Principle: Mill and Censorship. In E. J. Eisenach (Ed.), *Mill and the Moral Character of Liberalism* (pp. 115–30). University Park: The Pennsylvania State University Press.
VOA. (2011). Dalian PX Xiangmu Fuchan, Guangfang Beizhi Chu'erfan'er [Dalian PX Project Restored, The Government Promise Repealed]. Retrieved June 8, 2012, from www.voachinese.com/content/article-20111231-dalian-px-136472918/792448.html.
Walter, C., and Howie, F. (2012). *Red Capitalism: The Fragile Financial Foundation of China's Extraordinary Rise* (2nd ed.). Singapore: John Wiley and Sons Singapore Pte. Ltd.
Wang, H. (1997). *Wang Hui Zixuanji [Self-Selected Works of Wang Hui]*. Nanning: Guangxi Normal University Press.
Wang, H. (1998). Contemporary Chinese Thought and the Question of Modernity. *Wenyi Zhengming*(6), 7–22.
Wang, H. (2009). *The End of Revolution*. London: Verso.
Wang, H. (2010). *The Chinese Dream: The Rise of the World's Largest Middle Class and What It Means to You*. Brande: Bestseller Press.
Wang, H. (2011a). Zaiwen "Shenme de Pingdeng"? Lun Dangdai Zhengzhi Xingshi yu Shehui Xingshi de Tuojie [Revisiting "Equality of What"?—On the Disjuncture of Contemporary Political Forms and Social Forms]. *Beijing Cultural Review*(5), 66–81.
Wang, H. (2011b). Shangshengqi de Maodun, Tixixing Weiji yu Biange Fangxiang [Contradictions, Systematic Crisis and Direction of Reform in the Rise Period]. *Guowai Lilun Dongtai*(12), 80–89.
Wang, H., and Chen, Y. (2005). *Wenhua yu Gonggongxing [Culture and Public Sphere]*. Beijing: Shenghuo Dushu Xinzhi Sanlian Shudian.
Wang, H., and Xu, Y. (2006). "Qu Zhengzhi Hua de Zhengzhi" yu Dazhong Chuanmei de Gonggongxing ["Depoliticized Politics and the Public Nature of Public Media]. *Gansu Social Sciences*(4), 235–48.
Wang, J. (2010). *Brand New China: Advertising, Media, and Commercial Culture*. Cambridge: Harvard University Press.
Wang, J., and Wang, W. (2006). Shilun Dangbao yu Zhuliu Meiti [Tentative Talk on Party Newspapers and Mainstream Media] *Renmin Gongheguo Dangbao Luntan [ Party Newspapers Forum of the People's Republic]* (pp. 259–63). Beijing: Zhongguo Chuanmei Daxue Chubanshe.
Wang, L. (2008). Xifang yu Zhongguo de Xinwen Ziyou [Press Freedom in the West and China]. *Xinwen Yu Xiezuo*(6), 34–5.
Wang, S. (2008). *Baokan Shendu [Review Reading of Newspapers and Publications]*. Guangzhou: Guangdong Renmin Chubanshe.
Wang, S., and Wang, L. (2012, November 23). Wei Baipai Shijian Daoqian: Yige Lishixing Jinbu [Apologizing for Photo Orchestration: A Historical Progress], *Jiancha Daily*, p. 5. Retrieved from newspaper.jcrb.com/html/2012-11/23/content_114027.htm.
Wang, T. (2011). Jinqi Xi'an Ditie Xiao Wenti Duo, Wangyou Baoliao Ditiezhan Boli Baolie [Xi'an Subway Troubled by Minor Problems Lately, Netizens Reported Cracked Glass in the Station]. Retrieved October 15, 2011, from news.cnwest.com/content/2011-09/28/content_5284978.htm.
Wang, W. (2011). *Zuowei Laodong de Chuanbo: Zhongguo Xinwen Jizhe Laodong Zhuangkuang Yanjiu [Communication as a Labour Job: A Survey of the Working Conditions of Chinese Journalists]*. Beijing: Communication University of China.

Wang, X. (2003). A Manifesto for Cultural Studies. In C. Wang (Ed.), *One China, Many Paths* (pp. 274–91). London: Verso.
Weil, R. (1996). *Red Cat, White Cat: China and the Contradictions of "Market Socialism."* New York: Monthly Review Press.
Weisberg, J. (2012). Hairy Eyeball: China's New Censorship Model. Retrieved June25, 2012, from www.slate.com/articles/newsandpolitics/thebigidea/2012/05/sinaweibohanhanandchi nesecensorshipbeijingsnewideasforcrackingdownondebateanddissent.html.
Wen, J. (2010). Jianshe Fuwuxing Zhengfu: Chuangzao Tiaojian Rang Renmin Piping Jiandu Zhengfu [Constructing a Government of Service Type: Creating Conditions for the People to Criticize and Oversee the Government]. Retrieved October 11, 2010, from news.xinhuanet.com/politics/2010-03/05/content_13102646.htm.
Wennuanyangguang. (2009). "Kaitianchuang" Shijian Xianwei Renzhi de Benzhi—Zhizao Jia Fanduipai [Hardly Known Nature of the "Skylight Window" Drama: To Create False Opposition]. Retrieved September 20, 2010.
Whale, J. (1977). *The Politics of the Media*. Manchester: Manchester University Press.
White, L. T. (1999). *Local Causes of China's Intellectual, Legal, and Governmental Reforms*. Armonk: M.E. Sharpe, Inc.
Wolfsfeld, G. (2004). *Media and the Path to Peace*. Cambridge: Cambridge University Press.
Wu, F. (2011). Baijia Meiti Kai Tianchuang de Yuanyin he Yingxiang [Causes and Effects of the Skylight Windows Opened by A Hundred Newsprints]. Retrieved October 10, 2011, from www.epochtimes.com/gb/11/8/9/n3338870.htm%E4%BC%8D%E5%87%A1-%E7%99%BE%E5%AE%B6%E5%AA%92%E4%BD%93%E5%BC%80%E5%A4%A9%E7%AA%97%E7%9A%84%E5%8E%9F%E5%9B%A0%E5%92%8C%E5%BD%B1%E5%93%8D.
Wu, G. (2000). One Head, Many Mouths: Diversifying Press Structure in Reform China. In C.-C. Lee (Ed.), *Power, Money, and Media: Communication Patterns and Bureaucratic Control in Cultural China* (pp. 45–67). Evanston: Northwestern University Press.
Wu, G. (2008). Yushi Jujin, Gaijin Xinwen Xuanchuan [Keep Pace with the Times, Improve Jounalism and Propaganda]. *Xinwen Jizhe*(8), 4–6.
Wu, X., and Gao, H. (2010). Cong guanggao shuju kan zhongguo chuanmei chanye 30 nian. In B. Cui (Ed.), *Report on China's Media Industry (2009)* (pp. 400–10). Beijing: Social Sciences Academic Press (China).
Wu, X., and Jin, G. (2004). *Zhongguo chuanmei jingji yanjiu 1949–2004*. Shanghai: Fudan University Press.
Wu, Z. (2005). Dui Jianli Guangbo Dianshi Xin Tizhi de Sikao. *Beifang Chuanmei Yanjiu*(3).
Wu, Z. (2006). Lun youfa heyi tizhi de queli [On establishment of *youfa heyi*]. *Lishi dang'an*(3), 121–6.
Wulf, C. (2003). Religion and Rituals. In B. Qvarsell and C. Wulf (Eds.), *Culture and Education*. New York: Waxmann Verlag GmbH.
Xiao, Q. (2011). The Rise of Online Public Opinion and Its Political Impact. In S. L. Shirk (Ed.), *Changing Media, Changing China* (pp. 202–24). Oxford: Oxford University Press.
Xiao, Y. (2004). *Dalu Dangbao Jituanhua Fazhan zhi Yanjiu—Yi Renmin Ribao he Guangzhou Ribao Weili [Study on Conglomeration of the Official Newspapers in the Mainland: Case Studies on the People's Daily and Guangzhou Daily]*. (Master), National Chengchi University, Taipei.
Xiao, Y. (2005, September 9). Yulun Tongqing Sharenfan Wang Binyu Shige Weixian Xinhao [It Is a Dangerous Signal That Public Opinion Sympathizes with Murderer Wang Binyu], *China Youth Daily*. Retrieved from news.sohu.com/20050909/n226909975.shtml.
Xie, B., and Gao, M. (2013). Sustaining China's Media Economy: Tackling Sensationalism and Three Dilemmas. In C. Andressen, A. R. Mubarak and X. Wang (Eds.), *Sustainable Development in China* (pp. 93–110). London: Routledge.
Xie, H., and Wen, J. (2000). *Zhongguo Xiaokang Zhi Lu*. Beijing: Zhongguo Tongji Chubanshe.
Xie, R. (2008). Huigu 2008, Zhongguo Meiti Ling Meiguo Meiti Guamu Xiangkan [Looking Back on 2008, Chinese Media Amazed American Media]. Retrieved May 25, 2012, from world.people.com.cn/GB/57507/8600726.html.

## Bibliography

Xinhua. (2004). Jiaqiang Guanban Fenli He Huazhuan Baokan Guanli [Strengthening Administration of the Division of Administration and Management and Transferred Newspapers and Periodicals]. Retrieved June 27, 2012, from www.people.com.cn/GB/paper79/12077/1087267.html.

Xinhua. (2009). Official Probed over "People-or-Party" Blunder. Retrieved January 2, 2011, from www.chinadaily.com.cn/china/2009-06/22/content_8309791.htm.

Xinhua. (2011). Guomin Jingji he Shehui Fazhan Di Shi'er Ge Wunian Guihua Gangyao (Quanwen) [The Twelfth Five-Year Plan of National Economy and Social Progress (Full Text)]. Retrieved May 26, 2012, from www.gov.cn/2011lh/content_1825838.htm.

Xinhuanet. (2008). Xinhuawang Xiang Wangyou de Zhixianxin [Apology Letter from Xinhuanet to Netizens]. Retrieved May 30, 2012, from news.xinhuanet.com/newscenter/2008-09/26/content_10117833.htm.

Xiong, Y. (1999). *History of Shanghai [Shanghai Tongshi]* (Vol. 14). Shanghai: Shanghai People's Press.

Xu, G. (2004). Jiang Zemin Xinwen Sixiang de Hexin Neirong [The Core Content of Jiang Zemin's Thought of Journalism]. *Xinwen Zhanxian*(2), 4–6.

Xu, J. (2006). *Zhongguo Guanggao Shi [History of Advertising in China]*. Beijing: Zhongguo Chuanmei Daxue Chubanshe.

Xu, J. (2010). Wangyi Shiyu Youxi Nianhui, Banshu Jiama Wangyou Jianguan Lidu [Netease Absent at the CGIAC, GAPP Tighens up Supervision over Online Games]. Retrieved January 7, 2012, from game.people.com.cn/GB/48644/48662/10815231.html.

Yang, F. (2009). The Style and Contents of China Government in Steering E-Government Construction and Implementation. In J. Tubtimhin and R. Pipe (Eds.), *Global E-Governance: Advancing E-Governance through Innovation and Leadership* (pp. 84–93). Amsterdam: IOS Press BV.

Yang, L. (2006). China Mulls Emergency Management Law. Retrieved January 10, 2010, from news.xinhuanet.com/english/2006-06/24/content_4742725.htm.

Yang, L. (2009). Yufang Zhiwu Fanzui Bixu Baozhang Meiti de Zhengdang Quanli [The Media's Justified Rights Must Be Ensured to Prevent Crime by Taking Advantage of Duty]. Retrieved September 24, 2011, from www.gy.yn.gov.cn/Article/sflt/fglt/200910/15856.html.

Yang, M. (2007). What Attracts Mainland Chinese Students to Australian Higher Education. *Studies in Learning, Evaluation, Innovation and Development*, 4(2), 1–12.

Yang, T. (2004). Zhongyang Guanzhu Yulun Jiandu [The CCP Central Committee Pay Close Attention to Media Supervision]. *Liaowang*(31), 11–3.

Yang, W. (2014). Xi Jinping Chuxi Zhongyang Zhengfa Gongzuo Huiyi: Jianchi Yan'ge Zhifa Gongzheng Sifa [Xi Jinping Attending the Central Political and Legal Commission Meeting: Adhering to Strict Law Enforcement and Judicial Justice]. Retrieved February 20, 2014, from news.xinhuanet.com/politics/2014-01/08/c_118887343.htm.

Yao, F. (1990). *Zhongguo Bianji Shi [the editorial history of China]*. Shanghai: Fudan University Press.

Yao, L. (2011). Zhongguo Baoye Guanggao: 2010Nian Huigu 2011Nian Zhanwan [Advertising on Chinese Newspapers: Look Back on 2010 and into 2011]. *Zhongguo Baoye*(3), 27–32.

Yick, J. K. S. (1995). *Making Urban Revolution in China: The CCP-GMD Struggle for Beiping-Tianjin 1945–1949*. Armonk: M.E. Sharpe, Inc.

Yin, R. K. (2003). *Case Study Research: Design and Methods*. Thousand Oaks, CA: SAGE Publications, Inc.

Young, S. (2002). *Beyond Rawls: An Analysis of the Concept of Political Liberalism*. Lanham, MD: University Press of America.

Yu, H., and Deng, Z. (2000). *Zhongguo dangdai guanggao shi*. Changsha: Hunan kexue jishu chubanshe.

Yu, P.-k. (1975). *Research Materials on Twentieth-Century China: An Annotated List of CCRM Publications*. Washington D.C.: Association of Research Libraries.

Yu, Y.-l. (1991). Change and Continuity in CCP's Power Structure Since its 13th National Congress: A "Line" Approach In R. H. Myers (Ed.), *Two Societies in Opposition: The*

*Republic of China and the People's Republic of China After Forty Years* (pp. 57–74): Hoover Press Publication.
Yu, Z. (2008). Zhongguo Banbu Xin Tiaoli, Waiguo Jizhe Caifang Bubi Guanfang Peitong [China Issued New Regulation, Foreign Journalists No Longer Need to be Officially Escorted When Collecting News]. Retrieved August 5, 2010, from www.zaobao.com/special/china/cnpol/pages1/cnpol081019.shtml.
Yuan, J. (2000). *Xinwen Meijie Tonglun [General Discussions on Journalism]*. Beijing: Beijing Guangbo Xueyuan Chubanshe.
Zeng, G. (2009, November 6). Weihu Jizhe Quanyi, Baozhang Jizhe Liyi [Protect the Journalists' Rights and Safeguard the Journalists' Interests]. *China Press and Publication Newspaper*.
Zhan, J. (2005). Jingti Meiti de "Shuangchong Fengjianhua" [Be Aware of the 'Double-Feudalization' of the Media]. *Qingnian Jizhe*(3), 7–9.
Zhan, J. (2007). To Enhance Social Progress by Journalist Legislation: Reflection on the Eighth Journalist Day. *Youth Journalists*(21), 35–7.
Zhang, B. (Ed.). (2005). *2005 Zhongguo Zhejiang*. Beijing: Wuzhou Chuanbo Chubanshe.
Zhang, G. (2003, December 28). Shenzhen Ni Lifa Guiding Jizhe Xiangyou Wuguocuo Heli Huaiyiquan [Shenzhen Intend to Legalize Journalists' Rights to Reasonable No-fault Suspicion], *Nanfang Dushibao*. Retrieved from qol.qdc.com.cn/xwkd_out.asp?code=8281.
Zhang, M. (2009). Wanqing baoren de geming jia fengqing [Revolution and romance of the journalists in late Qing dynasty]. *Caijing Magazine*, 253(26), 147.
Zhang, M. Y., and Stening, B. W. (2010). *China 2.0: The Transformation of an Emerging Superpower—And the New Opportunities*. Singapore: John Wiley and Sons (Asia) Pte. Ltd.
Zhang, N. (1992). A Conflict of Interests: Current Problems in Educational Reform In A. Watson (Ed.), *Economic Reform and Social Change in China* (1996 ed., pp. 144–70). Abingdon: Routledge.
Zhang, S. (2006). *The Impact of ELT on Ideology in China (1980–2000)*. Wuhan: The Mid-China Normal University Press.
Zhang, S., Tian, Z., and Chen, J. A. (Eds.). (1995) Kangri Zhanzheng Da Cidian [Grand Dictionary of the Anti-Japanese War]. Wuhan: Wuhan Chubanshe.
Zhang, X. (1996). *Jiang Jieshi Quanzhuan [Full Biography of Chiang Kai-Shek]*. Zhengzhou: Henan People's Press.
Zhang, X. (2007). *The Origins of the Modern Chinese Press: The Influence of the Protestant Missionary Press in Late Qing China*. Abingdon: Routledge.
Zhang, Y. (1986). *Xianzheng Luncong [Tribune on Constitutionalism]* (Vol. 1). Beijing: Qunzhong Chubanshe.
Zhang, Y. (2007, February 1). Dianshiju Zenme Guan? [How to Administrate TV Shows?], *Nanfang Zhoumo*.
Zhang, Y. (2010). *Fumian baodao bushi huai dongxi: zhongguo xinwen shijian zhong de zhenmingti*. Taipei: Showwe Information Co., Ltd.
Zhao, X., and Ding, Y. (1992). *Minmeng Shihua [History of the Democratic League]*. Beijing: China Social Sciences Press.
Zhao, X., and Shen, P. (1993). Some Reasons Why the Party Propaganda Failed This Time *Chinese Democracy and the Crisis of 1989: Chinese and American Reflections* (pp. 313–32): State of New York Press.
Zhao, Y. (1998). *Media, Market, and Democracy in China: Between the Party Line and the Bottom Line*. Champaign: University of Illinois Press.
Zhao, Y. (2000). From Commercialization to Conglomeration: The Transformation of the Chinese Press within the Orbit of the Party State. *Journal of Communication*, 50(2), 3–26.
Zhao, Y. (2001). Media and Elusive Democracy in China. *The Public*, 8(4), 21–44.
Zhao, Y. (2003). Enter the World: Neo-Liberalism, the Dream for a Strong Nation, and Chinese Press Discourse on the WTO. In C.-C. Lee (Ed.), (pp. 32–55). London: RoutledgeCurzon.
Zhao, Y. (2004a). The State, the Market, Media Control in China. In P. Thomas and Z. Nain (Eds.), *Who Owns the Media?: Global Trends and Local Resistances* (pp. 179–212). Penang: Southbound Sdn. Bhd.

Zhao, Y. (2004b). Underdogs, Lapdogs and Watchdogs: Journalists and the Public Sphere Problematic in China. In E. X. Gu and M. Goldman (Eds.), *Chinese Intellectuals between State and Market* (pp. 43–74). London: RoutledgeCurzon.

Zhao, Y. (2005). Who Wants Democracy and Does It Deliver Food? Communication and Power in a Globally Integrated China. In R. A. Hackett and Y. Zhao (Eds.), *Democratizing Global Media: One World, Many Struggles* (pp. 57–80). Lanham: Rowman and Littlefield Publishers, Inc.

Zhao, Y. (2008a). *Communication in China: Political Economy, Power, and Conflict*. Lanham: Rowman and Littlefield Publishers, Inc.

Zhao, Y. (2008b). Weishenme Jintian Women Dui Xifang Xinwen Keguanxing Shiwang? [Why We Are Dissappointed Today by the Objectivity of the Western Journalism?]. *Xinwen Daxue, 9*(2), 9–16.

Zhao, Y. (2010). *2010 China Radio and Television Year Book*. Beijing: Zhongguo Guangbo Dianshi Nianjian She.

Zhao, Y. (2011). "Qieting Men" yu Ziyou Zhuyi Xinwen Tizhi de Weiji ["Hacking-Gate" and the Crisis of the Liberal Journalism]. *Beijing Cultural Review* (5), 118–22.

Zhao, Y., and Gu, Z. (2010). Television in China: History, Political Economy, and Ideology. In J. Wasko (Ed.), *A Companion to Television* (pp. 521–39): Blackwell Publishing Ltd.

Zhao, Y., and Hu, Z. (2011). Jiazhi Chonggou: Zhongguo Chuanbo Zhutixing Tanxun [Reconstructing Values: Seeking Subjectivity in Chinese Communication]. Xiandai Chuanbo (2), 13–21.

Zhi, Y. (2005). *New Media Imperial: Brand, Capital and Industrialization in the Competitive Environment [xin chuanmei diguo: jingzheng geju xia de pingpai, ziben he chanyehua]*. Beijing: China Waterpower Press.

Zhong, P. (1997). *Dangdai Zhongguo de Xinwen Shiye [Journalism of Contempory China]* (Vol. 2). Beijing: Dangdai Zhongguo Chubanshe.

Zhong, P. (2003). Zhengzhi wenming yu xinwen lifa [Political Civilization and Construction of the Law of Journalism]. *Lingdao Wencui [Selected works of the leadership]*(12).

Zhou, K. X. (2009). *China's Long March to Freedom: Grassroots Modernization*. New Brunswick: Transaction Publishers.

Zhou, P. A. (2012). Chuli Baipai Xinwenren Juyou Huashidai Yiyi [Punishing the Journalists Who are Responsible for the Photo Orchestartion Saga is of Epoch-making Significance]. *Zhou Peng'an's Blog*. Retrieved November 4, 2013, from blog.ifeng.com/article/21288024.html.

Zhou, X. (2011, July 31). Dang Zhongguo Meiti Youle Kaitianchuang de Yongqi [When the Chinese Media Have the Courage to Open Skylights]. Retrieved November 10, 2013, from www.epochtimes.com/gb/11/7/31/n3330395.htm.

Zhou, Y. (2008). *Capitalizing China's Media Industry: The Installation of Capitalist Production in TV and Film Sectors*. Ann Arbor: ProQuest Information and Learning Company.

Zhou, Z. (2008, February 11). Baozhang Ziyou Buzai Fa [It Is Not Up to the Law to Ensure Freedom]. Retrieved from blog.sina.com.cn/s/blog_4bdb1fa001008ex2.html.

Zhu, X. (1998, December 25). 1998: Ziyou Zhuyi Xueli de Yanshuo [1998: Discourse on Theory of Liberalism], *Nanfang Zhoumo [Southern Weekend]*.

Zhu, X. (2006). *Shuzhai li de Geming [Revolution in the Study]*. Kunming: Yunnan People's Press.

Zhu, Z. (2011). Jiemi Zhongguo Shoufu Liang Wengen de Rudang Licheng [Uncover the Journey of China's Number One Rich Liang Wengen to Join the Party]. Retrieved March 12, 2012, from business.sohu.com/20110927/n320716484.shtml.

Zhuang, R. (1993). Yi "Jiubao" Yundong [Memory of the "Saving the Newspaper" Movement]. In Wenhui Bao Baoshi Yanjushi (Ed.), *Cong Fengyu Zhong Zoulai*. Shanghai: Wenhui Bao Chubanshe.

Zhuang, S. (2003). Ban Zhongguo Zuihao de Baozhi: Nanfang Dushi Bao Zhubian Liaotian Shilu [Making the Best Newspaper in China: An Interview with the Chief Editor of Nanfang Metroplis Daily]. Retrieved February 20, 2012, from news.sohu.com/54/93/news213299354.shtml.

Zittrain, J., and Palfrey, J. (2007). Introduction. In R. Deibert, J. Palfrey, R. Rohozinski and J. Zittrain (Eds.), *Access Denied: The Practice and Policy of Global Internet Filtering* (pp. 1–4). Cambridge: The MIT Press.

# Index

accountability, 12, 17, 19, 23, 24, 30, 31, 33, 44, 59, 80, 102, 150
*the Administrative Approval Law*, 22, 37
administrative board, 141
administrative regulations, 3, 36, 37, 38
AdWords, 11
Australia, 6, 7, 38
authoritarianism, ix

Ba Jin, 134–135
*Beijing Youth Daily* (BYD), 101
*bianweihui*, 112, 141
*bianzhi*, 115, 116, 117
blackmail of Enlightenment, 9
bribery, 18, 24, 48, 61, 63, 77
British Broadcasting Corporation (BBC), 5

Cable News Network (CNN), 5
capital elite, 71, 150, 155, 157, 158
capitalism, 155; agent of, 153, 154; with Chinese characteristics, 158; without democracy, 70
capitalist economic base, xix, 71, 73, 142, 143, 149
censorship, 3, 5, 6, 16, 18, 19, 29, 54, 59, 123, 127
censorship apparatus, 6, 7, 53, 57, 59, 71, 124, 130, 162
Central Organization Department, 117
Central Propaganda Department (CPD), 116

Central Publicity Department (CPD), 4, 29, 45, 55, 66, 104, 137
Chen Yun, 66
*China Business View* (CBV), 135, 136–137
China Central Television (CCTV), 43, 88, 118, 144, 151
China Writers Association, 41
*China Youth Daily* (CYD), 88
Chinese Communist Party (CCP), 4, 36, 37, 54, 55, 70, 79, 101, 107, 117, 123, 153
Chomsky, Noam, 17, 82, 142–143, 163
class antagonism, 13, 15, 89, 95
class containment, 13, 89, 95
commercialization, 101, 120, 125, 141, 145, 152, 153
communism, 7, 24
conglomeration, 4, 101, 108, 110, 112, 120, 152, 153
*Constitution of the Republic of China*, 131
consumerism, 82, 84, 89, 93, 109, 118, 125
contrarieties, 143, 154
control: agenda, 89; consensus on, 62, 139, 153; market, 16, 33, 44, 64, 80, 90, 125, 145, 150; political, 15, 78, 108, 145
corporate governance, 4, 39, 44, 85, 102, 109, 111, 113, 119, 152
corruption, 24, 30, 43, 48, 64, 77, 78, 80, 81, 97, 129, 140, 151
countering accusation, 57, 60–62

credibility, 17, 18, 32, 33, 41, 49, 59, 60, 77, 97, 102, 150
crisis of rationality, 10, 160
the Cultural Revolution, 67, 134, 135, 157

*dazibao*, 66
*Decree of Government Information Openness*, 3, 58
de-legitimization, 158
democracy, 5, 8, 10, 23, 57, 95, 120, 124, 127, 130, 138, 152
democratic management, 157
democratization, 25, 163
Deng Xiaoping, 48, 63, 70, 104, 157, 158
de-politicization, 13, 19, 89, 92, 93, 96, 118, 154
de-theorization, 154
developmentalism, 73, 150, 159
dictatorship, 97, 129, 130, 132, 145, 152, 157
dilemma: ethical, 99n3; identity, 90; market, 84; subjectivity, 90–96; survival, 84–90, 97
disenfranchise groups, 13, 15, 17, 22, 33, 45, 71, 89, 93, 145, 153, 154
disjuncture of representation, 23, 80, 143, 154, 156, 161

editorial independence, 41, 62
e-government, 3, 58, 74n4
elite politics, 4, 9, 17, 18, 50, 64, 71, 72, 80, 145, 149
e-media, 163
enterprise management, 103, 109
*Epochtimes*, 5
ethical values, 91
exploitation, 44, 149, 159

factor of production, 85, 87, 88, 117
fake news, 79
financial autonomy, 103, 104, 105, 153
foreign capital, 101, 114, 116
freedom of information, 6, 10, 58, 97, 149
freedom of speech, 8, 58, 68, 127, 130
free labor, 87, 115, 116, 117
free market, 61, 62, 81, 85, 90, 97, 116, 142, 143

General Administration of Press and Publication (GAPP), 2, 36, 38, 39
General Administration of Press, Publication, Radio, Film, and Television (GAPPRFT), 1, 47
Germany, 7, 11
Global Integrity and Public Radio International, 31
Golden Shield Project, 3
Google, 11
Great Firewall, 3
Green Dam Project, 3, 65–66
*Guangzhou Daily*, 104, 106, 109, 112
Guangzhou Daily Press Group, 108, 112, 113
*Guofeng Daily*, 126
Guomindang (GMD), 59, 63, 123, 126, 127, 129, 130

Habermas, Jürgen, 10, 12, 33, 92, 97, 152, 156, 161
harmonious society, 2, 29, 149, 159
hegemony, 124, 142, 158
Hong Kong, 5, 6, 38, 101
Hu, Jintao, 2, 70, 159
Huang, Yanpei, 127, 129, 130
*Huaxi Metropolis Daily* (HMD), 41, 58, 106

idealism, 9, 92, 96, 97, 162
ideological consensus, 21, 127, 132, 153, 160, 163
incrementalism, 7
information control, 3, 5, 35, 53, 78, 81, 123, 149
initial public offering (IPO), 101, 102
Iraqi War, xv, 10, 61, 62

Jiang, Jieshi (Chiang Kai-Shek), 126, 127, 129
Jiang, Zemin, 4, 29, 34, 70, 155
*Jinri Zaobao*, 79, 80, 81–82, 83, 84–85, 88
*Jujian Yundong*, 127–129, 130, 131, 138, 145, 163
justification problem, 53, 65, 70, 142, 150

labor market, 87, 115, 117
labor relationships, 9, 85, 86, 87, 109, 115, 139, 149

Law of Response to Emergencies (Draft), 162
legal framework, 67
legalism, 37, 69, 150
the Legislation Law, 37
liberal democracy, 5, 8, 16, 120
*Literary Review*, 133
Liu, Zaifu, 133, 134

malpractice, ix, x, xix, 18, 43, 77–78, 80, 81–83, 96–97, 99, 151, 153
management board, 112, 141
management despotism, 47
Maoism, 25
Mao Zedong, 130, 158
market discourse, 5, 12, 14, 19, 22, 25, 41, 118, 153, 161, 163
market imperatives, 8, 152, 153
market logic, 13, 23, 80, 82, 84, 87, 89, 96, 119, 120, 145, 160
Marx, Karl, 19
Marx-Leninism, 158
mass line, 163
maxim of good will, 92, 96
Measures for the Administration of Press Cards (MAPC), 2, 17, 37, 39
mechanism of power, 58, 120, 143, 153
media activism, 124; pre-1949, 132, 138, 146; reform era, 123, 124, 127, 133, 139, 146, 152
media boom, 1, 61, 143
media group, 47, 107, 108, 109, 112
media transparency, 7, 25, 30, 33, 102, 150
meta-censorship, 56, 57, 62, 64, 69, 70, 72, 150, 153; censorship of censorship, 57
middle class, 13, 83, 89, 94, 129, 139, 151
military censorship, 54
Ministry of Foreign Affairs, 58, 61
Ministry of Industry and Information Technology (MIIT), 36, 39, 47, 65–66
Ministry of Railways, 136
Ministry rules, 36
Minor Party Group (MPG), 129, 157
modernity, 9, 19, 23, 156
moral blackmail, 64
moral censorship, 54
mothers reviewing group, 65

Nanfang Daily Press Group, 139, 141

National People's Congress (NPC), 2, 36, 37, 66, 162
negative news, 53, 71
neo-leftism, 19
neoliberal, 8, 13, 92, 117
netizen, 1, 58
New Democracy, 130, 157
News Corporation, 61
niche market, 10, 82, 97, 103, 125, 151, 153, 160
non-Party media, 107, 110, 119
normative documents, 36
NPC resolutions, 36

Obama, Barack, 59, 61
one-party rule, 80, 126, 154
openness, 2, 3, 14, 25, 30, 31, 42, 44, 59, 83, 98, 150, 162
opportunistic journalism, 82, 90
the Organization for Economic Co-operation and Development (OECD), 31

paid news, 18, 77
Party logic, 4, 23, 68, 84, 95, 119, 141, 145
Party media, 42, 53, 102, 107, 109
Party resolutions, 36
Party-state, 3, 12, 21, 24, 29, 35, 54, 58, 81, 102, 125, 149
*People's Daily*, 58, 61, 70, 79, 88, 101, 104, 105
people's dictatorship, 154
photo orchestration, 81
pluralism, 12, 34
polarization, 53, 155, 158
policy environment, 17, 33, 36, 39, 49
political censorship, 54
political conviction, 92, 125, 133, 140, 152, 153
positive self-presentation, 58–59, 138
post-Mao, 13, 16, 22, 24, 37, 53, 66, 108, 138, 149
post-publication censorship, 55
pragmatism: capitalist, 73; Kantian, 92; linguistic, 154
pre-emptive censorship, 54
press card, 38, 39
press freedom, 4, 6, 8, 16, 29, 60, 102, 127, 161

press law, 20, 35, 36, 66, 67
principal-agent, 81, 82–83, 96, 151
private ownership, 62, 81, 90, 96, 107
private sector, 86, 94, 150
privatization, 5, 7, 13, 80, 81, 82, 143, 151
professional ethics, 6, 42, 163
professionalism, 9, 64, 79, 81, 89, 118, 120, 125, 135, 139, 146, 151
Prussian censorship law, 20
public institution, 4, 32, 103, 109, 114, 115
public nature, 9, 17, 22, 33, 54, 62, 97, 143, 153, 161, 163
public sphere, 3, 8, 10, 23, 30, 80
push and pull effect, 6

*Qingwu Yundong*, 134

red capitalist, 71
refeudalization, 152, 156
the Reform era, 1, 29, 69, 70, 85, 97, 103, 123, 125, 143, 152, 157
relativism, 7, 91
religious censorship, 54
rule by law, 35, 37, 162
rule of law, 30, 34, 35, 36, 37, 57, 162

self-censorship, 3, 56
sensationalism, 24, 41, 48, 77, 85, 89
sensitive key words, 3, 56
*shendu*, 62–64
*Shenyang Daily*, 117
*sheweihui*, 109, 111, 112, 113, 140
*shezhang*, 112
skylight, 123, 124, 125, 126, 131, 132, 133, 135
smart phone, 2, 79
social stability, 14, 22, 30, 66, 149
*Southern Metropolis Daily* (SMD), 139, 140, 141
*Southern Weekend*, 47, 59, 60, 138
State Administration of Radio, Film and Television (SARFT), 36, 39, 47, 108
State Council, 2, 36, 37, 62
State Council Information Office, 38, 58
*State Integrity Investigation*, 31
state-owned media, 7, 22, 81, 96, 101, 156
state ownership, 80, 81, 97
state-party, 157

state-versus-media dichotomy, xv, xvi, 5, 10, 146, 150
statification, 23, 157
subjectiviation, 91, 92, 94
subjectivity, 9, 13, 81, 90–96, 143, 151, 153
superstructure, 21, 71, 101, 132
supervision by public opinion, 3, 12, 29, 37, 63, 99, 145
*suzhi*, 14–15, 89, 96

technological constructivism, 165
technological determinism, 165
Three Learning and Education Programs (TLEP), xix
Three Represents, 21, 23, 156, 158
Tiananmen Crackdown, 109, 132
toning down, 57, 62, 63
transparency: nominal, 7, 16; process, 7; substantive, 16, 18, 21
transparency illusion, 7, 16, 17, 18, 73, 149, 153
transparency of the media, 39, 44
*Transparency Report*, 11
transparency rhetoric, 3, 29, 57, 58, 149, 159
Two National Conferences, 79

United Front Work, 130, 157
United Kingdom, 6, 7, 11, 12, 40
United States, 6, 7, 8, 10, 31, 38, 61, 120, 129

Voice of America (VOA), 5

watchdog, 2, 30, 44, 50, 99, 142
*weibo*, 14, 15–16
Wen, Jiabao, 2, 34, 67, 159
Wen-Yong high speed train collision, 43, 123, 135, 136

Xi, Jinping, 3, 155
Xinhai Revolution, 126
*Xinhua Daily*, 126

Yan'an, 66, 127, 130, 132
*youfaheyi*, 105–106

Zhejiang Daily Press Group, 79, 80, 84

# About the Author

**Baohui Xie** lectures at the Centre for Asian Studies at the University of Adelaide, Australia. At the same time, he maintains associate professorship at Jiangxi Normal University, China. His research interests cover linguistics, second-language acquisition, media studies, and Chinese studies. For years, academic and non-academic debates over China's media have been focusing on such issues as censorship, ownership reform, commercialization and marketization, and talking about political problems with depoliticized delusions, though now is a time for re-directing the inquiries deeper into the real political representation of the Party-state and the media. To this paradigm shift, the author has been committed in his most recent research endeavor.